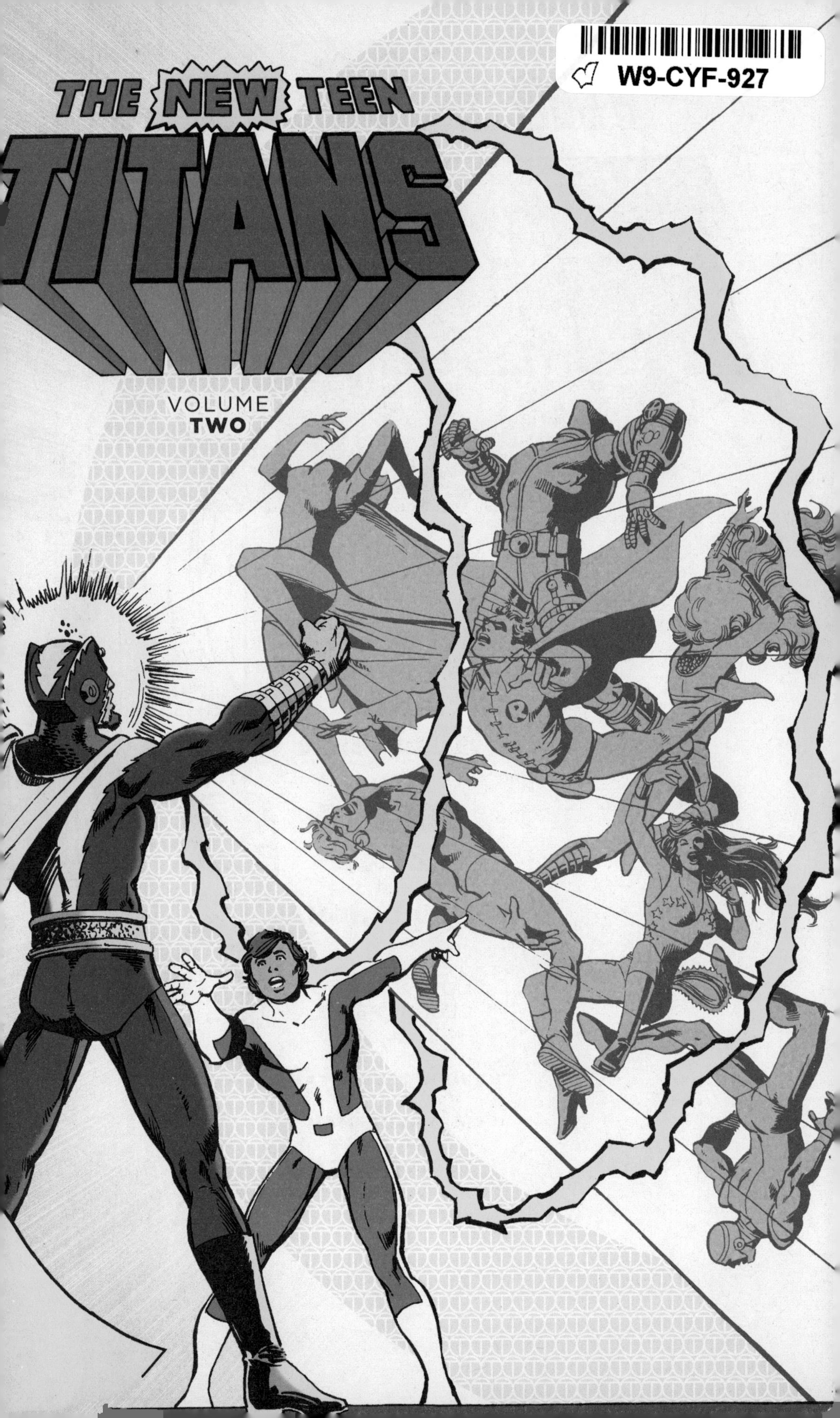
THE NEW TEEN
TITANS
VOLUME
TWO

THE NEW TEEN

TITANS

VOLUME TWO

WRITTEN BY
MARV WOLFMAN

ART BY
GEORGE PÉREZ
and
ROMEO **TANGHAL**

COVER ART BY
GEORGE **PÉREZ**

THE NEW TEEN TITANS
CREATED BY
MARV **WOLFMAN**
AND
GEORGE **PÉREZ**

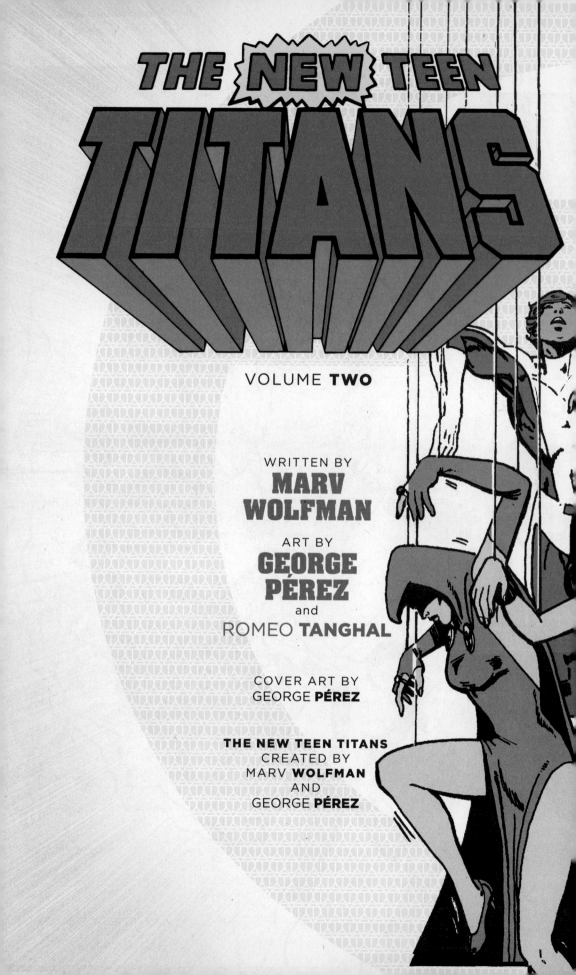

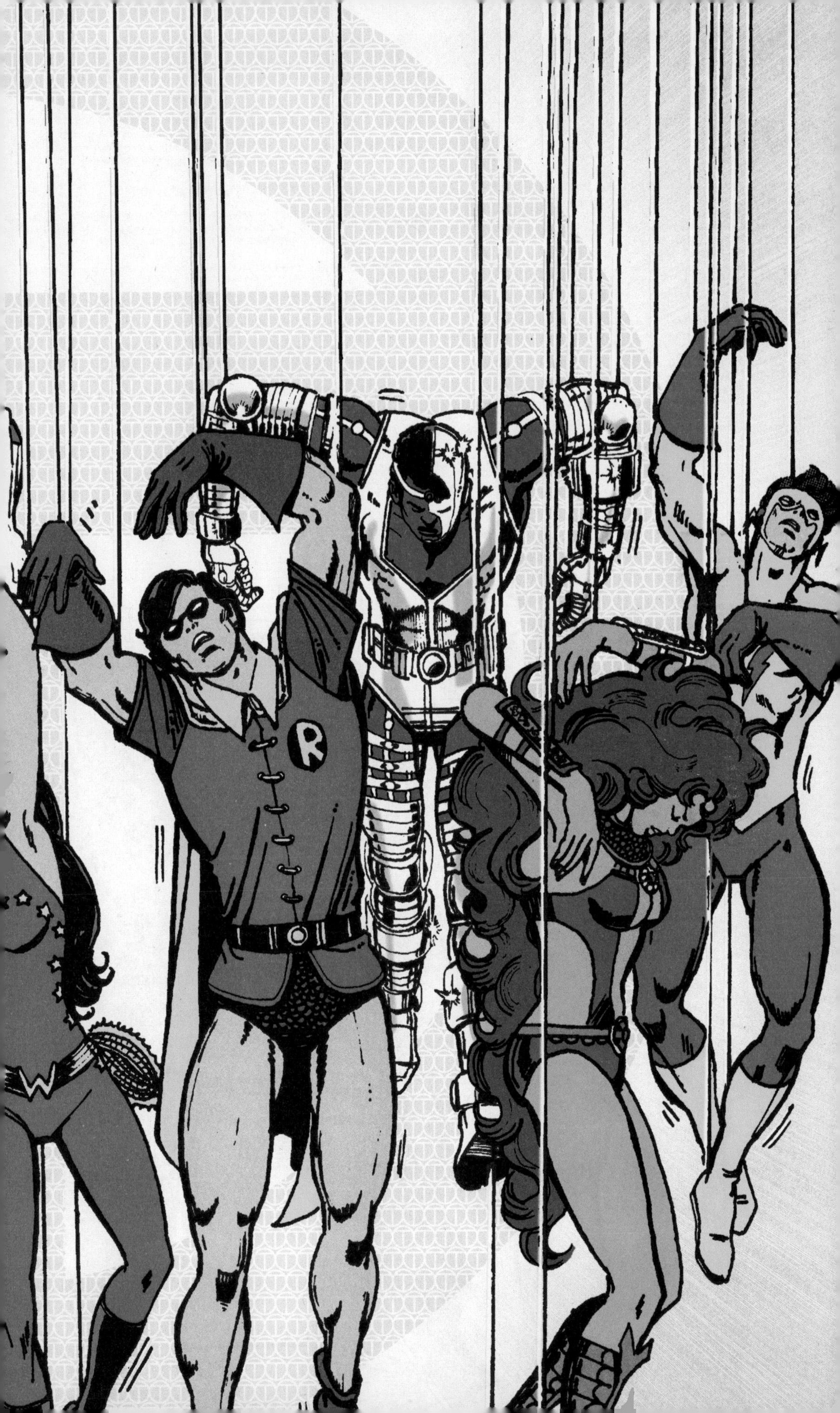

LEN **WEIN** Editor – Original Series
JEB **WOODARD** Group Editor – Collected Editions
SCOTT **NYBAKKEN** Editor – Collected Edition
STEVE **COOK** Design Director – Books
CURTIS **KING JR.** Publication Design

BOB **HARRAS** Senior VP – Editor-in-Chief, DC Comics
PAT **McCALLUM** Senior VP – Editor-in-Chief, DC Comics

DAN **DiDIO** Publisher
JIM **LEE** Publisher & Chief Creative Officer
AMIT **DESAI** Executive VP – Business & Marketing Strategy,
Direct to Consumer & Global Franchise Management
BOBBIE **CHASE** VP & Executive Editor, Young Reader & Talent Development
MARK **CHIARELLO** Senior VP – Art, Design & Collected Editions
JOHN **CUNNINGHAM** Senior VP – Sales & Trade Marketing
BRIAR **DARDEN** VP – Business Affairs
ANNE **DePIES** Senior VP – Business Strategy, Finance & Administration
DON **FALLETTI** VP – Manufacturing Operations
LAWRENCE **GANEM** VP – Editorial Administration & Talent Relations
ALISON **GILL** Senior VP – Manufacturing & Operations
JASON **GREENBERG** VP – Business Strategy & Finance
HANK **KANALZ** Senior VP – Editorial Strategy & Administration
JAY **KOGAN** Senior VP – Legal Affairs
NICK J. **NAPOLITANO** VP – Manufacturing Administration
LISETTE **OSTERLOH** VP – Digital Marketing & Events
EDDIE **SCANNELL** VP – Consumer Marketing
COURTNEY **SIMMONS** Senior VP – Publicity & Communications
JIM (SKI) **SOKOLOWSKI** VP – Comic Book Specialty Sales & Trade Marketing
NANCY **SPEARS** VP – Mass, Book, Digital Sales & Trade Marketing
MICHELE R. **WELLS** VP – Content Strategy

Cover color and interior color reconstruction by **JAMISON**.

THE NEW TEEN TITANS VOLUME TWO
Published by DC Comics. Compilation Copyright © 2015 DC Comics.
All Rights Reserved. Introduction Copyright © 2004 DC Comics.
All Rights Reserved. Originally published in single magazine form
in THE NEW TEEN TITANS 9-16. Copyright © 1981, 1982 DC Comics.
All Rights Reserved. All characters, their distinctive likenesses and
related elements featured in this publication are trademarks of
DC Comics. The stories, characters and incidents featured in this
publication are entirely fictional. DC Comics does not read or accept
unsolicited submissions of ideas, stories or artwork.

DC Comics, 2900 W. Alameda Avenue, Burbank, CA 91505
Printed by LSC Communications, Owensville, MO, USA. 10/8/18. Third Prin
ISBN: 978-1-4012-5532-9

Library of Congress Cataloging-in-Publication Data

Wolfman, Marv.
  The New Teen Titans. Volume two / written by Ge
Pérez and Romeo Tanghal.
    pages cm
  Summary: "When the series launched, writer Marv Wolfman (CRISIS ON
INFINITE EARTHS) and artist George Perez (FINAL CRISIS: LEGION OF T
WORLDS, Avengers) crafted a timeless story starring Robin, Kid Flash, W
Girl, Cyborg, Changling, Raven and Starfire--a group of young individuals
with great powers and strong personalities who learned their way in the w
through the strength of their friendship and the adventures they shared.
Collects NEW TEEN TITANS #9-16"-- Provided by publisher.
  ISBN 978-1-4012-5532-9 (paperback)
  1. Graphic novels. I. P?rez, George, 1954- II. Tanghal, Romeo. III. Title.
PN6728.T34W6383 2015
741.5'973--dc23
                                                            2015000600

TABLE OF CONTENTS

All stories by MARV WOLFMAN,
all cover art and story pencils by GEORGE PÉREZ,
and all story inks by ROMEO TANGHAL, except where noted.

Introduction by **MARV WOLFMAN** 6

LIKE PUPPETS ON A STRING! 9
From **THE NEW TEEN TITANS** #9, July 1981

PROMETHIUM UNBOUND! 35
From **THE NEW TEEN TITANS** #10, August 1981

WHEN TITANS CLASH! 61
From **THE NEW TEEN TITANS** #11, September 1981

CLASH OF THE TITANS! 87
From **THE NEW TEEN TITANS** #12, October 1981
Inks by FRANK CHIARAMONTE

FRIENDS AND FOES ALIKE! 115
From **THE NEW TEEN TITANS** #13, November 1981
Cover Inks by ROMEO TANGHAL

REVOLUTION! 143
From **THE NEW TEEN TITANS** #14, December 1981
Cover Inks by DICK GIORDANO

**THE BROTHERHOOD
OF EVIL LIVES AGAIN!** 171
From **THE NEW TEEN TITANS** #15, January 1982
Cover Inks by ROMEO TANGHAL

STARFIRE UNLEASHED! 199
From **THE NEW TEEN TITANS** #16, February 1982
Cover Inks by ROMEO TANGHAL

BIOGRAPHIES 228

INTRODUCTION

Books change as they grow. Or at least they should. As time goes on, the writer and artist begin to feel more confident with what they're doing. If they're lucky, they know they've got something that works so they don't mind taking chances. Most important, they know they've laid the proper groundwork so if one experiment fails, it won't spell instant disaster for the book.

That's TITANS #9-16 in a nutshell.

Back in 1981, sales of THE NEW TEEN TITANS started high, dropped with issues #2 and #3, then began to zoom higher and higher starting with issue #6. The readers were with us. They saw something special, something different was happening. And, most important, the Titans were attracting readers who hadn't bought a DC comic in years. We could have been content just writing and drawing the same stories month in and month out, but we weren't. The ever-amazing George Pérez and I both would get bored pretty quickly, and, trust me, the readers, sensing that, would not be far behind.

We knew this was the time for us to push the envelope. TITANS would hit its stride in what will be our third volume in this reprint series, but all the groundwork was laid in issues #1-8 and confidently pushed along in issues #9-16, the stories that are re-presented here.

George and I knew we had good characters in Robin, Wonder Girl, Changeling, Starfire, Cyborg and Raven. We had spent a lot of pre-publishing time creating and developing them. And, as ex-Marvel guys (Marv: *Spider-Man*, *Tomb of Dracula*, among others; George: *Avengers* and a zillion special projects) who loved DC Comics and its great history, we knew we could take the best of Marvel (action and soap opera) and blend it with the best of DC (plot and story) and do the kind of book we felt neither company was then producing.

George and I were, and remain, good friends. I think that was evident in the early stories and that kept us together as we struggled to expand upon the consistency we had developed. We would often start or finish each other's ideas, and all of it was without ego or the need to be number one. Our single goal was to make the book the star. Considering the number of Titans revivals that have since been attempted, I think we did exactly that.

The readers sensed our love for the stories and characters and TITANS quickly became DC's best-selling comic. Although what I'm about to bring up is business and not creative, I think it is still very important. DC introduced the idea of creator royalties at about the time of TITANS #11. Up until then we, and all other writers and artists in the business, did what we did for a standard page rate and nothing more. It was the same rate we'd get if our book sold or didn't sell. Well, THE NEW TEEN TITANS sold and we got royalties. Big royalties. Sometimes, other writers at the time would complain that we were getting royalties because we were put on a good-selling title and that they weren't getting extra money because they had been shoved off onto something that nobody cared about. When this happened, and it did more often than I'd now care to say, I always reminded them that at least two previous versions of the Titans had failed, and that because of those failures, as much as DC loved what we said we intended to do with the book, this new version of the Teen Titans was not expected to survive beyond six issues. Besides which, I said that George and I created the Titans only expecting our page rates. Period. What we did we did for love. That we benefited from our work later was gravy.

Which brings us back to the reason we're all here. TITANS #9-16.

After a major cosmic storyline and a one-issue, all-character, no-action story, we decided to take on a standard DC villain and see what we could do with it. Because I was a huge Green Lantern fan I wanted to use the Puppet Master from GREEN LANTERN #1. Our story is nothing special, but the issue exists to introduce a number of strong character arcs that would take years to culminate.

In issue #9 we set up Questor, Gar Logan's foil at home, even as we poured the cement for the upcoming Deathstroke/Changeling relationship. We also meet Sarah Simms and her school kids — introduced briefly in issue #8 — and spend time with Terry Long, Wonder Girl's future husband. At the time, some fans didn't like that Donna A) wasn't dating Dick Grayson, and B) was involved with a much older man. Speaking for myself, I thought Donna needed someone who was more mature. A less confident guy would never be able to survive in a relationship with the equally strong-willed and strong-armed Donna Troy.

Issue #10 brings back Deathstroke the Terminator, easily my favorite Titans bad guy, because deep down he wasn't all that bad. Well, he was for a while, but he got better. Deathstroke had more shades of gray than any other villain I had ever previously created, so it's not all that surprising that this issue — which really sets up the Terminator/Changeling feud — is resolved four years later in one of my very favorite stories entitled, appropriately enough, "Shades of Gray."

What can I say about issues #11 and #12 after "I don't care if 'Clash of the Titans' is the most overused comic book title ever" (heck, I even used it on an old *Fantastic Four* script)? It was the only title I could have used.

I was and am a huge mythology buff. I've got too many books on mythology, and not just of the Greek and Roman persuasion. Besides, how could I not have our teenaged Titans face the immortal Titans of myth? In many ways I think this two-part story helped cement the Titans' popularity. This is the issue where action and character all came together without any of the seams showing. The story also showed the Amazons of Paradise Island used, perhaps for the first time in a very long time, as real warriors and not just mannequins wearing flimsy long white gowns.

The best part about this story was that it got George Pérez excited about the ancient Greek myths. I may have helped light the mythological candle under him, but where he took it when he started writing and drawing his incredible run on WONDER WOMAN was all his. At any rate, this story was huge, with multiple sets of gods, great wars, good characterization and unbelievable art. I'm extremely proud of it.

Issue #13 begins the Titans' second year of publication and is blessed with one of the best George Pérez Titans covers ever. It's one of the few pieces of Titans art I always wished I owned (George kindly gave me the original art for the covers of the first and last Titans issues, which are framed together and hang proudly on my office wall next to the framed lithographed CRISIS ON INFINITE EARTHS poster sent to me by the unbelievable Alex Ross).

Modestly, I believe that in this three-part story we did for The Doom Patrol what we had previously done with the Titans; we took a group that wasn't fondly thought of up at the office and showed everyone how great the Patrol could be. I used to love the original D.P. stories that Arnold Drake, Bob Haney and Bruno Premiani spun for us way back when. The readers obviously agreed. The mail reaction to this story convinced DC to revive the Doom Patrol a short time later.

Issue #15 brings back and at the same time introduces one of my favorite villain teams ever, the Brotherhood of Evil. Influenced by the Arnold Drake originals, George and I created some new Brotherhood members that I think are every bit as good and goofy as the originals. I really like Plasmus, Houngan, Warp and Phobia.

Issue #16 closes out this second Titans collection. After so many multiple-part stories, I wanted to go back to several done-in-one issues.

In fact, in that issue's letter column I wrote, "We've already begun plans to 'scale down' the Titans a bit by pushing back the trip to Koriand'r's world until we've done some one-part, straighter stories." I felt then and now that sometimes comic-book stories, in an effort to always raise the stakes, keep getting larger and larger until there is nothing left for the readers to identify with. If all the people a super-hero meets have super powers of their own, it takes away the fragile layer of reality that we depend on. That's why characters like Sarah Simms, Terry Long and others exist: to ground the heroes in some manner of reality and to make the readers believe this could be happening right now around the corner, if only you can get there in time.

Long-running series need to be like roller coasters, with stories that move along faster than a speeding bullet followed by others that slow you down and remind you what you like about the characters even as you are being set up for the next major thrill. If you are constantly being shouted at you will eventually be numbed to every-thing. You gain perspective and have time for reflection only when there's some quiet.

Like #8's "Day in the Life" story, this issue is pretty much all character, all the time. We send Raven off to college, which she goes to, drops out from, then returns to several times during my 16-year run on the book. It also introduces Franklin Crandall, a man who... well, not to ruin it for anyone who hasn't read the story before, but Starfire falls deeply and wildly in love with him. Koriand'r's people have always been shown to be highly emotional, for good and bad. This story targets Kory's personality and I think it does it well. As far as I know, this issue has never been a big fan favorite, but it's always been one of mine.

That's it for the TITANS VOL. 2. I think George and I spent our second year solidifying our characters and our approach. Some of the stories are huge: Titans of Myth/Doom Patrol, while others are smaller, character-driven tales.

One year into the run, George and I are begin-ning to show confidence in what we were doing and the willingness to keep changing what we thought super-heroes stories had to be like.

I hope you enjoy these stories as much as we did.

— **MARV WOLFMAN**
2004

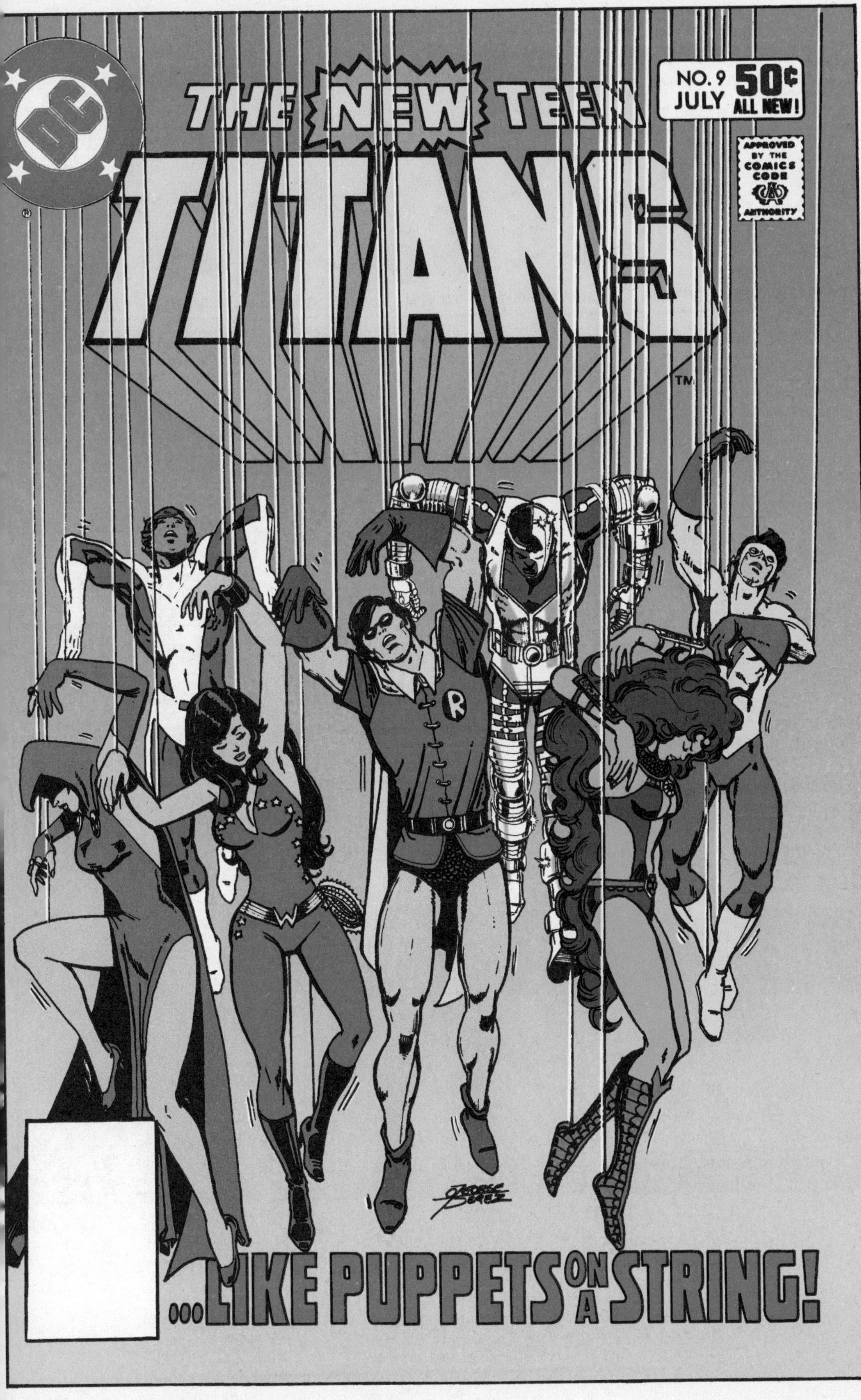
DC
THE NEW TEEN
TITANS
TM
NO. 9
JULY
50¢
ALL NEW!
APPROVED BY THE COMICS CODE AUTHORITY
...LIKE PUPPETS ON A STRING!

THEY ARE THE *BEST* THERE IS: *THE CHANGELING*, SHAPE-SHIFTER SUPREME; *CYBORG*, HALF MAN / HALF ROBOT; *KID FLASH*, SUPER-SPEEDSTER; *RAVEN*, MISTRESS OF MAGIC; *ROBIN*, THE TEEN WONDER; *STARFIRE*, ALIEN POWERHOUSE; AND *WONDER GIRL*, THE AMAZING AMAZON! TOGETHER THEY ARE...

THE NEW TEEN TITANS™

CHANGELING   CYBORG   KID FLASH   RAVEN   ROBIN   STARFIRE   WONDER GIRL

HEART TRIPPING WILDLY, HAROLD APPLETON LUNGES TOWARD THE OFFICE DOOR...

...AND SEES THE MINUSCULE MURDERERS RISING FOR THEIR FINAL ATTACK.

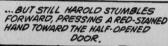

...BUT STILL HAROLD STUMBLES FORWARD, PRESSING A RED-STAINED HAND TOWARD THE HALF-OPENED DOOR.

...KNOWING ALL THE WHILE THAT IT IS FAR *TOO LATE.*

BILE WELLS UP IN HIS THROAT AS HE WHEELS, WIDE-EYED...

WHTT

MINIATURE ARROWS SLASH HIS FACE; BLOOD SPURTS WILDLY FROM OPENED VEINS...

SPAK

FHTTT

IN THE OUTER OFFICE, A SIX-INCH-TALL WOODEN SOLDIER RAISES HIS SWORD-ARM HIGH...

KHRAKK

BOOM!

AND WHEN HE FINALLY BRINGS IT DOWN, HAROLD APPLETON BREATHES HIS LAST.

1

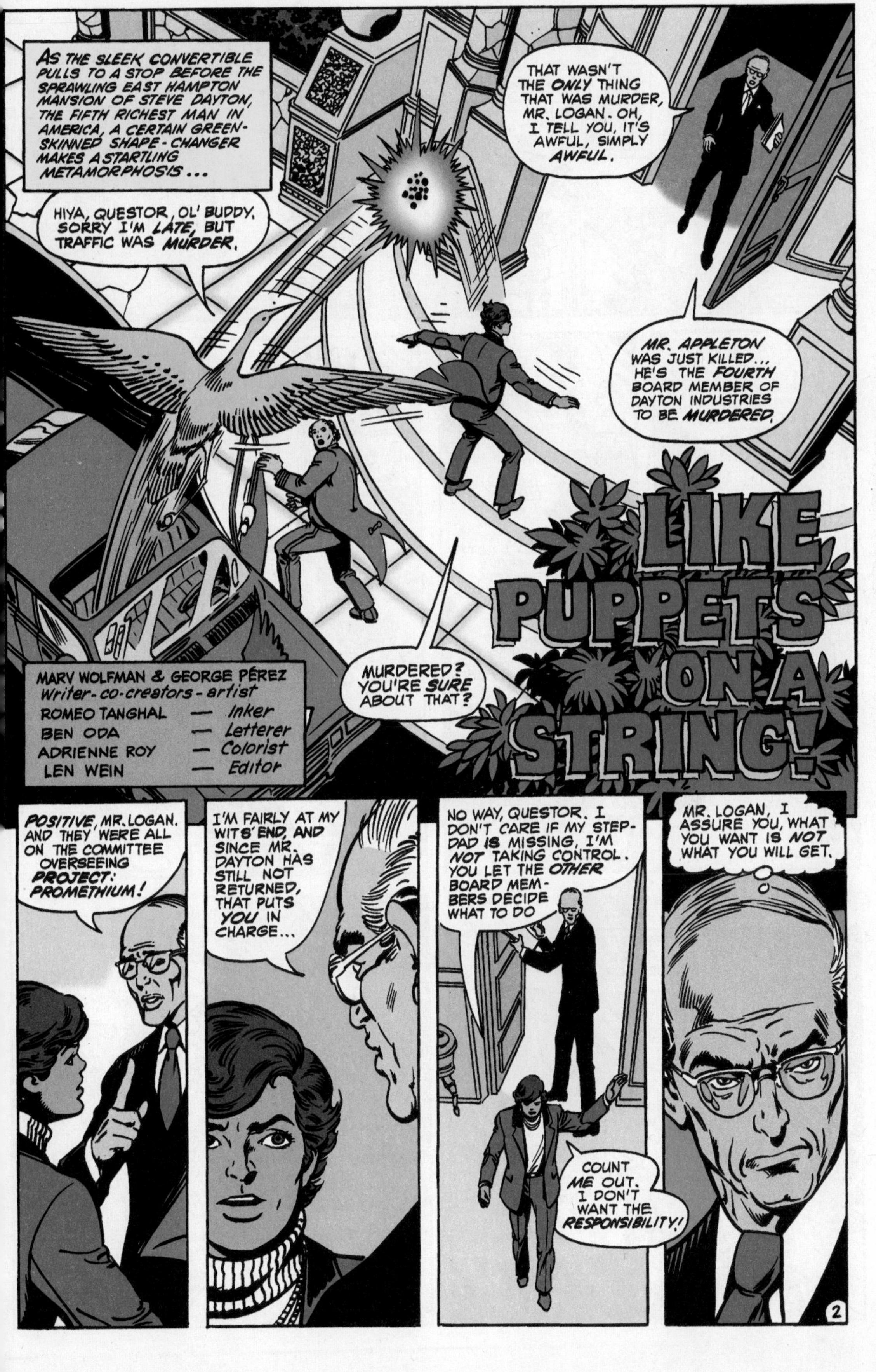
AS THE SLEEK CONVERTIBLE PULLS TO A STOP BEFORE THE SPRAWLING EAST HAMPTON MANSION OF STEVE DAYTON, THE FIFTH RICHEST MAN IN AMERICA, A CERTAIN GREEN-SKINNED SHAPE-CHANGER MAKES A STARTLING METAMORPHOSIS...
HIYA, QUESTOR, OL' BUDDY. SORRY I'M LATE, BUT TRAFFIC WAS MURDER.
THAT WASN'T THE ONLY THING THAT WAS MURDER, MR. LOGAN. OH, I TELL YOU, IT'S AWFUL, SIMPLY AWFUL.
MR. APPLETON WAS JUST KILLED... HE'S THE FOURTH BOARD MEMBER OF DAYTON INDUSTRIES TO BE MURDERED.
MURDERED? YOU'RE SURE ABOUT THAT?
LIKE PUPPETS ON A STRING!
MARV WOLFMAN & GEORGE PÉREZ Writer-co-creators-artist
ROMEO TANGHAL — Inker
BEN ODA — Letterer
ADRIENNE ROY — Colorist
LEN WEIN — Editor
POSITIVE, MR. LOGAN. AND THEY WERE ALL ON THE COMMITTEE OVERSEEING PROJECT: PROMETHIUM!
I'M FAIRLY AT MY WITS' END, AND SINCE MR. DAYTON HAS STILL NOT RETURNED, THAT PUTS YOU IN CHARGE...
NO WAY, QUESTOR. I DON'T CARE IF MY STEP-DAD IS MISSING, I'M NOT TAKING CONTROL. YOU LET THE OTHER BOARD MEM-BERS DECIDE WHAT TO DO
COUNT ME OUT. I DON'T WANT THE RESPONSIBILITY!
MR. LOGAN, I ASSURE YOU, WHAT YOU WANT IS NOT WHAT YOU WILL GET.
2

NUTS! EVERY TIME SOMETHING *GOOD* HAPPENS TO ME, SOMETHING'S GOTTA COME ALONG AND SCREW UP THE WORKS.

ALL I WANNA DO IS BE WITH THE OTHER *TITANS*, SO NATURALLY I GOTTA TAKE CHARGE OF DAYTON INDUSTRIES--

--WHICH IS MY *SECOND* MOST FAVORITE THING TO *DO* IN THE WORLD -- RIGHT AFTER *GARGLING RAZOR BLADES!*

IT'S ALL *YOUR* FAULT, POPS! YOU HADDA GO RUN OFF *LOOKIN'* FOR THE CREEPS THAT KILLED MY *STEP-MOM* -- AND THE *REST* OF THE *DOOM PATROL*...

...INSTEAD OF STAYIN' HERE WHERE *I* NEED YOU.

MAN, I GO LOOKIN' FOR A NEW *FATHER,* AND WHAT DO I GET? *STEVE DAYTON, ERRANT KNIGHT,* WHO--

KLIK

UH-OH. SUDDENLY MY CHEST HAIRS ARE BRISTLING! WHY DO I HAVE THE SINKIN' FEELING SOMETHING *AWFUL'S* GONNA--

OH, CRIPES!

SUDDENLY, A FLASH OF LIGHT, AN EERIE ALTERING OF SHAPES, AND...

FIGGERS! EVEN IN MY OWN *ROOM,* I'M A TARGET FOR *MURDER!*

SHOOOM!

AND RODNEY DANGERFIELD SAYS *HE'S* THE ONE WHO GETS NO RESPECT! SHEESH!

SKUNGH!

ONLY THIS ISN'T *FUNNY!* SOMEONE'S USING ME AS A LIVING *SKEET TARGET* -- AND THAT'S NOT EXACTLY *HIGH* ON MY LIST OF *LIKES!*

OKAY, SOMEONE WANTS TO KNOW ME AS *GAR LOGAN, DECEASED.* BUT WHO? *WHY?*

3

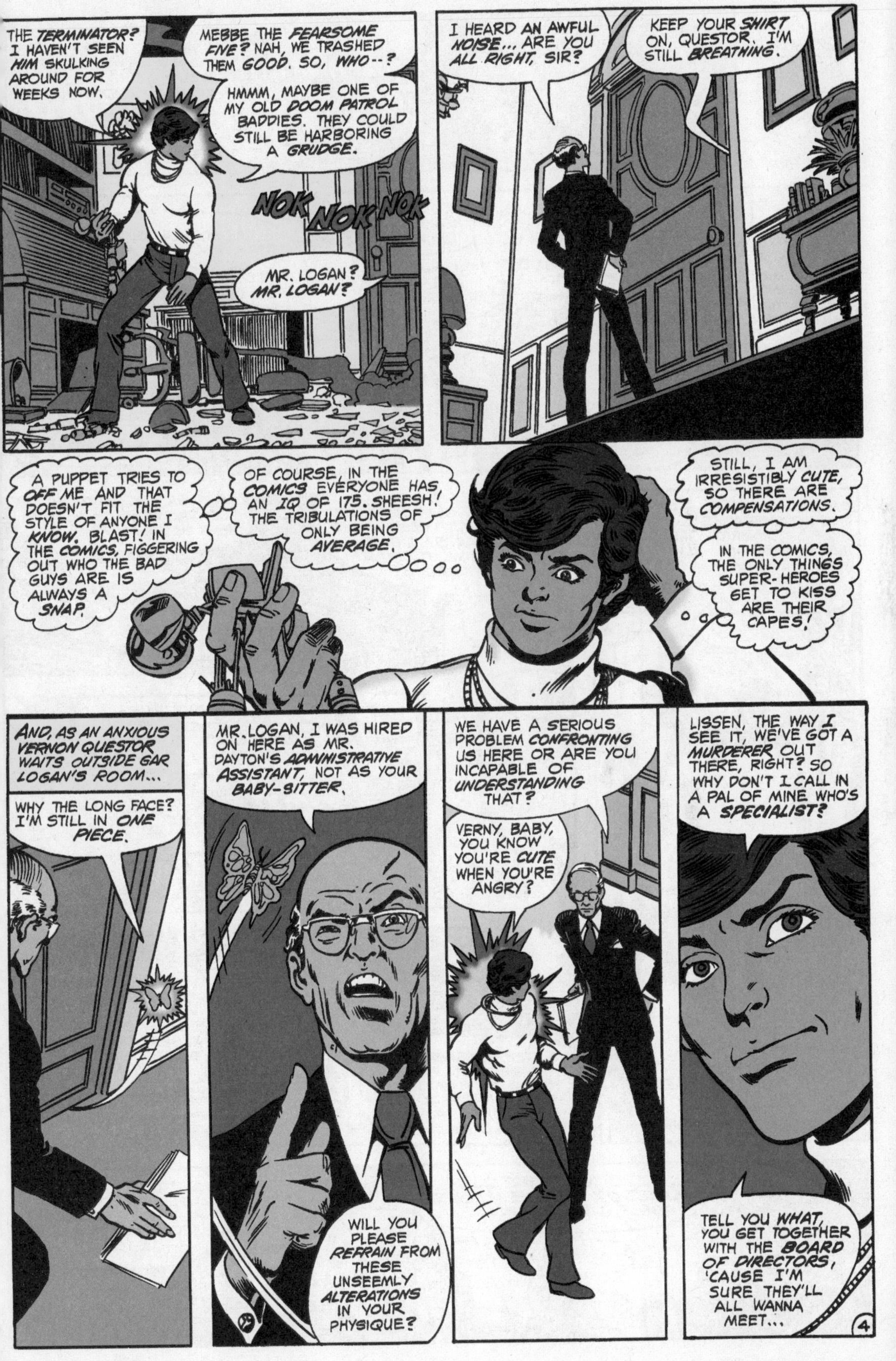

THE TERMINATOR? I HAVEN'T SEEN HIM SKULKING AROUND FOR WEEKS NOW.
MEBBE THE FEARSOME FIVE? NAH, WE TRASHED THEM GOOD. SO, WHO--?
HMMM, MAYBE ONE OF MY OLD DOOM PATROL BADDIES. THEY COULD STILL BE HARBORING A GRUDGE.
NOK NOK NOK
MR. LOGAN? MR. LOGAN?
I HEARD AN AWFUL NOISE... ARE YOU ALL RIGHT, SIR?
KEEP YOUR SHIRT ON, QUESTOR. I'M STILL BREATHING.
A PUPPET TRIES TO OFF ME AND THAT DOESN'T FIT THE STYLE OF ANYONE I KNOW. BLAST! IN THE COMICS, FIGGERING OUT WHO THE BAD GUYS ARE IS ALWAYS A SNAP.
OF COURSE, IN THE COMICS EVERYONE HAS AN IQ OF 175. SHEESH! THE TRIBULATIONS OF ONLY BEING AVERAGE.
STILL, I AM IRRESISTIBLY CUTE, SO THERE ARE COMPENSATIONS.
IN THE COMICS, THE ONLY THINGS SUPER-HEROES GET TO KISS ARE THEIR CAPES!
AND, AS AN ANXIOUS VERNON QUESTOR WAITS OUTSIDE GAR LOGAN'S ROOM...
WHY THE LONG FACE? I'M STILL IN ONE PIECE.
MR. LOGAN, I WAS HIRED ON HERE AS MR. DAYTON'S ADMINISTRATIVE ASSISTANT, NOT AS YOUR BABY-SITTER.
WILL YOU PLEASE REFRAIN FROM THESE UNSEEMLY ALTERATIONS IN YOUR PHYSIQUE?
WE HAVE A SERIOUS PROBLEM CONFRONTING US HERE OR ARE YOU INCAPABLE OF UNDERSTANDING THAT?
VERNY, BABY, YOU KNOW YOU'RE CUTE WHEN YOU'RE ANGRY?
LISSEN, THE WAY I SEE IT, WE'VE GOT A MURDERER OUT THERE, RIGHT? SO WHY DON'T I CALL IN A PAL OF MINE WHO'S A SPECIALIST?
TELL YOU WHAT, YOU GET TOGETHER WITH THE BOARD OF DIRECTORS, 'CAUSE I'M SURE THEY'LL ALL WANNA MEET...
4

YOU SUSPECT THAT SOMEONE INTENDS TO *STEAL* THIS PROMETHIUM?

OH, YES, INDEED. I EVEN KNOW *WHO* THAT PERSON MIGHT *BE*.

ALVIN, PLEASE PUNCH IN THE PROMETHIUM COUNCIL.

AH, HERE WE ARE. THAT TOP GENTLEMAN IS *JEREMY THORNTON*. HE WAS SLAIN LAST NIGHT, DISCOVERED BY HIS GRANDSON THIS MORNING. SO *TRAGIC*.

HAROLD APPLETON WAS KILLED THIS MORNING. HE WAS A FINE, FINE MAN. AND BEFORE THEM, ARTHUR KORDA AND SOREN WINSLOW WERE SLAIN.

YOU SAID YOU SUSPECTED WHO THE *KILLER* MIGHT BE?

AH YES, MR. *JORDAN WEIR*. HE WAS A *SCIENTIST* ON THE PROMETHIUM TEAM, AND A MAN WITH A *PRISON RECORD*, I FEAR.

WEIR... THE NAME SEEMS FAMILIAR.

IT MIGHT BE TO ONE IN *YOUR*--UHH-- PROFESSION. WHEN HE WAS A CRIMINAL, HE TENDED TO CALL HIMSELF THE *PUPPET MASTER*, THEN THE *PUPPETEER*!

THAT'S RIGHT. I REMEMBER *GREEN LANTERN* TELLING ME ABOUT HIM.* BUT HE SUPPOSEDLY GAVE UP HIS CRIMINAL CAREER YEARS AGO.

*GL FOUGHT THE PUPPETEER WAY BACK IN GL #1! --LEN.

MR. DAYTON HAS A RATHER--UHH-- *LIBERAL* POLICY REGARDING HIRING *EX-CONVICTS*. AND MR. *WEIR'S* BRILLIANCE...WELL, THAT MUCH IS *UNQUESTIONABLE*.

WELL, *SOMEONE* SHOULD HAVE QUESTIONED HIM AND I GUESS *THAT* NOW FALLS TO ME.

HOLD ON, LEGS. YOU'RE NOT GOIN' ANYWHERE WITHOUT *ME*. I GOTTA GET *OUTTA* THIS PLACE BEFORE I GO *BONKERS*!

OH, I DO HOPE I HAVEN'T MADE A *MISTAKE* IN THIS. SUPER-HEROES? HMPPH!

WHAT IS THIS WORLD COMING TO?

6

ROBIN GLIDES THROUGH NEW YORK'S EAST EIGHTIES ON A NYLON-THIN STRAND OF IMPOSSIBLY STRONG CORD, HIS ACTIVE MIND SORTING THROUGH A THOUSAND BITS OF STORED-AWAY INFORMATION...

THIS IS WEIR'S LAST KNOWN ADDRESS. WE MIGHT STILL FIND HIM HERE.

SURE! IF THAT GUY'S MURDERIN' THE FOLKS AT D.I., WE'D PROBABLY STAND A BETTER CHANCE OF FINDING VALERIE BERTINELLI THAN HIM.

C'MON, KILLERS DON'T HANG AROUND WAITING TO BE CAUGHT.

HE MIGHT, IF HE THINKS HE'S SMARTER THAN THE POLICE BESIDES, ONE THING BATMAN TAUGHT ME WAS NEVER OVERLOOK THE OBVIOUS.

WINDOW'S OPEN? ROBBIE, THIS COULD BE A TRAP.

I DUNNO, BUT SOMETHING JUST DOESN'T FEEL KOSHER.

GAR, TURN SLOWLY...WE'RE NOT ALONE.

REALLY? WHO'S WITH US? THE KUKLAPOLITAN PLAYERS?

NO! THE-MAN-WHO-IS-GOING-TO-KILL-YOU!

GAR-- DUCK!

YOU DUCK, PAL. ME, I'M GOIN' AFTER JERKO!

SHOK

NO!

C'MON, THE ONLY WAY TO STOP THIS CREEP IS TO STOP 'IM COLD!

BLEECH! WHAT'S THIS NERD MADE OUT OF ANYWAY?

PTUI

DIDN'T YOU HEAR THE MECHANICAL TONE TO HIS VOICE?

HE'S NOT REAL! AND THAT MEANS--

--WE'D BETTER GET THE BLAZES OUTTA HERE --AND FAST!

7

TOGETHER, THE TWO TITANS LUNGE FOR THE OPEN WINDOW...

WHY ARE WE TURNIN' TAIL? WE COULD'A STOPPED THAT SHMOE!

IS THIS AN ACT OR ARE YOU REALLY THIS THICK?

WE'RE DEALING WITH THE PUPPETEER...AND THAT PUPPET BACK THERE HAD TO BE A--

BLAMMO

DO I HAVE TO CONTINUE?

NOPE! I GET THE PICTURE....IN TECHNICOLOR, TOO.

HOLLLEEE! WHAT TH--?

MASTER! THEY ELUDED US... A SECOND TIME.

SHALL WE UNLEASH THE ASSAULT TEAM?

NOT YET, LITTLE ONE. BESIDES, IT MIGHT ALREADY BE TOO LATE FOR THAT.

IT APPEARS LOGAN HAS ALREADY INVOLVED THE TITANS.

AS THE H.I.V.E. WARNED YOU HE WOULD, PUPPETEER.

YOU FAILED TO GET US THE PROMETHIUM FORMULA...

FAILED? THIS IS ONLY A SETBACK, AND NOT EVEN A MAJOR ONE.

YOU WERE WARNED THAT IF LOGAN LIVED, THE TITANS WOULD INTERFERE WITH OUR PLANS.

WE TRIED TO DESTROY THAT GROUP EARLIER, KNOWING THAT PROJECT: PROMETHIUM WAS SOON TO BE COMPLETED. OUR AGENT, THE TERMINATOR, FAILED.*

HE FAILED. I WON'T.

* CHRONICLED IN TITANS #2.--LEN AGAIN!

8

BESIDES, THE SET-UP IN MY *HOME* WAS MERELY A TEST OF SKILLS THAT I *EXPECTED* THE TITANS TO EVADE. I SIMPLY WISHED TO OBSERVE THEM IN ACTION.

YOU SEE, I HAVE ALREADY *PERFECTED* A CERTAIN DEVICE WHICH WILL RENDER THEM ALL BUT *INOPERATIVE.*

I GUARANTEE THAT, BY TONIGHT, THE TITANS WILL BE *DEAD* --

--AND THEIR *ASSASSINS* WILL BE THE TITANS *THEMSELVES!*

HAW! HAW! HAW!

ACROSS TOWN, IN THE WEST SEVENTIES...

...ALL RIGHT, KIDS, LET'S PUT EVERY- THING *AWAY.*

CLASS IS *OVER.*

SOMETHING *WRONG,* RONALD?

AW, NO, MISS SIMMS. JUST, DO WE GOTTA GO *HOME?* I LIKE IT HERE WITH MR. STONE AN' THAT OTHER LADY AN' YOU.

C'MON, YOU WANNA *FREEZE* YER *BUTT* OFF? BUTTON UP OR YOU'RE AN *INSTANT POPSICLE.*

YOU STILL HAVEN'T EXPLAINED WHY YOU *ASKED* ME HERE, VICTOR.

HAVEN'T *GUESSED* YET, WITCH- LADY?

MISS RAVEN... MR. STONE, WELL, HE SAID YOU C'N MAKE PEOPLE FEEL BETTER JUST BY *TOUCHIN'* 'EM.

WELL, I DON'T HAVE A *HAND* AN' MY MOM AN' DAD, WELL, THEY DON'T HAVE THE *MONEY* FOR A NEW ONE.

NEW HAND? OH, A *MECHANICAL* ONE...?

OH, DEAR ONE, IF ONLY MY POWERS COULD *HELP* YOU... BUT THAT IS SO FAR *BEYOND* WHAT I CAN DO.

BUT, YOU'RE A *SUPER-HERO* AN' SUPER-HEROES CAN DO *ANYTHING.*

I WISH WE *COULD.* I WISH THERE WERE A WAY OF *STOPPING* ALL THE *HURTS* PEOPLE SUFFER, BUT WE *CAN'T.*

9

YET, STILL YOU BUILD *WALLS* AROUND YOU...ALMOST *DENYING* YOUR HUMANITY.

KLIK KLIK KLIK KLIK

LISSEN, I CALLED YOU DOWN TA TALK TO THOSE *KIDS,* NOT TA PLAY DR. BROTHERS WITH MY *HEAD,* GOT THAT?

SO WHY DON'T YOU JUST KEEP YOUR-- EH?

HOLD ON. SOMETHING'S...

WHAT *IS* IT, VI--

-- *VICTOR?!?*

"*PUPPET B-13...* ATTACH THE *NEURAL CONNECTORS!*"

CHRISTMAS! SOME KINDA *PUPPET*...MAKIN' LIKE THE *BOSTON STRANGLER!*

RAVEN, GET THIS THING *OFF'A*--

SPOOO   *OOMM!*

AAARGGHHH!

"*CONNECTION COMPLETE.* CONTROLLING ALL NEURAL ACTIVITY. BRAIN CIRCUITRY UNDER EQUAL CONTROL. THE *CYBORG IS MINE!*"

VICTOR? CAN YOU *HEAR*--?

STRANGE...HE'S *FALLEN,* YET I CAN SENSE NO *PAIN,* NO *DAMAGE.* STILL, AN EXPLOSION OF THAT *INTENSITY...*

"*RISE! RISE! AND DESTROY THE WOMAN!*"

HELPLESS, MINDLESS, LIKE A PUPPET ON A STRING, CYBORG RISES TO HIS FEET...

FROM THE BALLS OF CYBORG'S FEET, STEEL GRAPPLERS EMERGE, ANCHORING HIM TO THE HARD GROUND...

MIGHTY STEEL-JACKETED MUSCLES TENSE. HYDRAULIC-POWERED FINGERS DIG DEEP INTO THE MOIST WOOD.

11

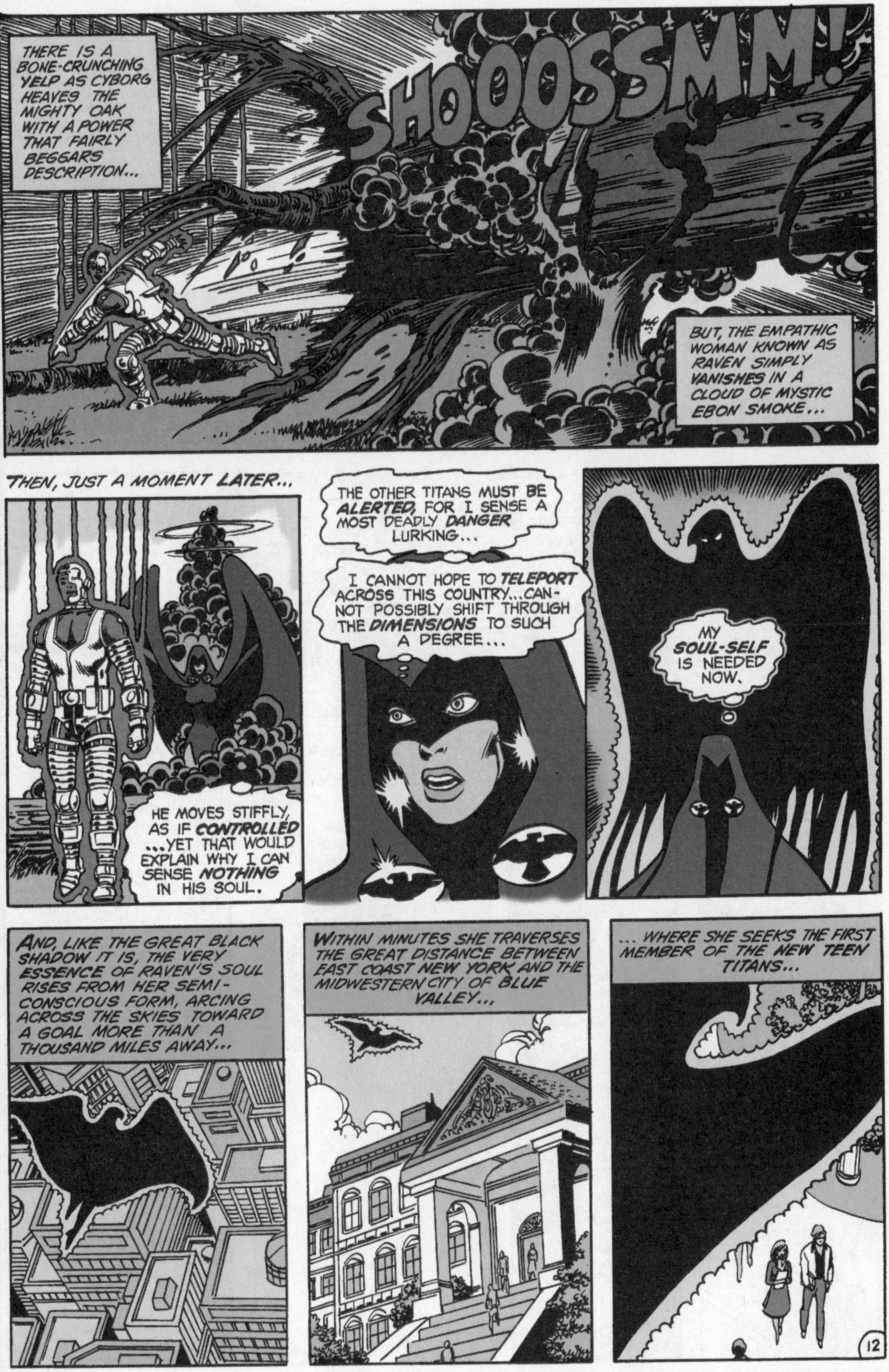
THERE IS A BONE-CRUNCHING YELP AS CYBORG HEAVES THE MIGHTY OAK WITH A POWER THAT FAIRLY BEGGARS DESCRIPTION...
SHOOOSSMM!
BUT, THE EMPATHIC WOMAN KNOWN AS RAVEN SIMPLY VANISHES IN A CLOUD OF MYSTIC EBON SMOKE...
THEN, JUST A MOMENT LATER...
HE MOVES STIFFLY, AS IF CONTROLLED ...YET THAT WOULD EXPLAIN WHY I CAN SENSE NOTHING IN HIS SOUL.
THE OTHER TITANS MUST BE ALERTED, FOR I SENSE A MOST DEADLY DANGER LURKING...
I CANNOT HOPE TO TELEPORT ACROSS THIS COUNTRY...CAN-NOT POSSIBLY SHIFT THROUGH THE DIMENSIONS TO SUCH A DEGREE...
MY SOUL-SELF IS NEEDED NOW.
AND, LIKE THE GREAT BLACK SHADOW IT IS, THE VERY ESSENCE OF RAVEN'S SOUL RISES FROM HER SEMI-CONSCIOUS FORM, ARCING ACROSS THE SKIES TOWARD A GOAL MORE THAN A THOUSAND MILES AWAY...
WITHIN MINUTES SHE TRAVERSES THE GREAT DISTANCE BETWEEN EAST COAST NEW YORK AND THE MIDWESTERN CITY OF BLUE VALLEY...
... WHERE SHE SEEKS THE FIRST MEMBER OF THE NEW TEEN TITANS...
12

THEN, HAVING FOUND WHAT SHE HAS COME FOR, HER ASTRAL IMAGE *DESCENDS* TOWARD THE GROUND...

OH, HEAVENS! *RAVEN!* SOMETHING MUST BE *UP.*

BUT IF SHE *CALLS OUT* TO ME, SHE'LL BLOW MY *SECRET IDENTITY!*

W-WALLY? WHAT *IS* THAT THING?

ONLY ONE CHANCE... GOT TO *PLAY* IT FOR ALL IT'S *WORTH.*

RUN, SUSIE-- I'M CALLING THE *POLICE!*

RAVEN DIDN'T *FOLLOW...* SHE MUST'VE *UNDERSTOOD,* THANK GOODNESS.

I JUST DON'T WANT THE *PROBLEMS* OF HAVING THE WORLD KNOW *KID FLASH* IS ALSO *WALLY WEST.*

HIS FINGER DARTS TO HIS SPECIAL RING, AND FROM WITHIN, A COMPRESSED COSTUME EXPANDS ON CONTACT WITH THE AIR...

THEN... RAVEN... ..WHAT IN BLAZES-- --IS *GOING ON?* WHY ARE YOU *HERE?*

THERE IS TROUBLE, WALLACE ...BEYOND ANY I HAVE EVER BE-FORE *ENCOUNTERED.*

I NEEDED THE *TITANS.* I NEEDED *YOU.*

I TOOK A *LEAVE OF ABSENCE.* YOU *KNOW* THAT! BUT SOME-THING HAS TAKEN *CONTROL* OVER *VICTOR.* HE TRIED TO *SLAY* ME.

OOOOKAYYY! THAT *CHANGES* THINGS!

YOU SEARCH OUT VICTOR WHILE *I* FIND DONNA AND THE PRINCESS. WE'LL LOCATE THE OTHERS IF THEY'RE *NEEDED.*

BUT BE *CAREFUL,* WALLACE-- HE'S *DANGEROUS!*

SO I'M A *SUPER-HERO* AGAIN. MAYBE IT'S JUST AS WELL. I STILL HAVEN'T DECIDED WHAT I *WANT...* TO BE *KID FLASH* OR JUST PLAIN *WALLY WEST.*

THE PROBLEM IS, CAN I *GO BACK* TO BEING A *REAL PERSON?* HAVE I BEEN A SUPER-HERO *TOO LONG?*

GOD, IF ONLY I COULD SEE INTO THE *FUTURE...* KNOW WHAT I SHOULD *DO...*

13

IN A SMALL RENTED NEW YORK PHOTO STUDIO...

GOTTA *TELL* YOU, KORIAND'R, I STILL HAVEN'T GOTTEN OVER THE FACT THAT YOU'RE AN *ALIEN.*

I MEAN, YOU'RE NOT A LITTLE GREEN MAN WITH *TENTACLES* OR ANYTHING.

WHY, *THANK YOU,* TERRY LONG, NEITHER ARE *YOU.*

TOUCHÉ! GUESS I *DESERVED* THAT, HUH?

TERRY, DO YOU AND DONNA *TALK* ABOUT SUPER-HEROING? ABOUT *FIGHTING?*

NO WAY! DONNA KNOWS *SO MUCH,* SHE'S SEEN AND *DONE* SO MUCH -- WE TALK ABOUT *EVERYTHING.* WHY?

I WAS WONDERING, DO YOU *LIKE* DONNA?

LIKE? I *LOVE* HER!

I WAS A LITTLE *TAKEN ABACK* WHEN SHE TOLD ME WHO SHE WAS, BUT...

YEAH. TERRY THOUGHT I WAS *OLDER*... LIKE *HIM.* HE'S *ANCIENT,* YOU KNOW. AT LEAST *29!*

NOW, IF YOU'VE FINISHED *SNOOPING,* KORY, I'LL SHOW YOU YOUR CONTACT PRINTS...

BUT...

DONNA... KORIAND'R. THE TITANS ARE IN *TROUBLE*...

RAVEN--?

BLAST! A PERFECT EVENING *BLOWN!*

TERRY, YOU WON'T *MIND*...?

SURE, BUT ONLY BECAUSE YOU WON'T BE *NEAR.* LOOK, I'VE GOT *PAPERS* TO GRADE. JUST BE *CAREFUL,* OKAY?

YOU *TOO,* LOVE. I KNOW HOW THOSE *COLLEGE CO-EDS* GET WHEN YOU *FLUNK 'EM!*

A MOMENT PASSES, AND...

WELL, WHAT DO YOU *THINK,* KORY? ISN'T HE A *DREAM?*

HE SEEMS A *NICE* MAN. DO YOU *LOVE* HIM?

HE'S KIND AND UNDERSTANDING, AND, KORY... HE CAN REALLY MAKE ME *LAUGH.*

I CAN'T THINK OF *ANYONE* I'D RATHER SPEND THE REST OF MY *LIFE* WITH.

AND, WATCHING, *TERRENCE LONG* SMILES AS THE TWO SLIM FIGURES FADE INTO THE AFTERNOON MISTS...

MEANWHILE, BACK AT A CERTAIN PUPPETEER'S LABORATORY...

SIMPLY PERFECT. *ANOTHER* OF YOUR TITANS FRIENDS HAS SHOWN UP, LOOKING FOR THE *CYBORG*, I WOULD ASSUME.

WELL, HIS METAL-CLAD FRIEND SHOULD BE *RETURNING* IN A MOMENT...

...WITH THE *SPECIAL WEAPON* I GAVE HIM.

I *TOLD* YOU, PAL-- YOUR *H.I.V.E.* BUDDIES WOULDN'T BE *DISAPPOINTED.*

THE *PUPPETEER* KNOWS WHAT HE'S *DOING!*

AND...

HERE COMES *RAVEN*... READY TO *REMERGE* WITH HER REAL *BODY.*

EVERY TIME I *SEE* HER, ALL MY DOUBTS *RETURN.*

HE TURNS IN A... *FLASH*. BUT, IT IS ALREADY *TOO LATE.*

IN AN INSTANT, HIS BODY IS NUMB. HE TRIES TO *VIBRATE* AT SUPER-SPEED TO *ESCAPE* THE ELECTRICAL HELL THAT HOLDS HIM IN A PAINFUL GRIP, BUT HE FINDS HE *CANNOT MOVE.*

I STILL DON'T KNOW IF SHE *CARES*... OR IF IT'S ONLY *ME*. I JUST DON'T UNDERSTAND OUR *RELATIONSHIP...*

AND, WHAT'S *WORSE*, SHE WON'T GIVE ME A SINGLE *CLUE.*

AHHHH, I AM *WHOLE* AGAIN!

BUT WHAT HURTS HIM EVEN MORE IS THE FACE OF HIS *COWARDLY ATTACKER* ...

STILL, THE *SHOCK* QUICKLY VANISHES...

I LOOKED *EVERYWHERE*, RAVEN, BUT *VICTOR'S* NOT *HERE*. ARE YOU SURE THIS IS THE *PLACE?*

AZAR PROTECT US! WALLACE-- *BEHIND YOU!*

...REPLACED A MOMENT LATER WITH THE BLANK STARE OF A MIND-CONTROLLED *KID FLASH.*

"ATTENTION: TWO TARGETS APPROACHING. GET READY!"

RAVEN, WHAT'S *GOING ON* HERE?

GET BACK, *BOTH* OF YOU, CYBORG AND KID FLASH ARE BEING *CONTROLLED* SOMEHOW.

"NOW! FIRE!"

WHOOMP!

IT IS *TRUE*, THEN... CYBORG IS NOW MY *ENEMY*.

EVEN IF SOMEONE IS *FORCING* HIM TO ATTACK ME, I CANNOT *ALLOW* THAT!

I MUST *FIGHT BACK*... WITH ALL MY *STAR-BORN POWER!*

BUT...

WHOOOMM!

I HAVE NO *CHOICE* NOW... I CANNOT ALLOW THEM TO *DEFEAT* ME.

SKREE

THE ALIEN PRINCESS IS *GRIM* AS SHE FIRES STARBOLT AFTER DESTRUCTIVE STARBOLT. BUT THEN, UNEXPECTEDLY...

X'HAL'S BLOOD!! MY *THROAT*--!

DONNA--DRAGGING ME DOWN WITH HER *MAGIC LASSO*--!

CAN'T FIGHT WITH IT *BINDING* ME...

HER *PUNCH*...NEVER FELT SUCH *POWER* BEFORE! SHE'S IM-POSSIBLY *STRONG!*

AGGHH!

KROOM!

STILL, I MUST *RESIST!*...

16

'BUT IT IS MUCH TOO LATE FOR RESISTANCE, FOR...

"WE HAVE THEM NOW. ONLY THE BLACK-CLOAKED ONE KNOWN AS RAVEN HAS RESISTED MY CONTROL!"

"SHE WILL FIND THE FINAL TWO TITANS... SHE WILL SEEK THEIR AID, BUT YOU, MY PUPPETS, YOU WILL FOLLOW HER...

"YOU WILL FIND THOSE OTHER TITANS ...AND YOU WILL DESTROY THEM AND THEN DESTROY YOURSELVES AS WELL!"

AND THEY WATCH IN OBEDIENT SILENCE AS RAVEN DRAPES HER CAPE ABOUT HER SLENDER FORM AND VANISHES...

...TRAVELLING 'TWIXT DIMENSIONS AS EASILY AS YOU MIGHT CROSS 'TWEEN STREETS...

AND, OBSERVING ALL THAT HAS TRANSPIRED...

THEY WILL FOLLOW HER, MASTER?

INDEED THEY WILL, LITTLE FRIEND...THEY'LL FOLLOW HER STRAIGHT TO OUR LAST TWO TITANS...

...ROBIN AND GAR LOGAN, THE ONE WHO BEGAN THIS LITTLE BATTLE IN THE FIRST PLACE.

THEY WILL BE DOWNED AND THEN, BEFORE WE DESTROY THEM ALL, WE'LL USE THEIR POWER TO TAKE POSSESSION OF PROJECT: PROMETHIUM ITSELF!

WE'VE WON, LITTLE ONE! WE'VE WON.

MEANWHILE, IN THE MANHATTAN OFFICES OF DAYTON INDUSTRIES...

...WEIR KILLED YOUR FIRST TWO BOARD MEMBERS TO INTIMIDATE YOU... TO FORCE YOU INTO GIVING HIM THE SECRET OF PROMETHIUM...

INTIMIDATION? C'MON, YOUNGSTER, THAT SOUNDS FAR-FETCHED TO ME. YOU CAN'T INTIMIDATE AN ENTIRE CORPORATION.

YOU CAN IF YOU POSSESS HIS POWER.

NONSENSE, LAD, POPPYCOCK! I REMEMBER WEIR... A SLIGHT MAN, HARDLY A THREAT.

NO, THOSE MURDERS WERE, WELL, SIMPLY COINCIDENCE, NOTHING TO CONCERN US.

DAYTON INDUSTRIES

CHANGE MY SOCKS! IT'S *RAVEN!*

GARFIELD! ROBIN! YOU MUST *COME* WITH ME *QUICKLY!*

THE *OTHERS* HAVE BEEN TAKEN OVER BY *FORCES UNKNOWN.*

TAKEN OVER? IT'S GOTTA BE *THE PUPPETEER...*THAT WAS HIS *M.O.** THE LAST TIME.

IF HE'S CONTROLLING THE TITANS, HE CAN MARCH RIGHT IN HERE AND *TAKE* THOSE PRECIOUS PLANS... UNLESS WE CAN DO SOMETHING *FAST!*

* *M.O. — METHOD OF OPERATIONS. — LEGAL LEN.*

TOO LATE, ROBIN. EVEN BEFORE YOU CAN *BEGIN* TO FORMULATE A PLAN...

UH-OH--IT ALL JUST HIT THE *FAN,* ROBBIE. THAT'S ONE'A STARFIRE'S *STARBOLTS!*

SKREEEEEEEEEEEEEK!

SHE'S OBVIOUSLY BEING *CONTROLLED!* HER MOVEMENTS ARE TOO *STIFF* TO BE NATURAL.

CHANGELING, CIRCLE *AROUND* HER WHILE I HIT FROM THE *FRONT!*

NO USE, SHE ISN'T EVEN *SLOWING DOWN.*

HIS HAND FLASHES TOWARD HIS UTILITY BELT, EXTRACTING HIS BATA-RANG IN LESS THAN A SECOND, THEN...

RAVEN, CLEAR EVERYONE *OUTTA* HERE. THE OTHERS HAVE TO BE RIGHT *BEHIND* HER!

HURRY, ALL OF YOU, WHILE STARFIRE'S ATTENTION IS TURNED TOWARD *ROBIN.*

THERE MUST BE NO DELAY-- *RUN FROM HERE NOW!*

OH, LORD... MY *LEG.* SHE REALLY WRECKED MY *LEG.*

C'MON! HELP ME GET JIM *OUTTA* HERE!

18

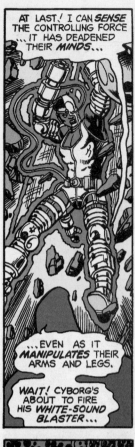

AT LAST! I CAN *SENSE* THE CONTROLLING FORCE ...IT HAS *DEADENED* THEIR *MINDS*...

...EVEN AS IT *MANIPULATES* THEIR ARMS AND LEGS.

WAIT! CYBORG'S ABOUT TO FIRE HIS *WHITE-SOUND BLASTER*...

CYBORG'S ATTACK COMES SWIFTLY, BUT THE MAID OF MYSTICISM VANISHES EVEN AS A MILLION DECIBELS OF WHITE SOUND BLASTS THE SPOT WHERE SHE HAD STOOD JUST INSTANTS BEFORE...

ONLY CHANCE IS TO GET CYBORG'S INNER CONTROLS ...*CRIPPLE* HIM...

BUT...

SO MUCH FOR *THAT* IDEA!

EVEN AS THE ACROBATIC ACE SOMERSAULTS TO SAFETY...

HOOBOY, THIS WAS DEFINITELY A BAAAAD *MISTAKE.*

NOT THAT I *MIND* PUTTING THE HUG ON STARRY, BUT I DON'T LIKE THE WAY HER *HANDS* ARE STARTIN' TO *GLOW!*

CHANGELING'S OCTOPODAL GRIP WEAKENS FOR A MOMENT AS HIS BODY TENSES, PREPARING ITSELF FOR MIND-NUMBING *STARBOLT* BLAST...

WHILE OUTSIDE, ANOTHER MINDLESS HUMAN MARIONETTE RACES UP THE SIDE OF DAYTON INDUSTRIES' CORPORATE HEADQUARTERS...

HE TRIES TO RESIST, BUT RESISTANCE IS *USELESS.* HE IS HELPLESS AGAINST THE PUPPETEER'S POWER.

AND SO, INSTEAD OF *RESISTING*, ALL HE DOES IS *JOIN THE FIGHT*...

JUST GREAT! NOW IT'S *TWO* AGAINST *ONE!*

NOW I'M REALLY GETTIN' *TICKED OFF!*

ONCE MORE THE CHANGELING'S FORM METAMORPHOSES AND...

IF I *HURT* WALLY, I'LL APOLOGIZE *LATER*, BUT RIGHT NOW I'M *FIGHTING* FOR MY *SKIN!*

AND THAT'S SOMETHING I'VE BECOME VERY *ATTACHED* TO THESE PAST YEARS!

MY CURRENT SKIN *EXCEPTED*, OF COURSE!

19

BUT, EVEN AS THE SHAPE-CHANGER'S GRIP CONSTRICTS, KID FLASH BEGINS TO WHIRL, HIS SPINNING SPEED GROWING FASTER, FASTER...

IN SECONDS, HE PASSES THE SPEED OF SOUND, YET EVEN THAT IS NOT FAST ENOUGH.

A MOMENT MORE PASSES AND THE CENTRIFUGAL FORCE SENDS THE CHANGELING SPINNING HELPLESSLY AWAY...

...BUT STILL KID FLASH SPEEDS ON... COMING CLOSE... CLOSE ...CLOSER TO THE VERY SPEED OF LIGHT ITSELF,...

HIS BODY TREMBLES WITH THE VIBRATIONAL FORCE THAT FAIRLY THREATENS TO TEAR HIM APART...

...BUT THEN ...WITH A HEART-RENDING EXPLOSION, HE SHATTERS ALL BOUNDS...

QUIT GABBIN'! DON'T YOU SEE I NEED HELP WITH A CAPITAL H!

I-- I'M FREE! LORD, I'M FREE!

OKAY, IT JUST TOOK A MOMENT TO CLEAR MY THOUGHTS.

NOW THAT I KNOW THE VIBRATIONAL FREQUENCY, I CAN REPEAT IT...USE MY SPEED TO FREE STARFIRE!

JUST DO IT BEFORE MY GOOSE IS COOKED... LITERALLY!

I...FELT MYSELF REGAINING CONTROL AS I BEGAN SPINNING,... I URGED MYSELF ON ...MOVED FASTER THAN THOSE FORCES COULD KEEP UP WITH.

VIC'S GOT ME PINNED TO THE WALL...HIS CYBORG STRENGTH MUCH TOO POWERFUL...

IT'S DIRTY FIGHTING, BUT I HAVE ONLY ONE CHANCE TO HIT HIM WHERE IT WILL DO THE MOST GOOD!

AND, FROM AFAR...

A HORRIFIED PUPPETEER WATCHES IN DESPAIR...

HE'S HALF-ARMORED... CAN'T HURT HIM THERE...

WHOOMP

20

VIC STONE'S EYES *BULGE*. HE STAGGERS, SWAYS, THEN FINALLY COLLAPSES...

HE'LL *LIVE*, BUT HE'LL PROBABLY NEVER *FORGIVE* YOU.

I'LL WORRY ABOUT *THAT* WHEN WE'RE *SAFE*.

C'MON, WE'RE NOT OUTTA THE COW CHIPS *YET*--

YOU KNOCKED HIM OUT.

--WE STILL HAVE TO PUT DOWN *WONDER GIRL*!

LISTEN TO ME, WONDER GIRL. WE'RE YOUR *FRIENDS*...YOU DON'T WANT TO HURT *US*!

ROBIN IS DIVERTING HER ATTENTION... *CONFUSING* HER. HER AMAZON INNER STRENGTH IS *FIGHTING* THE PUPPETEER'S POWER, BUT IT ISN'T *ENOUGH*!

SHE NEEDS *ME*!

RAVEN'S SOUL-SELF DRAPES ITSELF ACROSS THE AMAZON'S SHOULDERS WITH AMAZING GRACE. IT HANGS THERE, HOLDING THE SUDDENLY PARALYZED FIGURE IN AN UNSHATTERABLE SPELL...

TO EXPLAIN WHAT HAPPENS NEXT IS IMPOSSIBLE. YET, AS THE ASTRAL IMAGE AT LAST RISES...

...IT LEAVES A VERY DEFEATED WONDER GIRL IN ITS WAKE...

WONDER GIRL, ARE YOU ALL RIGHT? PLEASE, *SPEAK*...CAN YOU SPEAK...?

OOOOH, WHAT *HAPPENED*? WHAT DID I DO...?

THE SAME THING *ALL* OF US DID, LADY. WE GOT *USED*!

BUT WE'RE *FREE* NOW, FREE TO *FIGHT BACK*, READY TO DESTROY OUR FOES!

DESTROY'S A LITTLE TOO *PERMANENT* FOR ME, STARFIRE. THE *GENERAL IDEA*.

SO HOW DO WE FIND THE *PUPPETEER*? HE'S PROBABLY NOT LISTED IN THE YELLOW PAGES UNDER "BADDIES"!

YOU JUST FOLLOW *ME*, I'LL TAKE CARE OF THE *REST*!

21

AND, IN THE PUPPETEER'S PRIVATE LABORATORY...

THEY'RE *FREE*, MASTER.

I *KNOW!* I *KNOW!* BUT IT'S NOT THE TITANS I'M WORRIED ABOUT, IT'S THE *H.I.V.E.*

I *FAILED* THEM AND THEY DON'T *ACCEPT* FAILURE! *BLAST!* I KNEW I SHOULD NEVER HAVE *JOINED* THEM...

LITTLE ONE, I SUGGEST WE *PREPARE* OURSELVES. I WOULD ASSUME THE *H.I.V.E.* WILL BE SENDING THEIR *ASSASSINS* AFTER US...

I WENT STRAIGHT FOR SO LONG, *DAMN!* BUT THEY APPEALED TO MY *EGO*...TO MY *GREED.*

CRASH!!

THEY'RE *HERE!* WELL, THEY'LL LEARN I'M NOT *HELPLESS.* NOT HERE IN MY *PLAYROOM!*

HELPLESS, *NO*... STUPID, DEFINITELY *YES.*

WHY DO WE *STAND* HERE? LET US *TAKE* HIM!

YOU *HEARD* THE LADY, WEIR. I SUGGEST YOU *GIVE UP* BEFORE WE LET HER *LOOSE* ON YOU.

THE TITANS?!? B-BUT *HOW?* YOU *COULDN'T* HAVE FOUND ME!

SURE WE COULD, POPS! BY FOLLOWING YOUR *ENERGY VIBRATION RESIDUE*... IT LED US STRAIGHT *HERE*...

HMMM, THIS COULD BE *FORTUITOUS,* YOU KNOW. MY *H.I.V.E.* FRIENDS MIGHT NOT YET BE *DISAPPOINTED.*

YOU SEE, THIS WORKSHOP IS *MINE!* MY *SOLDIERS* ARE HERE...

...AND THEY ARE MOST ANXIOUS TO *MEET* YOU!

SOLDIERS READY! DESTROY THEM NOW!

THERE IS A MECHANICAL WHIRRING AS THE WALL BEHIND THE TITANS SLIDES OPEN...

GREAT HERA! I DON'T *BELIEVE* IT!

THOSE ARE *SOLDIERS?* BUT--?

THEY'RE NOT WHAT THEY *SEEM* TO BE, STARFIRE. REMEMBER WHAT *GAR* TOLD US *ATTACKED* HIM, THEY'RE MORE *DANGEROUS* THAN THEY MIGHT SEEM!

22

DESPITE WHAT THEY MAY *LOOK* LIKE, THEY AREN'T *KIDS' TOYS* OR *PUPPETS!*

THEY'RE *WEAPONS*-- WEAPONS DESIGNED TO *KILL!*

FWIPP

THEY FIGHT NOW, FREE OF ALL *RESTRAINTS...*

SPO

BLAM

STIPP

BAM

STARFIRE'S *STARBOLTS* LASH OUT WITH UNMERCIFUL ABANDON.

SKREEE

HER LUSH LIPS CURL UP IN CRUEL SAVAGERY.

THIS ALIEN PRINCESS COMES FROM A *WARRIOR RACE* AND THIS BATTLE IS SOMETHING SHE DEEPLY *RELISHES.*

THE OTHERS LASH OUT WITH EQUAL FEROCITY. THEY HAVE BRED THEM-SELVES TO HONOR *ALL* LIFE, BUT THESE TOYS, THESE MECHANICAL *PUPPETS,* ARE ONLY A *BLASPHEMY...*

SO THEY ATTACK WITH ALL THEIR *INCREDIBLE* POWER...

...BE IT *STRENGTH* OR *ENERGY...*

...OR EVEN A POWER THAT DEFIES ANY PLAUSIBLE *EXPLANATION...*

FOR SEVERAL INTERMINABLE MINUTES, THE BATTLE RAGES, THEN...

THERE AIN'T MANY LEFT, SHORT-PANTS! WE'RE SMASHIN' 'EM ALL!

DON'T CELEBRATE YET, CYBORG -- WE'RE STILL VASTLY OUTNUMBERED!

ATTACKED BY *TOYS!* THIS IS *INSANE!*

I'LL PUT UP WITH IT *NO LONGER!*

HER COLD EYES BLAZING WITH BATTLE-LUST, STARFIRE LETS LOOSE A DEADLY, DESTRUCTIVE SWEEP OF UNBRIDLED STARPOWER.

IN A SEARING, AGONIZING MOMENT, ALL DEFIANCE IS SUDDENLY, INSTANTLY ENDED...

THAT IS THE WAY ONE FIGHTS, MY FRIENDS, YOU FIGHT TO *WIN.* ANYTHING LESS IS *SENSELESS!*

I DON'T *UNDERSTAND,* THE PUPPETEER SEEMED TO BE *AFTER* US, BUT I THOUGHT HE WANTED SOME *PLANS* OR SOMETHING.

SO HE'S A *GREEDY* LITTLE DEVIL... HE WANTED *BOTH!*

SPEAKING OF HIM, WHERE THE HECK HAS THE PUPPETEER *FLED?* HE'S *GONE!*

WHERE? TO FIND HIM NOW, YOU HAVE TO LOOK FAR *ACROSS* TOWN, WHERE...

WE LOST *AGAIN,* MASTER. HAVE YOU FORMED YOUR *CONTINGENCY PLAN?*

YEAH, *YEAH.* JUST GET ME OUT OF THIS *CITY...*

AS FAR AWAY FROM THE *H.I.V.E.* AS YOU CAN, THEN I CAN PUT THE FINAL TOUCHES ON MY *ULTIMATE PLAN.*

BELIEVE ME, LITTLE ONE, THEY HAVEN'T HEARD THE *LAST* OF THE *PUPPETEER!*

ATTENTION! TARGET IS *WITHIN RANGE.*

THEN WHAT ARE YOU *WAITING* FOR, NUMBER *NINE? SHOOT!*

AND REMEMBER, THE *H.I.V.E.* DOES NOT TOLERATE *FAILURE...* FROM *ANYONE!*

24

WHILE...

DAYTON INDUSTRIES' LONG ISLAND LABORATORY IS USUALLY A PLACE OF CALM AND QUIET. WORK PROCEEDS WITH PATIENCE, TEMPERS RARELY FLARE.

BUT, A SABOTAGED FIFTEEN-CENT WASHER IN THE BASEMENT GENERATOR QUIETLY PRODUCES TOTAL CONFUSION AND PANIC...

...AND A VERY DEADLY SIX-ALARM FIRE.

EVERYONE OUT OF THERE! THE PLACE IS GOING UP LIKE TINDER!

HURRY! MOVE IT! WE'VE GOT TO EVACUATE!

FIGURES! EVEN THE MOST BRILLIANT SCIENTIST RUNS LIKE A MINDLESS CLOD WHEN CONFRONTED WITH FIRE.

IT DISRUPTS THEIR ORDER, AND WITHOUT ORDER THEY CAN'T POSSIBLY COPE.

SO, WHEN EVERYONE ELSE RACES ALONG LIKE CHICKENS WITHOUT HEADS--

--THE TERMINATOR CALMLY WALKS IN...

...AND THE PLANS FOR PROJECT: PROMETHIUM BECOME MINE FOR THE TAKING!

HA HA HA

HA HA

 NEXT ISSUE: PROMETHIUM: UNBOUND!

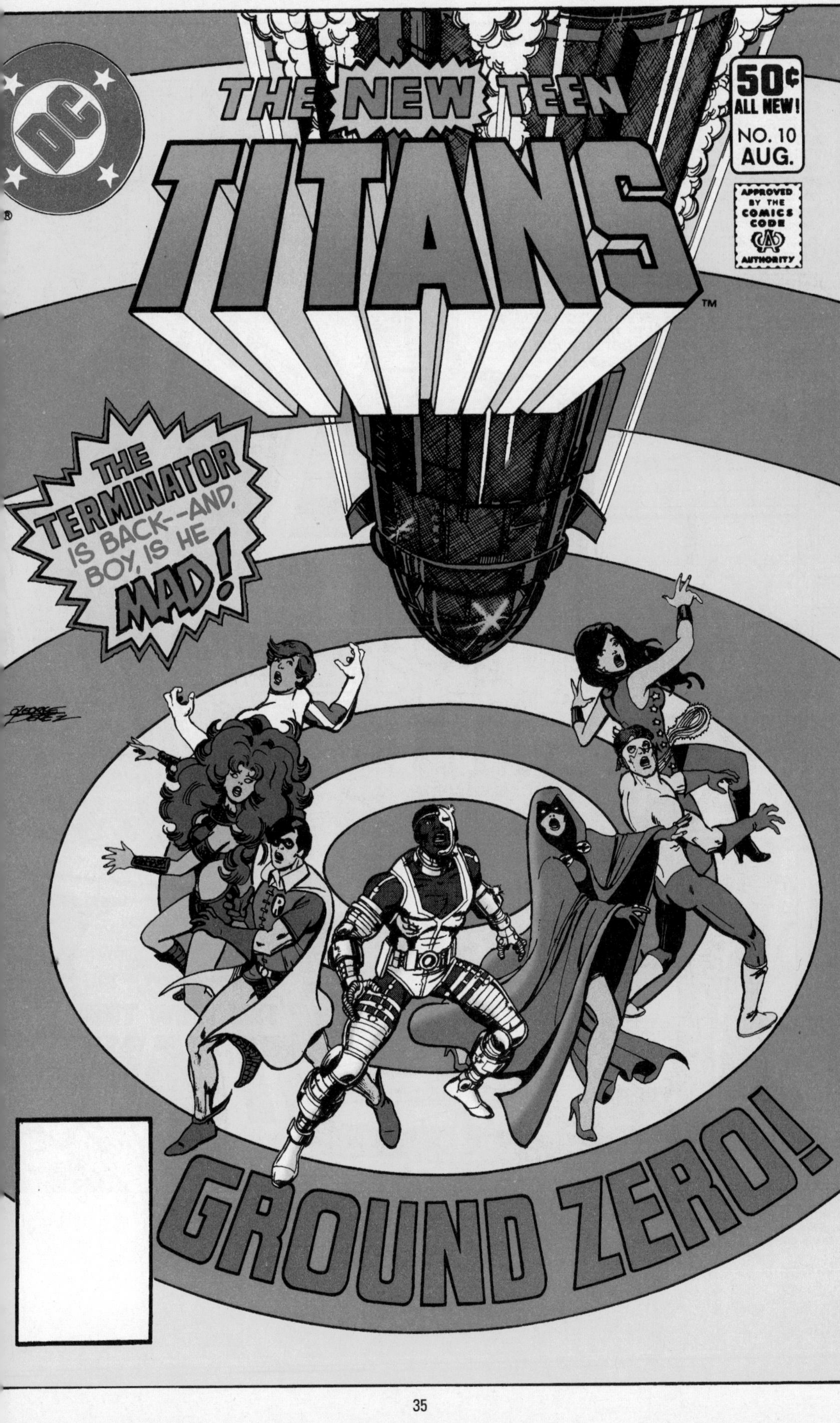
THE NEW TEEN TITANS
50¢ ALL NEW!
NO. 10 AUG.
APPROVED BY THE COMICS CODE AUTHORITY
THE TERMINATOR IS BACK--AND, BOY, IS HE MAD!
GROUND ZERO!

MARV WOLFMAN & GEORGE PÉREZ ✶ ROMEO TANGHAL ✶ BEN ODA ✶ ADRIENNE ROY ✶ LEN WEIN
WRITER -- CO-CREATOR -- ARTIST — EMBELLISHER — LETTERER — COLORIST — EDITOR

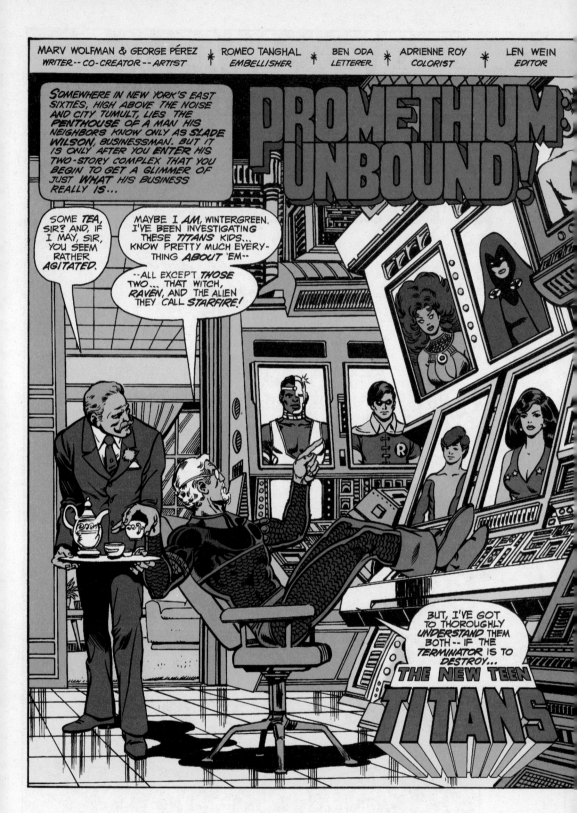

SOMEWHERE IN NEW YORK'S EAST SIXTIES, HIGH ABOVE THE NOISE AND CITY TUMULT, LIES THE PENTHOUSE OF A MAN HIS NEIGHBORS KNOW ONLY AS SLADE WILSON, BUSINESSMAN. BUT IT IS ONLY AFTER YOU ENTER HIS TWO-STORY COMPLEX THAT YOU BEGIN TO GET A GLIMMER OF JUST WHAT HIS BUSINESS REALLY IS...

PROMETHIUM UNBOUND!

SOME TEA, SIR? AND, IF I MAY, SIR, YOU SEEM RATHER AGITATED.

MAYBE I AM, WINTERGREEN. I'VE BEEN INVESTIGATING THESE TITANS KIDS... KNOW PRETTY MUCH EVERYTHING ABOUT 'EM--

--ALL EXCEPT THOSE TWO... THAT WITCH, RAVEN, AND THE ALIEN THEY CALL STARFIRE!

BUT, I'VE GOT TO THOROUGHLY UNDERSTAND THEM BOTH -- IF THE TERMINATOR IS TO DESTROY...

THE NEW TEEN TITANS

36

SURELY YOUR VARIOUS AGENCIES HAVE THE INFORMATION YOU REQUIRE?

IF THEY DID, WINTERGREEN, I WOULDN'T BE SITTING HERE NOW.

YOU SEE, I'VE GOT THESE TWO PROBLEMS... THE FIRST IS THAT CONTRACT I TOOK OUT WITH THE H.I.V.E.-- I SWORE I'D KILL THE TITANS ...AND I CAN'T GET OUTTA THAT.

THE OTHER IS HOW TO HANDLE THIS PROMETHIUM GAMBIT... AND GET BACK AT THE H.I.V.E. AT THE SAME TIME...

STILL BURNIN' OVER THE WAY THEY CONNED ME INTO WORKING WITH THEM.*

YEAH, TWO PROBLEMS... AND I'VE GOT TO FIND TWO ANSWERS-- QUICKLY!

MR. WILSON, SIR?

*AS SHOWN IN TITANS #2.--LEN.

DR. BENSON HONEYWELL, MY LAB CHIEF! YOU GO OVER THOSE PROMETHIUM PLANS YET, HONEYWELL?

OH, YES SIR, ALONG WITH MY ASSISTANT, BLEEKER.

QUITE FASCINATING, THIS PROMETHIUM, SIR... THE IDEA OF A CONTINUALLY-REGENERATING ENERGY SOURCE...ITS POTENTIAL FOR DESTRUCTION... INCREDIBLE, SIR...

EXCEPT, SIR, THERE IS SOMETHING YOU SHOULD KNOW... IT MAY VERY WELL ALTER YOUR PLANS...

DON'T KEEP IT TO YOURSELF, HONEYWELL. WHAT IS IT?

AND ON THAT QUESTION, WE PAUSE...

...AND RETURN TO OUR STORY SEVERAL DAYS LATER, IN THE MID-PACIFIC, WHERE A NAVY TRANSPORT SUDDENLY FINDS ITSELF IN THE MIDDLE OF AN UNDECLARED WAR...

BLOOM!

BAMMO!

SPOOOOOMM!

2

THE ATTACKING JETS CAME FROM NOWHERE. NOT EVEN THE CARRIER'S RADAR SPOTTED THEM BEFORE THE FIRST SALVO DROPPED AND EXPLODED.

PANIC WAS INSTANTANEOUS AS THE CARRIER'S FLEET OF BATTLE-READY FLIERS LAY IN SUDDENLY RUINED, TWISTED TANGLES OF STEEL.

WITHIN TWO MINUTES, FIFTEEN CREW MEMBERS WERE SERIOUSLY INJURED. THREE WOULD LATER DIE OF COMPLICATIONS.

...BLAST IT, GENERAL, WE'RE BEING ATTACKED! I DON'T KNOW WHO'S ATTACKING... I DON'T EVEN CARE!

I NEED HELP HERE ... AND I NEED IT NOW!

BUT MORE THAN A THOUSAND MILES AWAY, AT BASE OPERATIONS...

WE'RE TALKING ABOUT CARRIER F-16?

THAT'S IT, WILKINS. WE'VE GOT TO FIND OUT IF THE RUSSIANS ARE BEHIND THIS, OR...

W-WE CAN'T, SIR...COMMUNICATIONS... THEY JUST WENT DEAD, SIR.

AND, SIR... F-16... ISN'T THAT SHIP CARRYING...

...A THERMONUCLEAR WARHEAD?

WILKINS' SUPERIOR NODS GRIMLY AS HIS TREMBLING HAND REACHES FOR A BRIGHTLY-COLORED CRIMSON PHONE.

MEANWHILE, AS THE F-16 LIES LIMPLY IN THE VAST PACIFIC, UNDER THE CALM BLUE WATERS, SILENT AS A SCHOOL OF FISH, A SQUADRON OF TRAINED FROGMEN SWOOP TOWARD THE SMOLDERING HULK, ALL MINDS FOCUSED ON THE TASK AT HAND...

3

AND, BEFORE YOU BEGIN ASKING TOO MANY QUESTIONS, LET'S LOOK IN ON A VAST ESTATE IN LONG ISLAND'S FAMED EAST HAMPTON...

BUT, MR. LOGAN, WE NEED YOU IN THAT *BOARD MEETING*, WITH THE MAIN PLANS FOR PROJECT: PROMETHIUM *STOLEN*...

YEAH, YEAH, I KNOW... THEY COULD BE *DANGEROUS*. LOOK, WE'VE GOT *MICROFILM* COPIES...

THAT ISN'T THE *POINT*, SIR... MR. DAYTON PLACED YOU IN *CHARGE* OF HIS COMPANY ...YOU SHOULD--

QUESTOR, OLD BUDDY, I RESIGN, QUIT, BUG-OUT, LEAVEAY-VOUS, SHUFFLE OFF... IN SHORT, *YOU* TAKE OVER.

I GOT *BETTER* THINGS TO DO WITH MY TIME... AND RUNNIN' A MULTI-ZILLION-DOLLAR CORPORATION COMES *SECOND* ON MY LIST... AFTER *EVERYTHING ELSE*.

YOU WANT A *KID* RUNNING THAT PLACE, CALL *RICHIE RICH*. JUST LEAVE *ME* ALONE.

SHEESH!

TAKE IT *EASY*, SALAD-HEAD... YOU'RE GONNA *BLOW* A *GASKET*...

KNOCK IT OFF, STONE. DON'T YOU HAVE ANY-THING *BETTER* TO DO THAN HANG AROUND HERE...?

GO GET A TUNE-UP OR A *LUBE JOB* OR SOMETHING.

NAH I DIG PLAYIN' *"STAR ATTACK"* ON YER FIVE-FOOT TO.

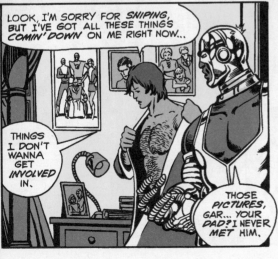

LOOK, I'M SORRY FOR *SNIPING*, BUT I'VE GOT ALL THESE THINGS *COMIN' DOWN* ON ME RIGHT NOW...

THINGS I DON'T WANNA GET *INVOLVED* IN.

THOSE *PICTURES*, GAR... YOUR *DAD*? I NEVER MET HIM.

THAT'S MY *STEP-DAD* ...HIM AND THE *DOOM PATROL*.

OH, YEAH... I KEEP FOR-GETTING YOU WERE A *BIG SHOT* WITH THEM A FEW YEARS BACK-- THE ONLY SUPER-HERO DRESSED IN *PAMPERS*, RIGHT?

NEVER WAS SURE HOW YOU GOT *INVOLVED* WITH 'EM, THOUGH.

4

HOW? COULDN'T HELP IT... Y'SEE, MY FOLKS WERE *BIOLOGISTS* WORKING IN AFRICA. WELL, I CAME DOWN WITH THIS CRAZY DISEASE CALLED *SAKUTIA*...

"TO SAVE ME, MY DAD USED SOME KIND'A GIZMO ON ME... ONLY IT TURNED ME INTO A LIVING LAWN... BUT GREEN WASN'T ALL IT MADE ME.

"ONLY I WAS ABOUT *TEN* AT THE TIME... AND TOO *DUMB* TO KNOW WHAT TO DO WHEN MY PARENTS WERE CAUGHT IN A STORM.

"WELL, A YEAR LATER, I WAS FOUND BY NILES CAULDER, THE BIG ENCHILADA OF *THE DOOM PATROL*..."

"NO, I FOUND I COULD ALSO CHANGE SHAPES... INTO ANIMALS. OTHER HEROES FLY, HAVE *SUPER-STRENGTH.* I BECOME A LIME-JELLO MONGOOSE! IT FIGGERS.

"BECAUSE OF ME... BECAUSE I COULDN'T HELP 'EM... THEY *DIED*...

FOR AWHILE I *HUNG AROUND* WITH THEM. BUT, WHEN ONE OF THEIR MEMBERS, RITA FARR -- *ELASTI-GIRL* -- GOT MARRIED TO *STEVE DAYTON*, THEY DECIDED THEY WANTED TO *ADOPT* ME.

"SHE THREATENED TO *OFF* THIS JOINT CALLED CODSVILLE, MAINE, POPULATION *14*... IF THE PATROL DIDN'T SACRIFICE THEMSELVES INSTEAD.

"FOR FOURTEEN PEOPLE THEY DIDN'T EVEN KNOW... THE PATROL, AND MY MOM -- *DIED*... JUST LIKE THAT."

SUDDENLY I HAD A WHOLE *NEW FAMILY.* GOTTA TELL YOU, IT WAS A *REAL GOOD FEELIN'!*

SO, NATCH, IT COULDN'T *LAST.* MADAME ROUGE, A *NASTY* IF YOU EVER SAW ONE, *CAPTURED* THE DOOM PATROL.

*FLASHBACKS COURTESY OF DOOM PATROL #'S 100 & 121.

5

MY STEP-DAD TOOK OFF, *SEARCHING* FOR ROUGE AND HER PARTNER... AND IN THAT TIME WE LEARNED *CLIFF STEELE, ROBOTMAN,* DIDN'T DIE.

SPEAKING OF CLIFF... I GOT A *MESSAGE* IN TO HIM. HOLD ON, WILLYA, VIC?

HEY, GREENIE, WHAT'S COOKIN'?

NOT *MUCH,* CLIFF. ANY *LUCK* IN FINDING MY *STEP-DAD?*

ZILCH! FOLLOWED HIM HERE TO *BRAZIL,* BUT HE TOOK OFF. SUPPOSEDLY GOT A LINE ON MADAME ROUGE IN *UGANDA.*

YOU SURE YOU WANNA KEEP *BANKROLLIN'* THIS HIDE-AN'-SEEK GAME?

BELIEVE IT, CLIFF... I WANT DAYTON *BACK* HERE.

OKAY, GREENS, IT'S YOUR *BUCKS.* BY THE WAY, TELL YOUR LAB GUYS *THANKS.* IF I GOTTA BE *TRAPPED* IN A ROBOT BODY, I REALLY PREFER *THIS* ONE.

SIGNIN' OFF, AND TAKE CARE, SQUIRT.

ROBOTMAN? HE'S ALMOST LIKE *ME.* IS THAT WHY LOGAN...?

CLIFF'S SOME *GUY,* ISN'T HE, VIC?

Y'KNOW, FOR AWHILE I DIDN'T EVEN WANNA *SPEAK* TO HIM ...SEEIN' HIM *REMINDED* ME OF MY *STEP-MOM* AND ALL MY PROBLEMS...

AND WHEN THE *TITANS* WERE FORMED... WELL, SEEIN' *YOU* SORTA *REMINDED* ME OF CLIFF... I REALLY *HATED* YOU FOR AWHILE BACK THEN.

BUT THEN I GOT TO *KNOW* YOU... WE BECAME *FRIENDS,* AND BECAUSE OF *YOU,* VIC... I WAS ABLE TO CALL *CLIFF* AGAIN...

...ABLE TO *LOOSEN* UP AND OFFER HIM A *JOB*...

WITHOUT *KNOWIN'* IT, PAL... YOU *HELPED* ME ...REALLY *HELPED* ME.

THANKS.

6

41

IN MANHATTAN, IN THE WEST EIGHTIES, MISS SARAH SIMMS SHOPS FOR HER SUPPER...

GAWD! 89 CENTS! IT WAS ONLY 75 CENTS LAST WEEK.

I SPEND SO MUCH MONEY, MY WALLET'S DYING OF MALNUTRITION!

MOM! HEY, IT'S MISS SIMMS, MY TEACHER AT THE SPECIAL SCHOOL!

HELLO, MISS SIMMS. I'M MRS. GRAHAM, JIMMY'S MOTHER. I HAVE TO SAY YOU'VE DONE WONDERS WITH JIMMY...

...AFTER HIS ACCIDENT I DIDN'T THINK HE'D EVER GET USED TO HAVING A PROSTHESIS INSTEAD OF A REAL HAND, BUT YOU...

...YOU TURNED HIM AROUND... AND I THANK YOU.... TRULY THANK YOU.

IT'S MY PLEASURE, MRS. GRAHAM ... REALLY.

WOW! I'M BROKE, BUT I'M HAPPY. IT'S WORTH SO MUCH TO SEE A KID LIKE THAT SO HAPPY AFTER WHAT HE'S GONE THROUGH.

GUESS I DON'T MIND NOT HAVING MONEY... BUT DO I REALLY HAVE TO BE SO BROKE ALL THE TIME?

OH, WELL ...

IT COULD BE WORSE, I GUESS...MOST OF THE GIRLS I GREW UP WITH AREN'T DOING ANYTHING THEY REALLY WANT TO DO...ANYTHING THEY ENJOY.

MY HOME MAY BE UNHEATED AND COLD, BUT I'VE GOT MORE THAN ENOUGH WARMTH INSIDE... WARMTH, HAPPINESS, AND CONTENTMENT.

LISTEN TO ME, I SOUND LIKE MISS MARY SUNSHINE. OH, WELL... MAYBE I AM... MAYBE I--

THEN, SUDDENLY, VICIOUSLY...

GOOD DAY, MISS SIMMS...

GOOD DAY, AND GOOD-BYE!

MMFMMF FFFM!

7

SOMEWHERE IN THE *MIDDLE EAST*, NIGHT: THE SLEEK PRIVATE JET LANDS AT THIS HIDDEN AIRSTRIP A HUNDRED MILES FROM THE NEAREST VILLAGE.

IT REFUELS WHILE WAITING FOR ITS *PASSENGERS* TO ARRIVE. SURROUNDING THE JET, ARMED GUARDS KEEP THEIR EYES PEELED FOR ANY UNWANTED *OBSERVERS*.

BELOW ARE TWO *UNWANTEDS*:

HARRY, IT MUST BE A *CONVENTION* DOWN THERE... EVERY BLAMED *TERRORIST* IN THE COUNTRY.

YOU THINK THEY'RE ARRANGING A *STRIKE?*

NAH, DON'T *THINK* SO ... IT LOOKS LIKE *BUSINESS* AND FROM THE *FLIGHT PLAN* WE SAW...

IT'S ABOUT TIME WE RADIOED *WASHINGTON*...I'VE GOT A BAD *PREMONITION.*

WHICH COMES *TRUE* JUST MOMENTS LATER, AS...

MMFMFF MMF

WASHINGTON'S *NOTIFIED*, HARRY... HARRY?

YOUR FRIEND IS *DEAD*, AMERICAN...

...AND YOU SHALL JOIN HIM-- *NOW!*

ARGGHHH!

LENINGRAD: BORIS BATTINOV, TERRORIST FOR THE *K.G.B.*, BOARDS A SMALL JET. HIS MISSION AND DESTINATION KNOWN ONLY TO A VERY FEW WITHIN THE *KREMLIN PRESIDIUM.*

KOREA: CHUNG LO OF KOREA'S CRIMINAL ORGANIZATION, *ZATZU*, CLUTCHES THE ATTACHE CASE FILLED WITH FIVE MILLION DOLLARS, SWISS, AS HE BOARDS HIS PRIVATE JET.

WHILE IN *LIBYA*, A CERTAIN FORMER HEAD OF STATE WITH DESIRES OF WORLD CONQUEST ALSO PREPARES TO FLY WESTWARD.

ALL THESE PEOPLE, AND MORE THAN ONE HUNDRED OTHERS LIKE THEM, ARE WINGING THEIR WAY SECRETLY TO AMERICA.

THEY ARE *NOT* COMING TO THROW A *PARTY.*

⑧

MEANWHILE, CUTTING A FLAMING SWATH ACROSS THE BLUE SKIES OF MANHATTAN COMES THE LITHE, GOLDEN FIGURE OF THE ALIEN PRINCESS KORIAND'R, ALSO KNOWN AS STARFIRE...

...HAVE TO TELL *DONNA* HOW MUCH I APPRECIATE THAT *MODELING JOB.*

AND THIS *IS* MY HOME NOW, FOR I HAVE NO REAL REASON TO *WANT* TO RETURN TO *TAMARAN...* THOUGH I DO MISS MY PARENTS...MY BROTHER.

STRANGE, THINKING OF *RYAND'R* MAKES ME THINK OF MY *SISTER.*

I THOUGHT I'D LONG AGO *BLOTTED* HER FROM MY MEMORY.

THAT TRAITRESS... FOR WHAT SHE DID TO *TAMARAN,* WHAT SHE LATER DID TO *ME...*

...I SWEAR I'D *SLAY* HER IN A MOMENT IF I HAD THE *CHANCE.*

THERE SHE IS. *BEAUTIFUL* KID, TOO.

WELL, GUESS *WHAT,* BABE. YOU JUST GOT ELECTED TO BE THE *FIRST* TITAN TO BE THE *LAST* TITAN.

BANG!

HUNH?

PERFECT... *DIRECT HIT!* AND WHY *NOT?* WHEN I GOT MY BRAIN POWER INCREASED 90%....

...IT NOT ONLY MADE ME *STRONGER* AN' *FASTER* THAN ANYONE ELSE ON EARTH--

--BUT IT INCREASED ALL MY *SENSES* A *THOUSANDFOLD!*

SO NOW-- THE *TERMINATOR* NEVER MISSES!

WORKING LIKE AN *EARTHLING* MAKES ME FEEL MORE *LIKE* THEM, LETS ME BE MORE *AT HOME* HERE ON EARTH.

9

SOMETHING *HIT* ME ...ATTACKED ME. THE *CITADEL?* HAVE THEY *FOUND* ME AGAIN?

I DON'T HAVE ANY OTHER *ENEMIES* HERE ON EARTH, OR--

KRAASH!

YOU? YOU'RE THE ONE WHO CALLED HIMSELF *THE TERMINATOR!*

YOU *REMEMBER,* GOLDIE? I SHOULD BE *FLATTERED!*

ANYWAY, BABE, I'VE GOT A LITTLE *MESSAGE* FOR YOU AND YOUR BUDDIES, AND I FIGGERED *THIS* WAY WAS CHEAPER THAN A *PHONE CALL.*

TERMINATOR, YOU ARE *MAD!*

YOU *ATTACKED* ME AND THINK I'M GOING TO SIT HERE LISTENING TO SOME *MESSAGE?*

SKREEEEEK

WELL, THE OTHERS AREN'T HERE TO *STOP* ME, TERMINATOR... NO ONE ELSE IS HERE TO *PREVENT* ME FROM *FIGHTING BACK!*

ON TAMARAN WE TRY TO *AVOID* THE FINAL BATTLE, BUT, WHEN WE FIGHT-- *WE FIGHT TO THE FINISH!*

BABE, THAT'S JUST WHAT I HAD *IN MIND!*

THE TERMINATOR'S HAND SQUEEZES THE RIFLE'S TRIGGER...

AND...

A DOZEN PELLETS, PERHAPS *MORE.* I NEED TO SPREAD MY STARBOLT BEAM *WIDE* ...SETTING UP A *FLAK PATTERN* TO ACT LIKE A *SHIELD!*

SPAM! SBTT! BLAM! SPTAM! SPAM!

THERE! THOSE LEADEN MISSILES *DETONATE* LONG BEFORE THEY *REACH* ME.

10

HE IS *DANGEROUS* AND MUCH *FASTER* THAN I REMEMBERED. I MUSTN'T ALLOW HIM TIME TO *COUNTER* MY ATTACK.

STILL, HE *AVOIDS* MY STARBOLTS AS IF THEY WERE *STANDING STILL.* HIS REFLEXES ARE *ASTOUNDING!*

OR HAVE I *SLOWED DOWN* THESE PAST YEARS? I HAVE NOT GONE THROUGH THE *RITUALS* TAUGHT TO ME BY THE *OKAARAN WARLORDS* SINCE THE CITADEL FIRST TOOK ME AS THEIR *SLAVE!*

YOU'RE *GOOD,* GOLDIE. I'LL GIVE YOU *THAT MUCH.* GOOD, BUT NOT GOOD *ENOUGH!*

ACKKK!

HIS PUNCH *HURT*...MUCH MORE THAN IT *SHOULD* HAVE. I HAVE TO RESUME MY *TRAINING*...EVEN HERE ON *EARTH!*

TERMINATOR, YOU DO NOT *WIN* A BATTLE BY *TALKING* YOUR OPPONENT TO DEATH!

DON'T *INTEND* TO, DEAR. WHEN IT *COMES DOWN* TO IT, I'LL WIN BECAUSE I'M *BETTER*...

...FASTER, AND DAMN *SNEAKIER!*

I DON'T *PLAY FAIR,* BEAUTIFUL!

SKRAKK!

BUT I *DO* PLAY FOR KEEPS!

11

HMMM, THE OTHERS ARE CLOSIN' IN ON US... WHICH *FIGURES.* PEOPLE ARE LIKE *VULTURES,* READY TO FEED ON THE *DEAD.*

ONLY THIS TIME THEY'LL HAVE TO *WAIT!*

I NEED *THIS* ONE TO PASS MY MESSAGE ON TO THE *OTHER* TITANS.

C'MON, GIRL--*WAKE UP.* I HAVEN'T GOT ALL DAY!

I *AM* AWAKE, TERMINATOR.!

AWAKE, AND OUT FOR *BLOOD!*

SKREEEEEEEEEEE

NOT AT ALL *BAD, GIRL*-- STILL, WITH MY POWER YOU NEED A BIT MORE TO DO ME IN!

YOU STILL *LIVE?* IMPOSSIBLE!

BABE, *FIRST* THING YOU GOTTA REALIZE IS-- *NOTHING'S* IMPOSSIBLE!

NOT MY STAYING *ALIVE* AGAINST YOUR *BEST* SHOT--

--OR EVEN MY *GETTING AWAY* ONCE I'VE DONE WHAT I SET OUT TO DO!

SKA BAMMM

12

47

HIS EXPLOSIVE DEVICE *MISSED* ME...AND NOW HE *RUNS*, THINKING HE'LL *ESCAPE!*

WHAT *ARROGANCE*... TO THINK I'D LET HIM ELUDE ME SO *EASILY* THAT--*EH?*

OH, MY GOD... *WATCH OUT!*

THAT *BUILDING!* OF COURSE...THE TERMINATOR WASN'T ATTEMPTING TO *DESTROY* ME WITH THAT BOMB--

--HE USED IT TO *DELAY* ME!

HE KNOWS I CAN'T CHASE HIM AND SAVE THOSE POOR *PEOPLE* AT THE SAME TIME.

HMMM, THEY'RE ALREADY *PANICKING*... LOSING *CONTROL* OVER THEIR ACTIONS.

AMAZING! YOU'D THINK THEY'D BE *TAUGHT* AS *CHILDREN* HOW TO HANDLE EMERGENCIES... BUT *NO*-- ALL THEY DO IS *REGRESS* INTO CHILDREN.

ALL OF YOU, PLEASE *LISTEN* TO ME... THERE IS NO REASON TO *RUN*...NO REASON TO *PANIC.* I CAN *HELP* YOU.

NO GOOD! THEY DON'T KNOW WHO I AM...AND MY STRANGE *APPEARANCE* ONLY SERVES TO FRIGHTEN THEM *MORE.*

THEREFORE I'VE GOT TO ACT MORE *QUICKLY* THAN I THOUGHT...

NEVER TRIED ANYTHING LIKE THIS *BEFORE*... BUT I HAVE TO *HARNESS* MY STARBOLT POWERS...PROJECT THEM IN AS *WIDE* A FIELD AS I CAN...

...AND REDUCE THIS STONE DEBRIS TO *ASH* BEFORE IT COMES HURTLING TO THE GROUND.

THE GREAT SHIMMERING RAY SPREADS WIDE... ⑬

AND... IT IS *OVER*, AND HE IS *GONE*. BUT--

--WHY DID HE *ATTACK* ME IN THE FIRST PLACE? AND WHY DIDN'T HE *KILL* ME WHEN HE HAD THE *CHANCE?*

AS THE ANSWER CAN-NOT BE DIS-COVERED WITH *STARFIRE*, LET'S MOVE ACROSS TOWN, WHERE...

WINTERGREEN, EVERYTHING PANNED OUT LIKE A *PROSPECTOR'S DREAM*. THE TRANSMITTER'S IN PLACE.

SIR... YOU HAVE A RATHER URGENT MESSAGE-- FROM *THE H.I.V.E.!*

AND... *TERMINATOR*, YOU STOLE PLANS TO WHICH WE HAD *PRIOR CLAIMS!* WE WISH THEM GIVEN TO US--*IMMEDIATELY*.

YOU'RE TALKING ABOUT *PROJECT: PROMETHIUM*, AREN'T YA? YEAH, I GOT THE PLANS, AND IF YOU *WANT* 'EM... WELL, THEY'RE UP FOR *BID*.

DO NOT TRY OUR *PATIENCE*, TERMINATOR. YOU ARE WORK-ING FOR *THE H.I.V.E.*, AND WE DO NOT ABIDE *INSUB-ORDINATION*.

PALLY, I WORK FOR *MYSELF*. OUR CONTRACT CALLS FOR ME TO *OFF* THE TITANS --- *NOTHING ELSE*.

AND, IF YOU REALLY *WANT* THOSE PLANS ... I'LL SEE YOU AT THAT *AUCTION*-- TOMORROW.

MEANWHILE, SOARING ACROSS THE NEW YORK SKIES...

OKAY, SO MAYBE I *AM* DUCKING IT, BUT YOU KNOW HOW EASILY I COULD *SCREW* THINGS UP?

BY THE TIME WE FIND *STEVE DAYTON*, HE COULD GO FROM THE FIFTH RICHEST GUY IN AMERICA TO LOOKING FOR HANDOUTS FROM *BAG LADIES*.

SO, UH-UH... I'M NOT TAKING OVER DAYTON ENTERPRISES FOR *ANYTHING*.

SEEMS TO *ME* YOU JUST DON'T WANT TO GET *INVOLVED*. YOU'RE NOT *HALF* AS DUMB AS YOU *THINK* YOU ARE.

THANKS! I KNEW YOU'D UNDERSTAND... *SHEESH!* LOOK, YOU AND THE *OTHER* TITANS... YOU'RE ALL *OLDER* THAN I AM...

YOU WERE *TRAINED*... EVEN *BETTER-EDUCATED*. ME, I SORT OF GOOFED AROUND HERE AND THERE ...AND *NOW*, WELL...

...I JUST DON'T WANNA TAKE THE CHANCE I'LL DO SOMETHING *WRONG*. 14

YOU'RE GONNA *HAVE* TO TAKE THAT RISK *SOMETIME*, GAR. YOU CAN'T ALWAYS *PROTECT* YOURSELF AGAINST *FAILURE*.

SURE I CAN. JUST WATCH ME. 'SIDES, WHO CAN CONCENTRATE ON *BUSINESS* WHEN THERE ARE ALL THOSE GORGEOUS *GIRLS* OUT THERE JUST *DYING* TO MEET ME?

GOTTA *ADMIT* IT, VIC -- THEY'RE A HECKUVA LOT *BETTER* TO CUDDLE UP WITH THAN BALANCE SHEETS AND YOUR TEXAS INSTRUMENTS COMPUTERS.

YOU DON'T HAVE A SERIOUS *BONE* IN THAT LETTUCE-GREEN *BODY* OF YOURS, *DO* YOU, LOGAN?

NOT IF I CAN GET AWAY *WITHOUT* ONE, STONEY.

IT'S *ABOUT TIME* YOU TWO SHOWED UP.

SORRY, WONDY-- BUT WE WERE STACKED UP OVER FIFTH AVENUE.

EVERYWHERE I TURN-- *COMEDIANS*! SHEESH!

'SIDES, WHAT'S THE BIG *PROBLEM?* THIS IS JUST A REGULARLY SCHEDULED MEETING, ISN'T IT?

DON'T *BET* ON IT, STIFF-JOINTS. LOOK AT ROBBIE'S *FACE*. HE LOOKS LIKE HE JUST SWALLOWED A WHOLE *LEMON!*

GARFIELD, BE *SERIOUS!* THIS IS AN *EMERGENCY*.

YOU KNOW YOU'RE *STUNNING* WHEN YOU POUT? LET'S *SHUCK* THIS DIVE AND *BOOGIE*.

EYES *IN*, LOGAN ... WE'VE GOT *WORK*.

TWO ORDERS OF BUSINESS: FIRST, WALLY AND RAVEN WERE INVESTIGATING THE *THEFT* OF THE PROJECT: PROMETHIUM PLANS.

WE SEARCHED DAYTON INDUSTRIES, BUT I COULD SENSE *NOTHING* WHATSOEVER.

15

50

WHOEVER MADE OFF WITH THEM WAS GOOD... A PRO.

SECOND--AND I THINK THERE'S A LINK HERE--STARFIRE WAS ATTACKED BY THE TERMINATOR ON HER WAY HERE...

...AND A GOVERNMENT FRIEND OF MINE, KING FARADAY, TELLS ME THAT ABOUT ONE HUNDRED OF THE WORLD'S MOST FEARED TERRORISTS ARE HEADING FOR THIS COUNTRY...

SUDDENLY...

GREETINGS, OLD FRIENDS.

GREAT HERA! WHAT--?

THAT VOICE...IT'S COMING FROM ME?

DON'T YOU RECOGNIZE IT? THAT'S THE TERMINATOR!

BEFORE STARFIRE TELLS YOU OF OUR RECENT ENCOUNTER, LET ME EXPLAIN...

YOU ARE SEARCHING FOR THE PLANS OF THE PROMETHIUM BOMB. I HAVE THEM.

AND I AM GOING TO BE SELLING THEM TO THE HIGHEST BIDDER--TOMORROW.

BUT, TO DO SO, I NEED TO PROVE THE EFFECTIVENESS OF THE WEAPON, WHICH IS WHERE YOU WILL COME IN.

YOU WILL BE MY TARGETS...AND WHEN YOU ARE DEAD, I WILL HAVE PROVEN THE POWER OF PROMETHIUM.

OF COURSE, I REALIZE YOU NEED A REASON TO VOLUNTEER ON THIS OBVIOUS SUICIDE MISSION.

THEREFORE, CYBORG-- ARE YOU LISTENING? --I HAVE KIDNAPPED A FRIEND OF YOURS ...SARAH SIMMS.

WHAT? H-H-HE'S-- HE'S GOT SARAH?

I'LL KILL HIM! I SWEAR I'LL KILL HIM!!

IF YOU FAIL TO SHOW UP, I'M AFRAID HER PRETTY FEATURES WILL BE REDUCED TO CINDER AND ASH.

I DO TRUST YOU WILL ALL ATTEND. DIRECTIONS WILL ARRIVE IN THE MORNING. I'LL SEE YOU ALL TOMORROW!

16

HE'S GOING *CRAZY!* I CAN BARELY HOLD HIM *STILL!*

BE *CALM,* MY FRIEND...LET YOUR ANGER FADE IN-TO ME...FEEL CALM...QUIET...

...I--I LIKE SARAH...SHE'S...THE FIRST *REAL* PERSON WHO DIDN'T LOOK AT ME AN' FLINCH...DIDN'T BACK AWAY...LIKED ME *DESPITE* WHAT I'VE BECOME.

IT'S NOT LIKE WE'RE *LOVERS* OR SOMETHING...JUST *FRIENDS*...AND THAT SCUM TERMINATOR HAD NO RIGHT TO *INVOLVE* HER IN THIS.

I DON'T *LIKE* THIS...EITHER *SHE* DIES OR *WE* DO. IT'S JUST WHAT HAPPENED TO THE *DOOM PATROL!*

IT'S NOT *FAIR* THAT IT'S HAPPENING *AGAIN!*

AND, AS THE EMPATH'S GENTLE WORDS HAVE THEIR EFFECT...

FOR EIGHTEEN HOURS THEY WAIT; THEY PLAN. THEN AS SOON AS DIRECTIONS ARRIVE AT TITANS TOWER, THEY ARE OFF...

...WE CAN'T GIVE IN TO THESE DEMANDS. IF WE DO, ANY JOKER CAN KIDNAP SOME-ONE AND ORDER US AROUND.

THEIR SUPERSONIC T-JET RIPS ACROSS THE AMERICAN SKIES, AND, LESS THAN TWO HOURS LATER, THEY ARE SOARING OVER THE MAGNIFICENCE OF THE GRAND CANYON...

GREENIE, WE'RE *NOT* GIVIN' IN ...JUST *BUYING TIME.*

REMEMBER, WE KNOW THE *SECRET* OF *PROMETHIUM*...AND WE'VE ALSO FIGURED OUT THE SECRET OF HIS *BOMB,* SO AS CYBORG *SAID,* WE MAY BE *PLAYING* HIS GAME...

...BUT WE'RE PLAYING WITH *OUR RULES.*

YEAH, I *KNOW* IT, ROB--BUT I STILL DON'T HAVE TO *LIKE* IT.

AND, AS THE TITANS EMERGE FROM THEIR JET...

SARAH! THANK GOD, YOU *OKAY?*

HE HASN'T *HURT* ME, VICTOR...BUT I *STILL* DON'T UNDERSTAND WHAT'S GOING ON!

WHAT'S *GOING ON,* BLONDIE, IS A LITTLE *TRADING.*

17

52

US FOR *YOU*, SARAH. SO, WE'RE *HERE*... LET HER *GO*.

FIRST, I WANT TO *CLEAR UP* A FEW THINGS... NO *GAMES*, NO *DOUBLE-CROSSES*. YOU BECOME *TARGETS* AT GROUND ZERO...

...OR MISS *SIMMS* HERE GETS A SECOND *MOUTH*.

WE'RE *HERE*. OBVIOUSLY, WE *AGREE*. LET HER *GO*, TERMINATOR.

SURE, SURE... *TAKE* HER.

H-HE GRABBED ME IN MY *APARTMENT*... BROUGHT ME *HERE*...

IT'S OKAY, BABE ...IT'S *OKAY*... YOU'LL BE *ALL RIGHT* NOW.

OH, VIC... THANK *GOD*.

THEY MOVE AWAY FROM THE *OTHERS*, TOWARD THE *T-JET*, WHERE...

YOU STAY *HERE*, INSIDE THE *JET*. ANYONE COMES AFTER YOU, PRESS THE *RED CONTROL BUTTON*.

THE AUTO-PILOT'LL *SCOOT* YOU BACK TO *NEW YORK*.

BUT WHAT ABOUT *YOU*, VIC?

I'LL BE *OKAY*... JUST DO AS I SAY. *PLEASE*.

THE GIRL IS *SAFE*. THERE IS NO LONGER ANY REASON TO GO ALONG WITH THIS *FARCE*.

WE'RE NOT *FIGHTING* HIM, KORY. WE GAVE OUR *WORD*.

SO? HE'S A *KILLER*. HE DOESN'T *DESERVE* COOPERATION.

PLEASE, KORY... THAT WILL BE *ENOUGH*.

EVENING, AND THE GRAND CANYON COMES ALIVE WITH THE SHIMMERING GLOW OF THE SETTING SUN...

...THAT'S *RIGHT*, FRIENDS AND BIDDERS: THE *PROMETHIUM BOMB*, BUILT FROM THE PLANS OF *PROJECT: PROMETHIUM*.

WHERE *MOST* BOMBS EXPEND THEIR DESTRUCTIVE ENERGIES IN *SECONDS*, THIS ONE CONTINUES TO *BUILD* ITS FORCE... *EXPAND* ITS DESTRUCTIVE RANGE...UNTIL YOU *SHUT IT DOWN*.

YOU WANT *POWER* IN YOUR COUNTRY, THIS WILL *GIVE* IT TO YOU. NOW, *I* COULD USE IT, BUT I'M A *SIMPLE* SOUL...

TO ME, POWER COMES *SECOND*... AFTER *GOLD*, AND IT'S FOR *GOLD* THAT I'M *AUCTIONING* OFF THESE PLANS.

18

WELL, NOW DON'T GO *SHY* ON ME, GENTLEMEN ... SHALL WE HEAR THE *OPENING BID?*

TERMINATOR, WE HAVE ALL PREVIOUSLY *AGREED--* WE WANT *PROOF* OF THIS WEAPON'S POWER.

YOU PROMISED US A *DEMONSTRATION.*

AND THE *TERMINATOR* IS A MAN OF HIS *WORD.* *GROUND ZERO* HAS ALREADY BEEN *SELECTED* ...AND WE EVEN HAVE *HUMAN TARGETS* SO YOU CAN OBSERVE THE *EFFECTS.*

PLEASE *NOTE,* THEY ARE THE NEW *TEEN TITANS,* AND ONCE THEY ARE *DEAD,* MY CONTRACT WITH YOU *H.I.V.E.* PEOPLE WILL BE *COMPLETED.*

ANYWAY, GENTLEMEN, THE MOMENT YOU HAVE BEEN *WAITING* FOR IS *AT HAND.*

AND PLEASE REMEMBER, BIDDING MUST BE COMPLETED WITH GREAT *HASTE*...

"THE AMERICAN AUTHORITIES WILL SURELY INVESTIGATE THE EXPLOSION. THUS WE HAVE LESS THAN *FIFTEEN* MINUTES IN WHICH TO CONCLUDE OUR BUSINESS.

"SETTLE BACK. THE FUN IS JUST *BEGINNING.* I DON'T KNOW ABOUT YOU...

"...BUT, FRANKLY I CAN'T WAIT!"

19

OBSERVE, FOR IT HAPPENS ALL AT ONCE:

A GREAT GREY CLOUD RISES AMIDST A COLUMN OF LIVING FIRE.

THE DESERT SANDS, TOO, COME ALIVE, BLAZING WITH THE HEAT OF A HUNDRED SUNS,

THEN THE DEAFENING ROAR OF A THUNDERCLAP: ONE MILLION DECIBELS OF EAR-SHATTERING AGONY.

THE IMPENETRABLE DARKNESS, THE INSUFFERABLE HEAT AND FIRE, THE MIND-NUMBING NOISE... IT MUST HAVE BEEN THIS WAY AT THE VERY DAWN OF CREATION...

BUT, CREATION CONTINUED AND EVOLVED. THIS, HOWEVER, WITHERS AND QUICKLY DIES...

...WITH ONLY THE RIPPLES OF A GLASSY DESERT TO MARK THAT IT HAD EVER BEEN.

KIND OF SHAKES YOUR **BOOTS**, DOESN'T IT?

NOW THEN, THE **BIDDING**?

THE H.I.V.E. OPENS THIS BID, TERMINATOR...

...WITH THE LIVES OF OUR **COMPETITORS**!

IF THERE ARE NOW NO **OTHER** BIDS, IT SEEMS WE HAVE **WON**.

YOU MAY KEEP THEIR **GOLD**, TERMINATOR...WE WILL KEEP THE **MONEY** WE BROUGHT WITH US.

WE BELIEVE THAT IS RATHER **EQUITABLE**, ISN'T IT?

20

NOW, TERMINATOR, GIVE US THE *PLANS*...

WAIT! H-HE'S G-GONE!

BUT NOT *FORGOTTEN!*

SO, YOU BOYS WANTED ME TO *GIVE IT* TO YOU, HUH?

SURE, FELLAS, I'D BE *GLAD* TO!

THIS WORKED OUT JUST *PERFECT*. Y'SEE, I KNEW YOU'D *DOUBLE-CROSS* THE OTHERS...

...WHICH WON'T EXACTLY *ENDEAR* THE *H.I.V.E.* TO THE CRIMINAL WORLD.

I ALSO WANTED *BACK* AT YOU FOR THE WAY YOU SUCKERED ME INTO THAT *CONTRACT*.

YOU CREEPS HELPED KILL OFF MY *KID*.

HE MAY'VE BEEN A *MORON*, BUT HE WAS *MY* MORON.*

WELL, NOW I GOT *YOUR* MONEY, TOO. NOT *BAD* FOR AN AFTERNOON'S WORK.

*TEEN TITANS #2. --LEN.

BUT HOW MUCH CAN YOU *SPEND* FROM BEHIND BARS, TERMINATOR?

WELL, WELL... I REALLY SHOULD BE *SURPRISED*, SHOULDN'T I?

REALLY SHOULD SHOUT OUT -- "THE TITANS-- *ALIVE!* BUT *HOW?*"

ONLY SOMEHOW I'M *NOT* SHOCKED. HOW'D YOU *DO* IT, BUDDIES?

IT WASN'T ALL THAT *DIFFICULT* ...ONCE DAYTON INDUSTRIES TOLD US THE *TRUTH* ABOUT PROMETHIUM.

WITH THAT AND SOME *OTHER* INFO WE HAD... WE WERE ABLE TO PIECE TOGETHER WHAT *REALLY* HAPPENED.

21

"WE WERE READY AS SOON AS THE BOMB WAS DROPPED.
"RAVEN CREATED CLOUD COVER WHILE KID FLASH USED HIS SUPER-SPEED TO ZOOM UPWARD TO THE BOMB. AT THE SAME TIME, STARFIRE USED HER STARBOLTS ... SETTING UP FLAMES WHICH SPREAD ACROSS THE DESERT.
"YOU SEE, WE WERE DUPLICATING THE EFFECTS OF THE BOMB... ONE BY ONE... SMOKE, FIRE...
"CYBORG USED ONE OF HIS HAND ATTACHMENTS TO CREATE A SONIC THUNDER-CLAP WHILE I DIRECTED ALL THE ACTIONS...
"SPECIFICALLY, KID FLASH. YOUR BOMB USED FISSIONABLE MATERIALS--IT EXPLODES ONLY WHEN THE MATERIALS MEET.
"KID FLASH'S VIBRATIONS PREVENTED THEIR COMING TOGETHER...
"TURNING A POTENTIALLY DANGEROUS DEVICE INTO A DUD WHICH WONDER GIRL WAS BRACED TO CATCH AS IT FELL.
22
"IT TOOK ALMOST ONE MINUTE FOR THE SMOKE TO CLEAR, BUT, BY THE TIME IT DID, WE HAD GONE.
"YOUR BIG MISTAKE, TERMINATOR, WAS STEALING THE PLANS FOR SOMETHING THAT HAD NOT BEEN PERFECTED.
WE KNEW YOUR PROMETHIUM BOMB WAS A PHONY... AND WE REASONED THAT IT WAS YOU WHO STOLE THAT NAVY ATOM BOMB.
AND ONCE WE KNEW THAT, WE KNEW HOW TO COUNTER YOUR ATTACK.
SO YOU KNEW MY WHOLE AUCTION GIMMICK WAS PHONY, EH? CLEVER ...BUT, FORTUNATELY, PAL, SO AM I.
SAY HELLO TO MY MERCENARY ARMY... THEY'RE JUST DYING TO KILL YOU!
SEE, PAL, I HAD 'EM READY... JUST FOR PROTECTION.
YOU NEVER LEARN, DO YOU?
TITANS--LET'S MOVE IT!

IT BEGINS WITH AN EXPLOSION OF VIOLENCE.

EACH TITAN MOVES INTO ACTION WITHIN SECONDS.

23

EACH TITAN KNOWS EXACTLY WHAT MUST BE DONE.

OOPS, TERMY'S TAKING IT ON THE LAM... GETTING OUT WHILE THE GETTING'S GOOD.

NO ONE ELSE SEEMS TO SEE HIM, SO I GUESS HE'S MINE.

WANNA PAY YA BACK ANYWAY FOR RECREAT-ING THE PATROL'S FAREWELL.

'SIDES, YOU'LL PROBABLY SURVIVE MY GOING AFTER YA. IF CYBORG GOT YA, YOU'D BE INSTANT DOG MEAT!

WHICH IS A-OK WITH YOURS TRULY. HEY, UGLY... THE DANCE ISN'T OVER... IT'S NOT TIME TO LEAVE.

DON'T BELIEVE IT, SHAPE-CHANGER... I'M NOT THE BEST THERE IS BECAUSE OF MY LOOKS!

MY REFLEXES HAVE BEEN SCIENTIFICALLY INCREASED ...MY STRENGTH IS THAT OF TEN MEN...

SO'S YOUR *BREATH*, BUT WHO'S *COMPLAININ'*?

LOOK, WHY DON'TCHA MAKE IT *EASY*? GIVE UP AND MAYBE, JUST *MAYBE*, THEY'LL LET YOU *OUT*-- IN *FIFTY-SIXTY* YEARS.

NEVER, CRETIN! NEITHER *YOU* NOR ANY OF YOUR FRIENDS CAN *STOP* ME. I'M MORE THAN A MATCH FOR *ALL* OF YOU.

IT ENDS WITH THE MUFFLED FALL OF BEATEN *FOES*.

EACH *TITAN* HAS PROVEN HIMSELF *WORTHY*.

WOK

DON'TCHA EVER GET TIRED OF BEING *WRONG* ALL THE TIME?

LOOK, MAYBE YOU DON'T KNOW THE *WORDS* TO SAY. HOWZABOUT-- "I *SURRENDER*." MEBBE "*UNCLE!*" "*GIVE!*" "*WHITE FLAG!*" ANY OF THOSE WILL *DO*.

C'MON, *SAY* IT... IT'S *EASY*. I... *S-U-R-R-E-N-D-E-R!* ONLY FOUR LITTLE *SYLLABLES*.

CHANGELING, THAT WAS YOUR FINAL *JOKE*. YOUR LIFE IS NOW *OVER!*

EACH *TITAN* HAD DONE WHAT HAD TO BE DONE.

59

WHILE, ELSEWHERE...

ANOTHER BATTLE ENDS AS WELL...

BUT ITS RESULTS ARE NOT NEARLY SO PLEASANT.

GAR LOGAN SCREAMS...

...AND WHEN THE SCREAMING STOPS, HE FALLS.

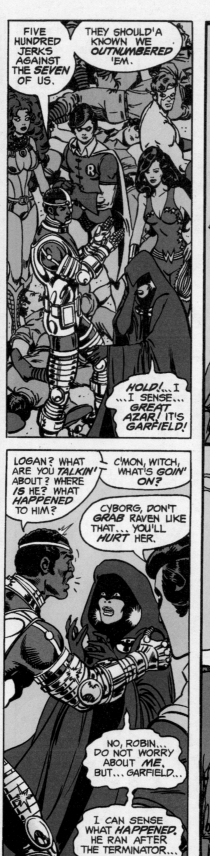

FIVE HUNDRED JERKS AGAINST THE *SEVEN* OF US.

THEY SHOULD'A KNOWN WE *OUTNUMBERED* 'EM.

HOLD!... I ...I SENSE... *GREAT AZAR!* IT'S *GARFIELD!*

LOGAN? WHAT ARE YOU *TALKIN'* ABOUT? WHERE *IS* HE? WHAT *HAPPENED* TO HIM?

C'MON, WITCH, WHAT'S *GOIN'* ON?

CYBORG, DON'T *GRAB* RAVEN LIKE THAT... YOU'LL *HURT* HER.

NO, ROBIN... DO NOT WORRY ABOUT *ME*, BUT... *GARFIELD*...

I CAN SENSE WHAT *HAPPENED*. HE RAN AFTER THE TERMINATOR...

...BARELY *BREATHING.*

N...*NO!* GOD, I...IT'S TOO LATE... *TOO LATE.*

THERE WAS A *FIGHT*... TERMINATOR *SHOT* GARFIELD WITH ... SOMETHING...

GARFIELD LOGAN...THE CHANGELING... HE'S--*DEAD!!*

OH, GREAT AZAR *HELP* US... I...I SENSE GARFIELD LYING THERE... HIS PULSE RATE... *SLOWING*...

DO WE REALLY HAVE TO SAY IT? TO BE CONTINUED!

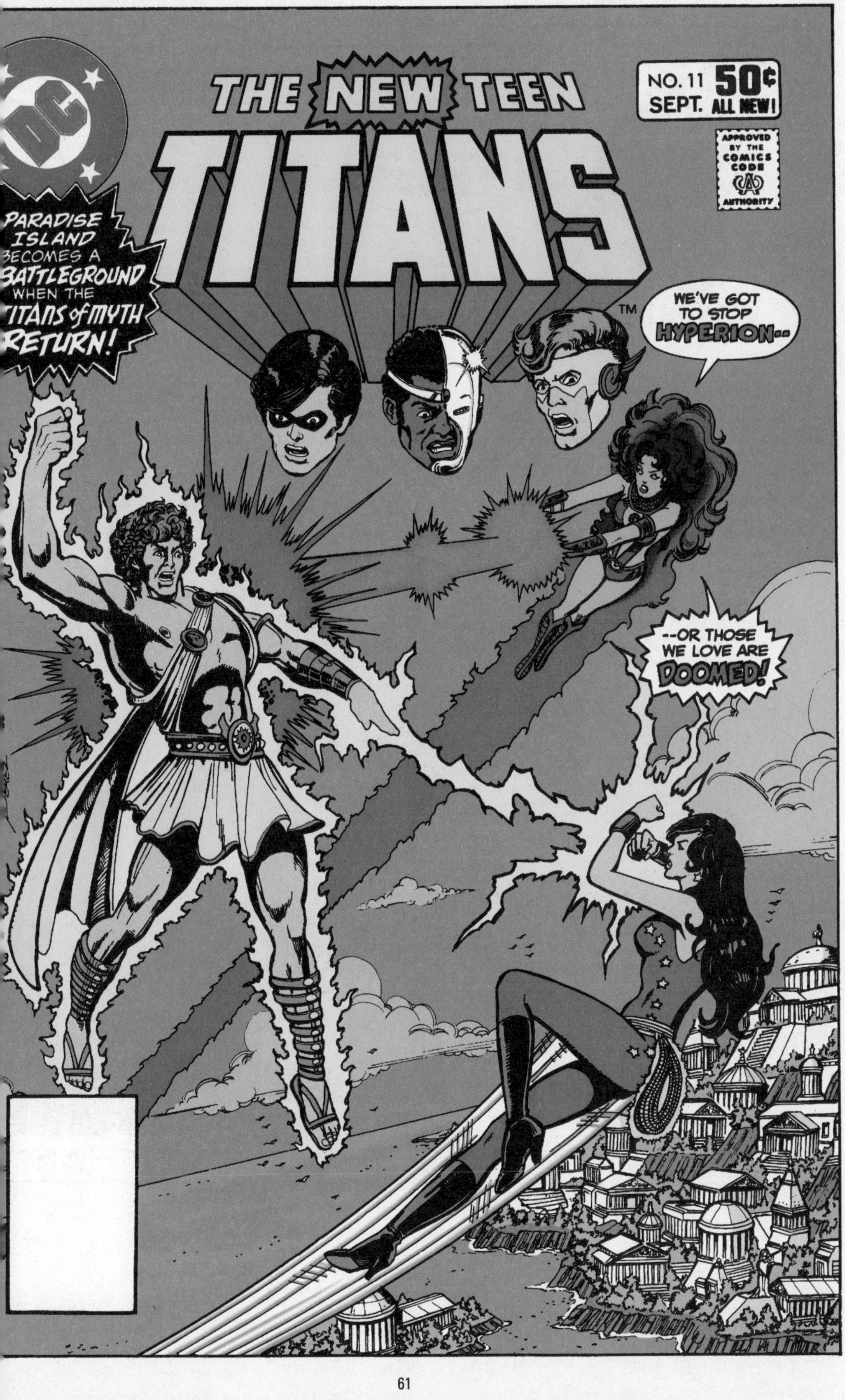
THE NEW TEEN TITANS
NO. 11 50¢ SEPT. ALL NEW!
APPROVED BY THE COMICS CODE AUTHORITY
PARADISE ISLAND BECOMES A BATTLEGROUND WHEN THE TITANS of MYTH RETURN!
WE'VE GOT TO STOP HYPERION--
--OR THOSE WE LOVE ARE DOOMED!

THE TITANS' T-JET STREAKS ACROSS THE AMERICAN PLAINS THEN ARCS HIGH OVER *NEW YORK CITY,* SETTING A FAST AND FURIOUS COURSE DUE EAST.

C'MON! *HURRY* IT, MAN. WE AIN'T GOT MUCH *TIME!*

GAR'S *DYIN'* BACK HERE!

YOU THINK I DON'T *KNOW* THAT, VIC? I'M ON *FULL-THROTTLE!*

PARADISE ISLAND: LEGENDARY HOME OF THE AMAZONS. THERE LIES THE ONLY POSSIBLE SALVATION FOR GARFIELD LOGAN, ALSO KNOWN AS THE CHANGELING. BUT THERE ALSO LIES POSSIBLE DESTRUCTION, NOT ONLY FOR THE HUMAN RACE, BUT FOR THE VERY GODS THEMSELVES!

WHEN TITANS CLASH

AN OVERUSED TITLE, PERHAPS. BUT THIS TIME IT'S MEANT IN *EARNEST!*

MARV WOLFMAN & GEORGE PÉREZ . ROMEO TANGHAL . COSTANZA . ADRIENNE ROY . LEN WEIN
writer-co-creators-artist   embellisher   letterer   colorist   editor

IC'S FALLING TO PIECES BACK THERE. DIDN'T KNOW HE AND GAR WERE SO CLOSE. THEY SEEM LIKE SUCH *OPPOSITES!*

THEY ARE, AND MAYBE THAT'S *WHY*. THEY *COMPLEMENT* EACH OTHER. EACH ONE'S WEAKNESSES ARE THE OTHER'S STRENGTHS!

BESIDES, WHAT IS IT THEY SAY ABOUT OPPOSITES *ATTRACTING...?*

...YOU'RE *SURE* OF THAT, RAVEN? HE'S STILL ALIVE?

HIS *HEART* DOESN'T BEAT, BUT HIS *BRAIN* STILL PULSES WITH LIFE.

AND HE'LL *STAY* THAT WAY, VIC -- IN THIS *SUSPENDED ANIMATION CHAMBER* WE BORROWED FROM *S.T.A.R.* LABS.

BUT IF HIS HEART'S STOPPED, HOW CAN WE BRING 'IM *BACK?*

GOD, I NEVER REALLY THOUGHT ABOUT ONE OF US ACTUALLY *DYIN'!* NEVER THOUGHT US *SUPERHERO* TYPES HAD ANY PROBLEMS LIKE THAT!

OUR ONE CHANCE, VIC -- IS THE AMAZONS' *PURPLE RAY...* IT WAS FIRST CREATED BY *WONDER WOMAN* HERSELF,* THEN MODIFIED, IMPROVED UPON BY PAULA VON GUNTHER, THE AMAZONS' GREATEST *SCIENTIST.*

* FIRST SHOWN IN *WONDER WOMAN #1.* --LEARNED LEN.

"PURPLE RAY"? IT SOUNDS LIKE SOMETHIN' OUTTA *STAR TREK!*

BUT IT'S NOT *FICTION*, VIC, AND IT'S NOT A *PANACEA.* THE RAY'S *FAILED* AS OFTEN AS IT'S *WORKED.*

IT COMES DOWN TO *THIS*, VIC -- IT'S OUR ONLY *HOPE...* AND FOR IT TO WORK, WE'VE GOT TO *PRAY!*

2

WHAT REALLY RUBS ME *WRONG* IS THAT THE TERMINATOR *ESCAPED* US AFTER SHOOTING GAR.

DON'T WORRY, WALLY. WHEN THIS IS *OVER*, WE'LL *FIND* HIM!

HOLD IT, DICK-- LOOK *AHEAD*! THAT STRANGE *CLOUD-BANK*--

AND NOW MY INSTRUMENTS HAVE GONE DEAD! *DONNA?*

DON'T *WORRY* ABOUT IT, DICK... THIS IS THE WAY THROUGH THE *BERMUDA TRIANGLE* TO PARADISE ISLAND. WE'LL BE PERFECTLY *SAFE.*

THE CLOUDS WERE PUT HERE BY THE GODDESS ATHENA TO PROTECT THE AMAZONS FROM *MAN'S WORLD!*

"MAN'S WORLD"? YOU GIRLS GOT A *HATE* ON FOR MEN, OR SOMETHIN'?

NOT *HATE*, VICTOR-- *FEAR!* MEN *ENSLAVED* THEIR WOMEN FOR TOO MANY YEARS.

PARADISE ISLAND IS A PLACE WHERE THE AMAZONS CAN LIVE *WITHOUT* MEN... AND LIVE IN *PEACE!*

A PLACE WHERE *SCIENCE* IS DEDICATED TO *LIFE*, NOT TO WAR!

WE'RE COMING THROUGH THE *CLOUDS* NOW... AND MY INSTRUMENTATION IS *RETURNING!*

IT'S BEEN SO LONG SINCE I'VE BEEN HERE, BUT ALREADY I FEEL *EXCITED!*

THERE-- DO YOU *SEE* IT-- HOME!

HOME--? THAT AIN'T NO *HOME*, GIRL! THAT'S *DISNEYLAND GONE MAD!*

THIS IS *INCREDIBLE*, DONNA. THE SKIES ARE SO *BLUE* HERE, THE AIR--EVEN THROUGH THE TITANS' JET-- FEELS SO *WARM!*

NOT SINCE I WAS TAKEN FROM *TAMARAN* HAVE I SEEN ANYTHING THAT COMES SO CLOSE TO *PARADISE* ITSELF!

PRETTY OR NOT, GIRL-- I DON'T LIKE LEAVIN' GAR *BEHIND.*

I'VE TOLD YOU, VICTOR, *MEN* CANNOT SET FOOT UPON PARADISE ISLAND--NOT WITHOUT ALL THE AMAZONS INSTANTLY *LOSING* THEIR POWERS AND IMMORTALITY.

THAT WAS THE DECREE OF THE *GODS...* AND IT CAN-NOT BE *DISOBEYED!*

YOU'LL TAKE CARE OF HIM, WON'T YOU?

DO YOU REALLY HAVE TO *ASK?*

HE MAY GET ON MY *NERVES* AT TIMES, BUT I *LIKE* GAR VERY MUCH.

HE'S A FRIEND, A *GOOD* FRIEND, AND I'LL DO EVERYTHING I *CAN.*

KORY, YOU TAKE GAR AND *FLY* HIM DOWN... MAKE CERTAIN HE DOESN'T TOUCH THE *GROUND.*

I UNDERSTAND, DONNA.

LET'S GO THEN. THE FASTER WE *MOVE,* THE BETTER OUR CHANCE FOR *SUCCESS!*

DONNA TROY, WONDER GIRL, GLIDES ON THE AIR CURRENTS CROSSING PARADISE ISLAND--WHILE STARFIRE, PROPELLED BY SOLAR POWER, FLIES OF HER OWN ACCORD...

AS FOR RAVEN, SHE MOVES AS ONLY A MYSTIC CAN...

HOLA, DAUGHTER!

IT HAS BEEN *TOO* LONG!

I MISS YOU *ALWAYS,* MOTHER, BUT--

I KNOW...YOU BELONG IN *MAN'S WORLD.* ONCE, THOUGH, I WISH ONE OF MY DAUGHTERS WOULD *STAY* HERE. THERE ARE TIMES I GROW *LONELY.*

MOTHER... IS PAULA *READY* FOR US?

SHE *IS!*

OF COURSE, THERE CAN BE NO *DELAY.* COME...EVERYTHING HAS BEEN *PREPARED.*

THERE THEY *GO,* AND HERE WE STAY. MAN, I FEEL SO BLASTED *USELESS!*

IF ANYTHIN' *HAPPENS* TO THAT WALKIN' SALAD...

YOU KNOW THEY'LL DO WHAT THEY *CAN,* VIC...JUST AS WE'VE GOT *OUR* WORK TO DO.

GAR'S BEEN SEARCHING FOR HIS ADOPTIVE FATHER, *STEVE DAYTON,* AND DAYTON'S BEEN SEARCHING FOR THE ONES WHO KILLED HIS *WIFE--* AND DESTROYED THE *DOOM PATROL!*

IT'S ABOUT TIME WE *HELPED* GAR... AND IT'S ABOUT TIME WE DID SOMETHING TO *FIND* THOSE KILLERS!

BESIDES, SUPERGIRL'S *ALSO* WORKING OUT OF NEW YORK THESE DAYS-- SO, THE CITY SHOULD DO WELL ENOUGH WITHOUT *US* AROUND.

THE T-JET ROCKETS OFF TOWARD AFRICA...

WHILE... FAR BELOW THE MYSTICALLY-ENSHROUDED LAND OF PARADISE ISLAND, THERE IS A WORLD MORE *STRANGE* THAN ANY WORLD EVER *SPECULATED* UPON BY MAN...

IT IS A WORLD DARK AND TAINTED WITH THE SOULS OF THOSE TWICE DAMNED.

A WORLD OF INCALCULABLE MADNESS, A WORLD OF IMPOSSIBLE EVIL. IT IS A PURGATORY BEYOND ALL PURGATORIES...THE GREATEST HELL OF ALL.

THIS IS A WORLD OF BURNING BRIMSTONE AND SULPHUR, SPOKEN OF ONLY IN MUTED WHISPERS-- EVEN BY THE GODS THEMSELVES.

THIS IS TARTARUS... A LAND FEARED EVEN BY THE DEAD.!!

5

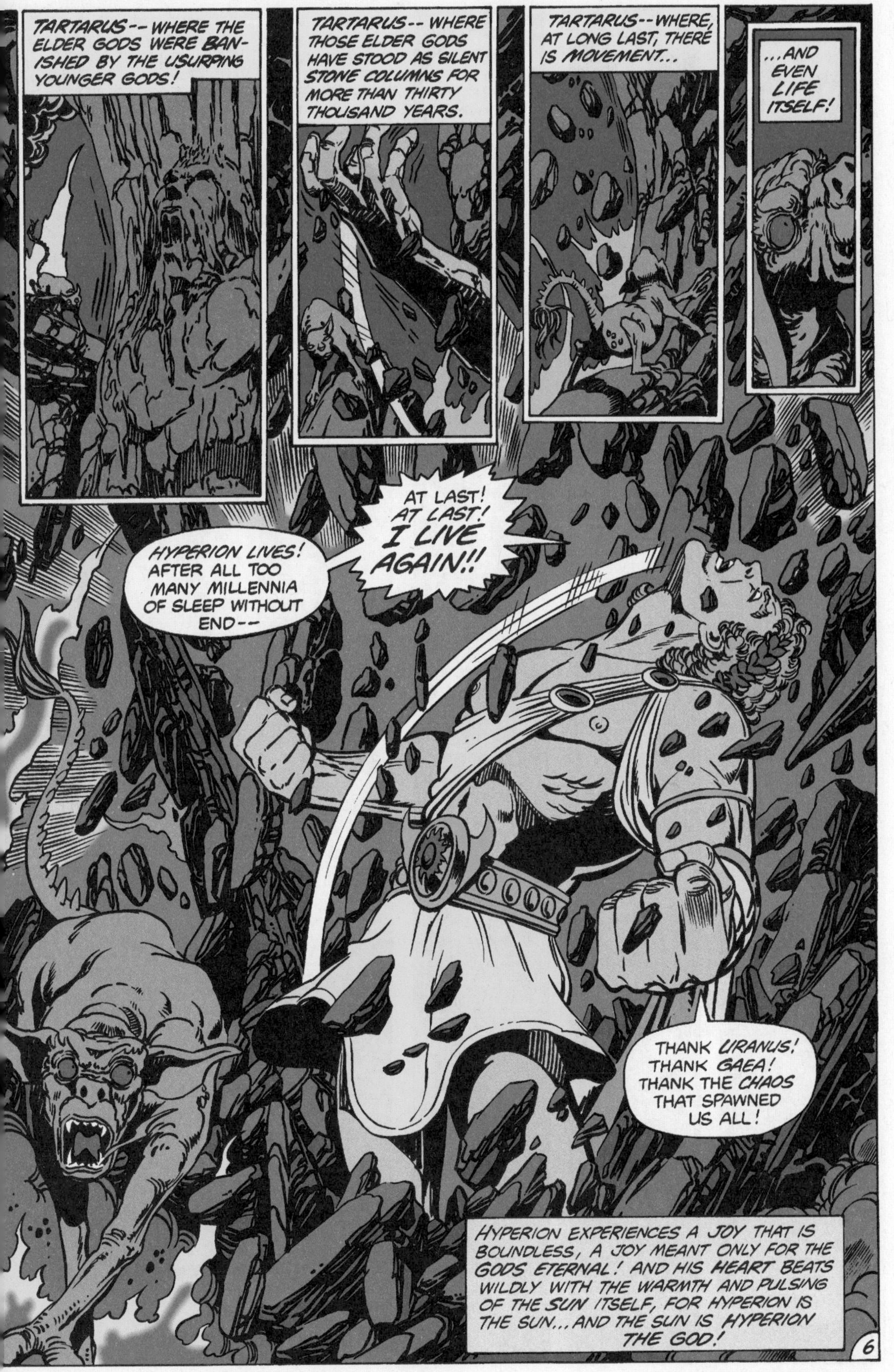
TARTARUS-- WHERE THE ELDER GODS WERE BANISHED BY THE USURPING YOUNGER GODS!
TARTARUS-- WHERE THOSE ELDER GODS HAVE STOOD AS SILENT STONE COLUMNS FOR MORE THAN THIRTY THOUSAND YEARS.
TARTARUS--WHERE, AT LONG LAST, THERE IS MOVEMENT...
...AND EVEN LIFE ITSELF!
AT LAST! AT LAST! I LIVE AGAIN!!
HYPERION LIVES! AFTER ALL TOO MANY MILLENNIA OF SLEEP WITHOUT END--
THANK URANUS! THANK GAEA! THANK THE CHAOS THAT SPAWNED US ALL!
HYPERION EXPERIENCES A JOY THAT IS BOUNDLESS, A JOY MEANT ONLY FOR THE GODS ETERNAL! AND HIS HEART BEATS WILDLY WITH THE WARMTH AND PULSING OF THE SUN ITSELF, FOR HYPERION IS THE SUN... AND THE SUN IS HYPERION THE GOD!
6

I LIVE, YES..., BUT HOW *USEFUL* AM I WHEN I AM SO TERRIBLY *WEAK*?

I NEED *STRENGTH*! I NEED MY POWER *RENEWED*!

I, WHO AM THE LIVING *PERSONIFICATION* OF THE SUN ITSELF MUST BATHE ANEW IN ITS *LIFE-GIVING RAYS.*

I MUST LET ITS WARMTH *REKINDLE* MY BEING.

GAEA, MY MOTHER, YOUR MIGHTY SON RETURNS TO THE *SKIES!* OH, HOW I FEEL *RE-NEWED!* OH, HOW MY *POWER* RUSHES TO ME ONCE MORE!

CHAOS BE *PRAISED!* GAEA AND URANUS BE *LOVED!* THE SWEET BREATH OF *LIFE* THAT YOU BESTOWED UPON THIS GRAND WORLD EARTH IS *MINE* AGAIN!

AND THE AIR IS STILL AS SWEET, STILL AS FULL OF *HOPE!*

BEHOLD, ALL WHO CAN SEE MY FORM AND HEAR MY WORDS-- *BEHOLD!* HYPERION IS *FREE,* AND HYPERION IS ONCE MORE A GOD AMONGST GODS!

7

THE AIR WITHIN PAULA'S LABORATORY CRACKLES WITH AN ELECTRONIC HUM. THEN...

OUR PURPLE RAY IS *SOLAR-POWERED*... AND SOMETHING IS DISTURBING... NO, *INTERCEPTING* THE SOLAR COLLECTORS.

YOUR *PURPLE RAY*, PAULA... IT SHUT ITSELF *OFF!*

WHAT'S *GOING ON* HERE?

QUEEN HIPPOLYTE, PLEASE COME HERE--*LOOK!*

INTERCEPTING? OUT THERE, BUT-- *HOLD!* DO YOU SEE IT, DAUGHTER?

I *DO*, MOTHER, ALTHOUGH IT'S SO *FAINT*. IT'S A *SILHOUETTE*-- OF A *MAN?*-- FLYING BEFORE THE *SUN?*

IS IT *POSSIBLE?*

IT IS *THERE!*

THEN THERE IS ONLY ONE THING I CAN *DO*-- AND THAT'S *INVESTIGATE!*

IF WHOEVER THAT IS IS *FRIENDLY*, I'LL ASK HIM TO *MOVE!*

IF HE PROVES A *THREAT*, HE'LL RUE THE DAY HE ENTERED OUR *SKIES!*

IT *IS* A MAN...OBLIVIOUS TO MY *PRESENCE* HERE.

BUT NOT FOR *LONG!*

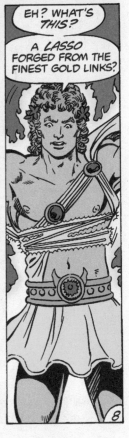

EH? WHAT'S *THIS?*

A *LASSO* FORGED FROM THE FINEST GOLD LINKS?

8

AND *THERE*... THE ONE WHO *WIELDS* IT!

CHAOS BE PRAISED! SHE'S A *WOMAN*, AND A *BEAUTIFUL* ONE AT THAT!

WELL, YOU'VE SNARED YOURSELF A *GOD*, MY DEAR...

AND NOW THAT YOU *HAVE* ME...

...DO YOU INTEND TO *HAVE* YOUR WAY WITH YOUR PRIZE?

HERA HELP ME! I SHOULD BE *CONTROLLING* YOU--HOW COULD...

HERA? YOU CALL UPON THAT UPSTART *CHILD* FOR HELP? WHY, YOU DON'T NEED THAT TRAITRESS...

NOT WHEN YOU CAN HAVE *HYPERION* HIMSELF!

MFMMFM FFMM

SHE IS *STARTLED*, THIS AMAZON...

BUT, BECAUSE SHE *IS* AN AMAZON, TRAINED FROM CHILDHOOD IN THE ART OF WARFARE, SHE REACTS...

...INSTANTLY, TERRIBLY!

GET YOUR HANDS OFF ME!

WHOMP!

OH, NO-- HE'S FALLING TO THE *ISLAND*... BUT, IF HE TOUCHES *GROUND*...

I CAN'T LET HIM FALL... I'VE GOT TO *SAVE* HIM!

WHAT? HIS EYES ARE OPEN...

AND THEY ARE ONLY FOR *YOU*, MY MAGNIFICENT MORTAL!

WHEN A *GOD* FEELS LOVE, THE WORLD BURNS BRIGHTER THAN THE *SUN* ITSELF!

GREAT ZEUS! HE'S GLOWING SO BRIGHTLY... *CAN'T SEE!*

9

THROUGHOUT TIME THE GODS HAVE TAKEN *MORTALS* TO LOVE, MORTALS WHOSE *BEAUTY* TRANSCENDS THE BOUNDARIES 'TWEEN GOD AND MAN.

AND ALWAYS HAVE THE MORTALS RESPONDED *IN KIND...*

FOR WHO CAN DENY A *GOD?*

WHO CAN RESIST THE *INNER LIGHT* THAT MAKES US SO MUCH *MORE* THAN MAN?

WE ARE GODS. INDEED, I AM A GOD *ABOVE* GODS...AND I CALL FOR *YOU...*

AND I *WANT YOU...*

AND, I WILL NOT BE *CONTENT* SO LONG AS A CREATURE AS *BEAUTIFUL* AS YOU, AS *MAGNIFICENT* AS YOU, IS NOT TOTALLY MINE TO *POSSESS.*

COME TO ME, JOIN WITH ME, TAKE MY HAND AND *KNOW* SUCH THINGS AS FEW *OTHER* MORTALS HAVE BEEN FORTUNATE ENOUGH TO *SHARE.*

YOU WILL BE *FULFILLED* IN WAYS NO MERE MORTAL COULD ASPIRE TO.

SHE IS ENTHRALLED, IS WONDER GIRL, ENTHRALLED BY AN ETERNAL POWER AND MAGNIFICENCE BEYOND ANY SHE HAS EVER KNOWN.

AND SHE FINDS SHE CANNOT *DENY HER* EMOTIONS, OR DENY WHAT SUDDENLY MEANS SO *VERY MUCH* TO HER.

WHILE...

LOOK...DONNA IS IN *TROUBLE.* KORIAND'R--?

TROUBLE? IT LOOKS TO ME LIKE THEY'RE IN *LOVE!*

71

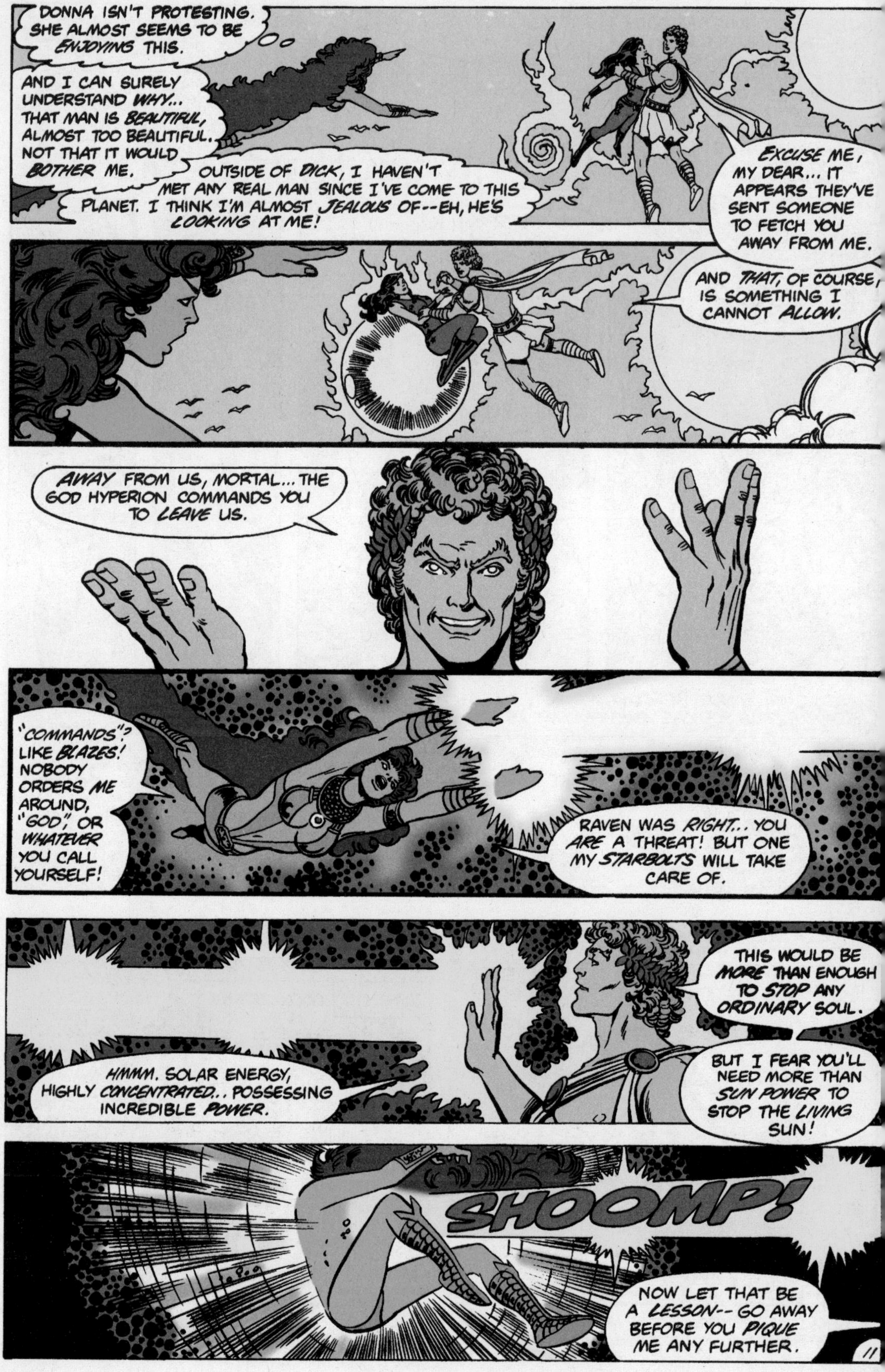
DONNA ISN'T PROTESTING. SHE ALMOST SEEMS TO BE ENJOYING THIS.
AND I CAN SURELY UNDERSTAND WHY... THAT MAN IS BEAUTIFUL, ALMOST TOO BEAUTIFUL. NOT THAT IT WOULD BOTHER ME.
OUTSIDE OF DICK, I HAVEN'T MET ANY REAL MAN SINCE I'VE COME TO THIS PLANET. I THINK I'M ALMOST JEALOUS OF--EH, HE'S LOOKING AT ME!
EXCUSE ME, MY DEAR... IT APPEARS THEY'VE SENT SOMEONE TO FETCH YOU AWAY FROM ME.
AND THAT, OF COURSE, IS SOMETHING I CANNOT ALLOW.
AWAY FROM US, MORTAL... THE GOD HYPERION COMMANDS YOU TO LEAVE US.
"COMMANDS"? LIKE BLAZES! NOBODY ORDERS ME AROUND, "GOD," OR WHATEVER YOU CALL YOURSELF!
RAVEN WAS RIGHT.. YOU ARE A THREAT! BUT ONE MY STARBOLTS WILL TAKE CARE OF.
HMMM. SOLAR ENERGY, HIGHLY CONCENTRATED.. POSSESSING INCREDIBLE POWER.
THIS WOULD BE MORE THAN ENOUGH TO STOP ANY ORDINARY SOUL.
BUT I FEAR YOU'LL NEED MORE THAN SUN POWER TO STOP THE LIVING SUN!
SHOOMP!
NOW LET THAT BE A LESSON-- GO AWAY BEFORE YOU PIQUE ME ANY FURTHER.
11

STUNNED, STAR-FIRE FALLS LIKE A LEADEN WEIGHT...

WHILE ON THE SHORES OF PARADISE ISLAND, AMAZONS AT THE READY MOVE QUICKLY INTO ACTION...

CYRENE, LEDA-- YOU RESCUE THE OUT-WORLDER! TARPEIA, YOU ALERT OUR QUEEN!

ATHENA PRESERVE US, CHRYSE! LOOK! THE AIR-WALKER IS PREPARING FOR BATTLE!

HYPERION, IF THAT IS TRULY YOUR NAME-- RELEASE YOUR MENTAL HOLD ON THAT GIRL! SHE BELONGS TO US!

DOES SHE NOW? DO YOU HAVE OWNERSHIP PAPERS, WRAITH?

CAN YOU PROVE SHE IS YOUR SLAVE?

AND, EVEN IF YOU COULD, DO YOU BELIEVE A TITAN ACCEPTS MEANING-LESS CONTRACTS BETWEEN MORTALS AS GOSPEL?

HIS EYES GLOW WITH GOLDEN LIGHT; GREAT BEAMS SHIMMER FORTH...

AND, IN SECONDS, THEY DO THEIR AWFUL WORK...

AARGHHH!

WHAT DID YOU DO TO HER, HYPERION? SHE WAS MY FRIEND.

SHE IS NOT HURT, AT LEAST NOT PERMANENTLY ...BUT IT WILL BE A LONG WHILE BEFORE SHE ATTACKS ME AGAIN, EH?

BUT FORGET HER--AND FORGET YOUR MORTAL PAST. FOR NOW, YOU WALK WITH HYPERION...

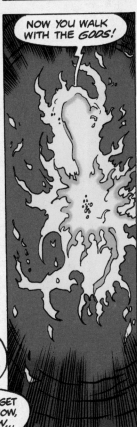

NOW YOU WALK WITH THE GODS!

MY STRENGTH IS FULL ONCE MORE, AND I HAVE MY MISSION BEFORE ME. COME, AND TOGETHER WE SHALL FIND GLORY!

IT IS AN ALL-ENVELOPING FLAME WHICH CONSUMES THEM. A FLAME WHICH BURNS BRIGHTLY FOR A MOMENT, HOLDS A MOM-ENT MORE, THEN IS GONE, TAKING WITH IT WONDER GIRL AND THE MAN-GOD CALLED HYPERION!

12

BUT, FAR BELOW...

UNHHH! NEVER HAVE I *FELT* ANYTHING LIKE THIS *BEFORE!*

TO SUMMON MY SHATTERED *SOUL-SELF* IS PURE *AGONY!*

KORIAND'R, ARE YOU *ALL RIGHT?*

MY INSIDES FEEL AS IF THEY ARE *BURNING.*

WHILE...

CAN HE *TRULY* BE *HYPERION* AS HE CLAIMS?

A *TITAN* RETURNED TO EARTH? IF THAT IS SO, PANTHIA, THEN I FEAR THE HORRORS WE HAVE JUST *SEEN...*

...WILL *PALE* BEFORE WHAT IS YET TO COME!

THE WARMTH OF PARADISE ISLAND *FADES* HERE DEEP IN THESE SHADOW-SHROUDED PITS. INDEED, ANY WARMTH THAT IS FELT AT ALL COMES NOT FROM THE SUN *ABOVE,* BUT FROM THE STYGIAN PURGATORY THAT AWAITS THESE TWO FAR, FAR *BELOW...*

YOU REALLY *ARE* HYPERION? YOU'RE ONE OF THE ORIGINAL *TITANS!?*

INDEED, MY DEAREST ONE...ONE OF *TWELVE,* I AM.

INDEED, TARTARUS HAS BEEN OUR *PRISON* FOR THIRTY THOUSAND OF YOUR YEARS...BUT *DEAD?* NAY, A TITAN CAN-NOT BE *SLAIN*--

--NOT EVEN BY THOSE TRAITOR GODS WHO WERE OUR *CHILDREN!*

BUT, AT LAST, I WAS *FREED,* AND NOW YOU AND I WILL *FREE* MY BROTHER AND SISTER *TITANS!*

THEN, TOGETHER, WE WILL MARCH INTO *OLYMPUS* AND TAKE THAT REALM AS *OUR OWN!*

INDEED, MY DEAREST ONE...ONE OF *TWELVE,* I AM.

TITANS....! MY FRIENDS AND I-- WE TOOK OUR *NAME* FROM YOU!

BUT, ACCORDING TO ALL THE *MYTHS,* YOU WERE *DESTROYED,* SENT TO THE HELL KNOWN AS *TARTARUS!*

AND YOU, MY BEAUTIFUL, MY MAGNIFICENT CREATURE --YOU WILL STAND AT MY SIDE AS AN *IMMORTAL REBORN!*

SHE WILL BE *DEAD,* SUN GOD! AS WILL *YOU!*

GREAT GAEA!

13

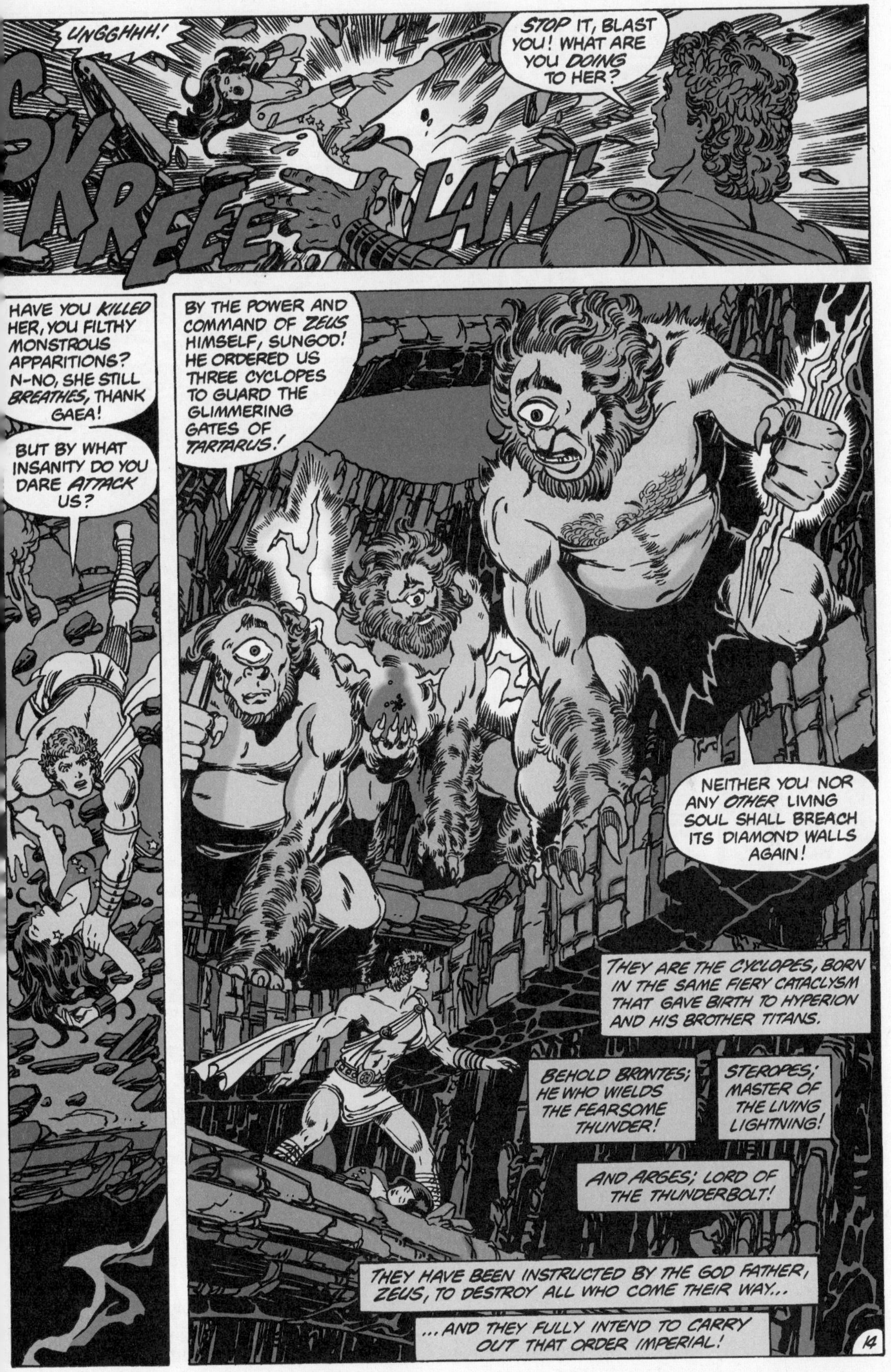
UNGGHHH!
STOP IT, BLAST YOU! WHAT ARE YOU DOING TO HER?
SKREEE-LAM!
HAVE YOU KILLED HER, YOU FILTHY MONSTROUS APPARITIONS? N-NO, SHE STILL BREATHES, THANK GAEA!
BUT BY WHAT INSANITY DO YOU DARE ATTACK US?
BY THE POWER AND COMMAND OF ZEUS HIMSELF, SUNGOD! HE ORDERED US THREE CYCLOPES TO GUARD THE GLIMMERING GATES OF TARTARUS!
NEITHER YOU NOR ANY OTHER LIVING SOUL SHALL BREACH ITS DIAMOND WALLS AGAIN!
THEY ARE THE CYCLOPES, BORN IN THE SAME FIERY CATACLYSM THAT GAVE BIRTH TO HYPERION AND HIS BROTHER TITANS.
BEHOLD BRONTES; HE WHO WIELDS THE FEARSOME THUNDER!
STEROPES; MASTER OF THE LIVING LIGHTNING!
AND ARGES; LORD OF THE THUNDERBOLT!
THEY HAVE BEEN INSTRUCTED BY THE GOD FATHER, ZEUS, TO DESTROY ALL WHO COME THEIR WAY...
...AND THEY FULLY INTEND TO CARRY OUT THAT ORDER IMPERIAL!
14

STEROPES--? IS HE DEAD, GIRL?

HE TRIED *KILLING* THE MAN I...*LOVE.*

SHE HESITATES ON THAT SINGLE WORD...IT IS A WORD UNSPOKEN TILL NOW...

BUT, SPOKEN AT LAST, SHE ALLOWS THE SUDDEN EMOTION TO WARM HER TREMBLING HEART. THEN...

STAND BACK, MY BEAUTIFUL AMAZON... THERE IS NO NEED TO SOIL YOUR SWEET HANDS ON THAT VERMIN.

IT APPEARS SUDDENLY, THIS GLOWING, GROWING FIREBALL...

Y-YOU'RE *ALIVE?* THANK HERA! WHEN I THOUGHT YOU HAD DIED, MY RAGE COULD NOT BE CONTROLLED!

...AND WHEN IT ABRUPTLY CONSUMES ITSELF, IT CONSUMES ARGES AS WELL...

THEN *CALM* YOURSELF, MY LOVE. STEROPES' *LIGHTNING* COULD NO MORE KILL AN IMMORTAL THAN *ZEUS* HIMSELF WILL STAY MY HAND FROM *DESTROYING* HIM AND HIS RENEGADE GODS!

I'M SO *AFRAID,* HYPERION... AND SO UNCERTAIN...I DON'T KNOW WHAT'S *HAPPENING* TO ME...

YOU WANT *ANSWERS?* WELL, THEN, YOU SHALL *HAVE* THEM!

THEN YOU WILL UNDERSTAND WHY I HAVE *RETURNED* TO THIS WORLD, AND WHY THERE SHALL SOON COME A *WAR* THAT WILL SHAKE THE VERY *COSMOS!* [16]

WHILE ON PARADISE ISLAND...

MY FRIENDS! MY SISTERS! MY FELLOW *WARRIORS!* YOU HAVE ALL HEARD THE WORDS OF *KORIAND'R...*

...AND YOU KNOW WHAT DEADLY *PERILS* AWAIT!

WE AMAZONS HAVE LONG BELIEVED IN *PEACE,* BUT WE HAVE ALSO TRAINED SINCE BIRTH IN THE ARTS OF *WAR!*

HERE ON THIS ISLAND HIDDEN FROM MAN, WE HAVE *AVOIDED* THE BATTLES OF THE OUTSIDE WORLD--BUT NOW, MY SISTERS, THE *BATTLE* COMES TO *US!*

BUT THIS BATTLE IS NOT WITH *MAN* NOR HIS TERRIBLE *WAR* MACHINES-- --THE BATTLE WE FACE IS WITH THE WRATH OF THE *ELDER GODS* THEMSELVES!

IT IS MY DAUGHTER WHO HAS BEEN TAKEN, AND GLADLY WOULD I MARCH *ALONE* TO RECLAIM HER IF I MUST.

WE WILL MARCH INTO *HELL* ITSELF, AND NOT ONE OF US MAY *SURVIVE!*

I ASK YOU, NOT AS YOUR *QUEEN,* BUT AS YOUR SISTER IN PEACE...*JOIN* ME. BUT, BEFORE YOU ANSWER, CONSIDER *THIS!*

KNOWING ALL THIS--WILL YOU, MY VALIANT SISTERS, *MARCH* WITH ME?

THERE IS NO PAUSE, NO HESITATION...

WE FIGHT AS ONE!

FOR HIPPOLYTE!

FOR PARADISE ISLAND!!

17

TO MARCH INTO HELL, WHERE EVEN NOW A GRIM-FACED HYPERION BEGINS HIS RECOUNTING...

BEFORE MAN, EVEN BEFORE THE BIRTH OF THE FIRST PLANET, THERE IS CHAOS...THE ENDLESS GULF OF NOTHINGNESS.

THEN, BORN FROM CHAOS WAS THE FIRST LIFE, SHE WHO WOULD BE MOTHER TO US ALL, SHE WHO WAS CALLED GAEA!

THERE IS MUCH TO UNDERSTAND HERE. THERE IS THE PAST AND, AS ALWAYS, THE PAST IS BUT PROLOGUE TO ALL THAT IS TO COME.

CHAOS, ROILING, TROUBLED, GROWING MORE AND MORE FURIOUS.

FROM GAEA CAME URANUS, WHO WAS TO BE HER HUSBAND AND FATHER OF ALL THE GODS.

BROAD OF SHOULDER, POWERFUL IN STANCE, HE WAS THE BUILDER OF THE HOME.

AND WHERE THEY LIVED, THERE WAS PEACE.

BUT THEN, FROM GAEA WERE BORN THE FIRST GODS-- MY BROTHERS AND SISTERS--

--WE WHO ARE CALLED THE TITANS! FOR LIKE GREAT TITANS WE STRODE THE UNIVERSAL SEAS, RULING ALL THAT WE SURVEYED!

IN ALL, THERE WERE TWELVE OF US!

18

"TO GAEA WERE ALSO BORN THE THREE CYCLOPES, AND OTHER HIDEOUS MONSTERS BEYOND MORTAL COMPREHENSION.

"BUT THESE BIRTHS UPSET URANUS, AND HE BANISHED ALL TO THE PITS OF TARTARUS.

"HE INTENDED TO KILL BOTH MONSTER AND TITAN ALIKE...

"...BUT GAEA HAD OTHER PLANS FOR HER CHILDREN.

"SHE ENLISTED ONE OF HER SONS, MY BROTHER, CRONUS, THE EARTH GOD-- AND CRONUS SLEW OUR FATHER WITH ONE BLOODY STROKE OF HIS SWORD.

"FROM THEN ON THERE WAS PARADISE ON EARTH, PARADISE FOR ALL.

"MAN AND WOMAN WERE BORN TO EARTH, AND FOR UNTOLD AGES MAN AND GOD WALKED IN PEACE AND HARMONY.

"THIS, THEN, WAS THE GOLDEN AGE, AND AN AGE OF MAGNIFICENCE UNRIVALED, TO THIS DAY.

"BUT CRONUS WAS TOLD BY ORACLE THAT ONE OF HIS OWN CHILDREN WOULD END HIS REIGN...

"SO HE WHO HAD KILLED HIS OWN FATHER NOW SWALLOWED HIS CHILDREN...

"ALL BUT ZEUS, HIS ELDEST BORN.

"ZEUS, WHO WAS TAKEN INTO HIDING BY RHEA, CRONUS' WIFE AND SISTER BOTH.

"AND THUS, IN HIDING, ZEUS GREW IN POWER...

"...AND RETURNED TO DEFEAT US TITANS IN BATTLE...

"...THEN CAST US INTO THE PITS OF TARTARUS WHERE WE WERE TO STAY FOR ALL THESE MANY YEARS!

19

WE WERE *BANISHED*, ALL TWELVE OF US INCLUDING THIA, MY SISTER AND WIFE, FORMED INTO *STONE COLUMNS*...

BUT, EVEN CAST IN STONE, I SENSED THIA HAD *VANISHED* DURING OUR BANISHMENT...SHE WAS GONE, LEAVING ME ALONE WITH NOTHING MORE THAN MY *THOUGHTS* TO KEEP ME COMPANY...

BUT THOUGHTS SERVED ME *WELL*, MY DARLING. FOR AS I STOOD SILENT, *THANATOS*, HE WHO IS *DEATH* HIMSELF, LED THOSE *NEWLY* DEAD PAST MY PRESENCE...

"...AND I REACHED INTO THEIR HEARTS, AND PLUCKED THE DYING EMBERS OF *SUNLIGHT* I FOUND THERE AND TOOK THEM TO MY BOSOM.

SO MANY *YEARS* IT TOOK, EACH HEART ADDING TO THE LAST, THEN, AT LAST, I HAD *REGAINED* ENOUGH OF MY POWER--

--AND I BURST *FREE*, FREE TO GREET THE WORLD ANEW!

AND FREE TO FIND *YOU*-- WHOSE BEAUTY FILLS ME WITH *LOVE*.

BUT NOW I MEAN TO FREE MY *FELLOW* TITANS, AND TOGETHER BANISH ZEUS AND HIS ILK. THEN, MY DEAREST, MY DARLING--

--THEN WE WILL CREATE *PEACE* AGAIN ON EARTH.

THERE SHALL COME A NEW GOLDEN AGE...BRIMMING WITH *LOVE*...

...LIKE THE LOVE THAT BINDS US *NOW!*

SHE IS AN *AMAZON*, TRAINED FROM CHILD-HOOD IN THE WAYS OF WAR.

BUT, NOW, SHE IS ONLY A *WOMAN*...A WOMAN HELD TIGHTLY IN THE ARMS OF AN IMPOS-SIBLE LOVE.

20

BUT AS WONDER GIRL EMBRACES THE SUNGOD, FAR ABOVE, AT THE ENTRANCE TO THESE DARKENED PITS...

THERE, MY SISTERS --THE FIRST OF OUR FOES LIES AHEAD!

FORWARD --TO VICTORY!

BUT, WHAT MANNER OF VICTORY IS POSSIBLE AGAINST THIS MONSTROUS DEFORMITY THAT ALSO CALLS ITSELF THE SON OF GAEA...FIFTY HEADS IT BOASTS...ONE HUNDRED POWERFUL ARMS...

ALREADY FIVE AMAZONS LIE DEAD, AND MORE WILL DIE, UNLESS I CAN STOP IT!

NO, KORIAND'R --DON'T! THERE IS ANOTHER WAY!

RAVEN, I WON'T HIDE NOW...AND I WON'T HOLD BACK MY FULL POWER.

I DO NOT ASK YOU TO, BUT THE CREATURE CANNOT BE SLAIN... SO LISTEN.

IN HURRIED WHISPERS, THE MYSTIC MISTRESS EXPLAINS TO THE GRIM, ALIEN PRINCESS, THEN...

THE GAMES OF AVOIDING BATTLE ARE BEGINNING TO GRATE AT ME, RAVEN. I WANT TO LASH OUT WITH ALL MY POWER... JUST ONCE.

BUT ALL THAT I WAS TAUGHT BY THE OKAARAN WARLORDS TELLS ME THAT THIS TIME AT LEAST YOUR PATH IS BEST!

KORIAND'R'S STARBOLTS CREATE A WALL OF SOLID FLAME, A WALL THROUGH WHICH EVEN THIS MANY-HEADED MONSTER FEARS TO PASS...

HIPPOLYTE LEADS HER ANXIOUS ARMY ONWARD, DOWN THROUGH CAVERNS AS DARK AS INFINITE SPACE, TO A POINT WHERE ALL REALITY SEEMINGLY ENDS. TWO DAYS PASS IN THE INTERIM...

OUR QUEST HAS BEEN IN VAIN, QUEEN HIPPOLYTE -- LOOK THERE!

21

PHILEGETHON! THE RIVER OF FIRE!

AND *BEYOND* THAT, QUEEN, A WALL OF *SOLID DIAMOND!*

NOT EVEN MY SOUL-SELF CAN *PENETRATE* IT!

AND MY DIMENSION-SPANNING *TELEPORTATIONAL* POWERS CANNOT GET ME THROUGH. I'VE TRIED A DOZEN TIMES AND *MORE...*

...AND I HAVE *FAILED* IN MY EVERY EFFORT.

BUT WE CAN'T HAVE COME ALL THIS WAY FOR *NOTHING.*

THAT WOULDN'T BE *FAIR!*

PERHAPS *YOUR* POWERS CANNOT HELP US, RAVEN, BUT WE ARE STILL FAR FROM *HELPLESS!*

THIS SWORD, GIVEN TO ME THREE THOU-SAND YEARS AGO BY *ATHENA,* GODDESS OF WISDOM--

-- CAN ONLY BE USED *ONCE* BEFORE THE SWORD FOREVER RETURNS TO ITS SCABBARD ON *MOUNT OLYMPUS!*

BUT *ONCE* IS ALL I *NEED!*

I MUST HAVE MY *DAUGHTER* BACK!

SKRAK

WHILE FAR BEYOND THE DIAMOND BARRIER...

HOW MUCH *LONGER,* HYPERION? IT'S BEEN *DAYS!*

TO BREAK THE SPELLS AND MAGIC OF ZEUS REQUIRES *TIME...* BUT VERY *SOON* NOW THEY WILL BE FREE. HAVE *PATIENCE,* MY DARLING.

SHE WATCHES, FOR-GETTING ALL BUT THIS ONE BEING.

SHE FEELS A SUBLIME THRILL AS HYPERION'S MIGHTY POWERS INSINUATE THE LIVING STONE...

22

AND SHE IS OVERWHELMED IN WHAT SHE SEES NEXT. THERE IS A BURST OF RADIANT LIGHT, AND BEFORE HER SUDDENLY STANDS NOT ONE, BUT ELEVEN MAGNIFICENT TITANS!

IAPETUS AND THEMIS, GODS OF JUSTICE!

CRIUS AND MNEMOSYNE, GODS OF MEMORY!

COEUS AND PHOEBE, THE MOON GODS!

CRONUS AND RHEA, THE EARTH GODS!

OCEANUS AND TETHYS, THE SEA GODS!

AS ONE, THE RAISE THEIR HANDS HEAVEN-WARD, AS IF THEY OWNED ALL THEY CAN TOUCH, AND SUDDENLY THE TRUTH BECOMES ASTONISHING-LY CLEAR...

AFTER THIRTY THOUSAND YEARS, THE TITANS WALK THE EARTH!!

GAEA BE PRAISED, HYPERION... YOU'VE FREED US!

WE HAVE WAITED LONG -- EH, OCEANUS?

TOO LONG, BUT THERE IS NOW TIME TO MAKE IT ALL UP!

OH, BLESS CHAOS FOR OUR FREEDOM AT LAST!

THERE WILL BE TIME ENOUGH TO FROLIC LIKE CHILDREN.

RIGHT NOW THERE IS WORK THAT NEEDS TO BE DONE!

GIVE US A MOMENT TO REJOICE, CRONUS ...SURELY THAT COULD NOT HURT...

IT CAN, MY WIFE... FOR THE GOD YOU SAVED, THE CHILD I WISHED DEAD, WILL DO ANYTHING TO KEEP US FROM USURPING HIS JEWELED THRONE!

TO SUCCEED, WE MUST PLAN!

23

BUT...

THAT *NOISE*...? HAS ZEUS DISCOVERED US *ALREADY?*

WE ARE NOT YET *READY* TO FIGHT! OUR POWERS MUST BE *RENEWED!*

THERE'S *NO TIME* FOR THAT NOW... WE DEMAND WHAT YOU'VE *TAKEN* FROM US.

GIVE US BACK OUR *TEAMMATE* OR BE READY TO *FIGHT!*

HMMM. THESE WARRIORS ARE ALL *WOMEN.* THEY CANNOT COME FROM *OLYMPUS.* MY SON, *ZEUS,* IS TOO MUCH THE *MISOGYNIST* TO CREATE A FEMALE FIGHTING FORCE!

THEY ARE *MORTALS!* THEY WILL PROVE *EASY* TO KILL!

YOU'LL *TALK* INSTEAD OF *BATTLE* WITH YOUR DAUGHTER'S KIDNAPPERS? *SLAY* THEM, HIPPOLYTE--DON'T MAKE *SPEECHES!*

NO, CRONUS... WE HAVEN'T COME TO *FIGHT*... NOT IF YOU RETURN MY *DAUGHTER* TO US. SHE IS *ALL* WE SEEK, NOTHING *MORE.*

BUT THEY AREN'T HOLDING ME *AGAINST* MY WILL, KORIAND'R.

IN FACT, I'VE WILLINGLY *JOINED* WITH THEM, NOT ONLY WITH MY *SOUL*... BUT WITH MY *HEART!*

PLEASE TRY TO *UNDERSTAND* ME, MOTHER... FRIENDS, THIS IS WHAT I *WANT.*

24

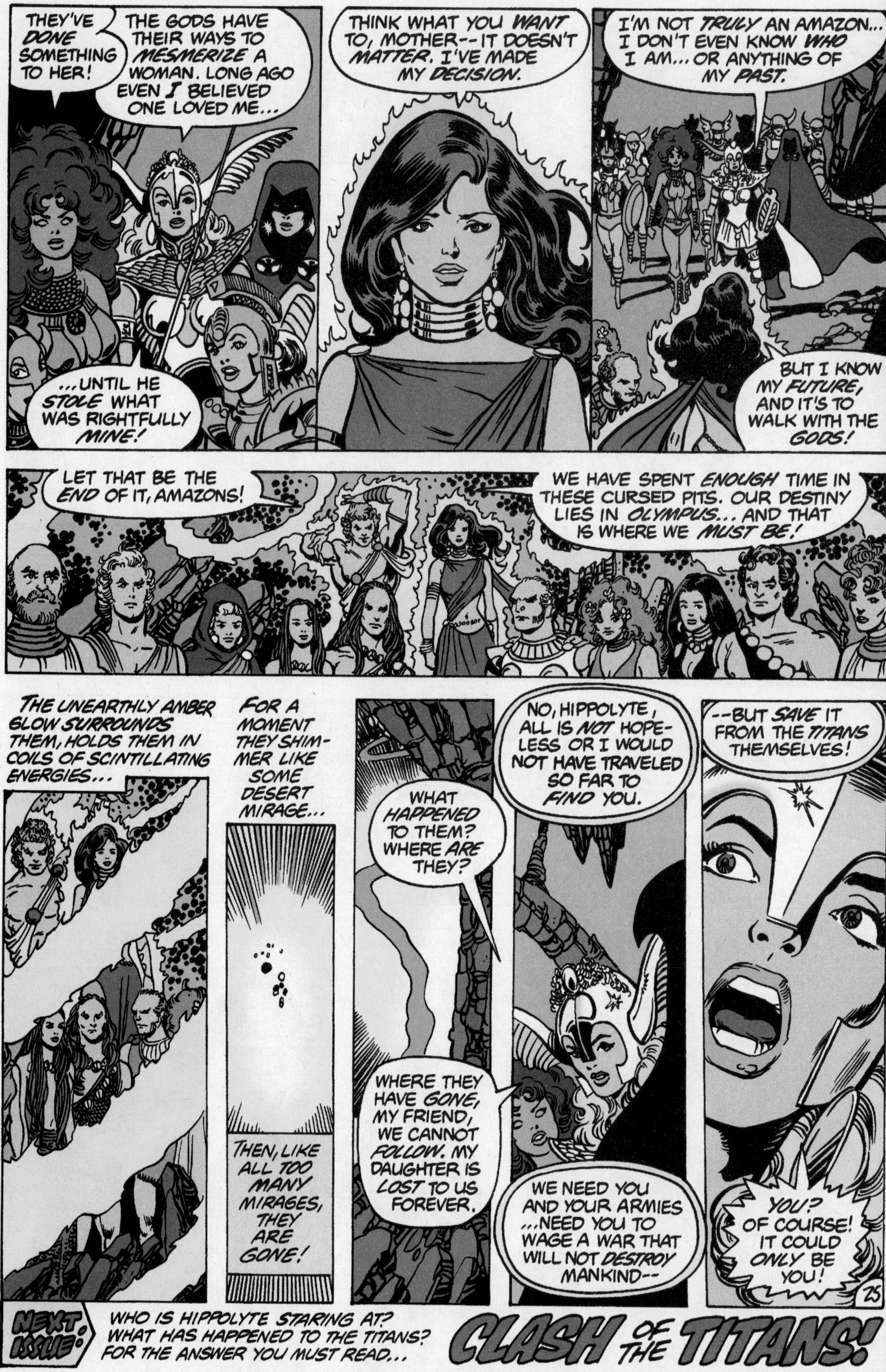

THEY'VE DONE SOMETHING TO HER!
THE GODS HAVE THEIR WAYS TO MESMERIZE A WOMAN. LONG AGO EVEN I BELIEVED ONE LOVED ME...
...UNTIL HE STOLE WHAT WAS RIGHTFULLY MINE!
THINK WHAT YOU WANT TO, MOTHER--IT DOESN'T MATTER. I'VE MADE MY DECISION.
I'M NOT TRULY AN AMAZON... I DON'T EVEN KNOW WHO I AM... OR ANYTHING OF MY PAST.
BUT I KNOW MY FUTURE, AND IT'S TO WALK WITH THE GODS!
LET THAT BE THE END OF IT, AMAZONS!
WE HAVE SPENT ENOUGH TIME IN THESE CURSED PITS. OUR DESTINY LIES IN OLYMPUS... AND THAT IS WHERE WE MUST BE!
THE UNEARTHLY AMBER GLOW SURROUNDS THEM, HOLDS THEM IN COILS OF SCINTILLATING ENERGIES...
FOR A MOMENT THEY SHIMMER LIKE SOME DESERT MIRAGE...
THEN, LIKE ALL TOO MANY MIRAGES, THEY ARE GONE!
WHAT HAPPENED TO THEM? WHERE ARE THEY?
WHERE THEY HAVE GONE, MY FRIEND, WE CANNOT FOLLOW. MY DAUGHTER IS LOST TO US FOREVER.
NO, HIPPOLYTE, ALL IS NOT HOPELESS OR I WOULD NOT HAVE TRAVELED SO FAR TO FIND YOU.
WE NEED YOU AND YOUR ARMIES ...NEED YOU TO WAGE A WAR THAT WILL NOT DESTROY MANKIND--
--BUT SAVE IT FROM THE TITANS THEMSELVES!
YOU? OF COURSE! IT COULD ONLY BE YOU!
25
NEXT ISSUE:
WHO IS HIPPOLYTE STARING AT? WHAT HAS HAPPENED TO THE TITANS? FOR THE ANSWER YOU MUST READ...
CLASH OF THE TITANS!

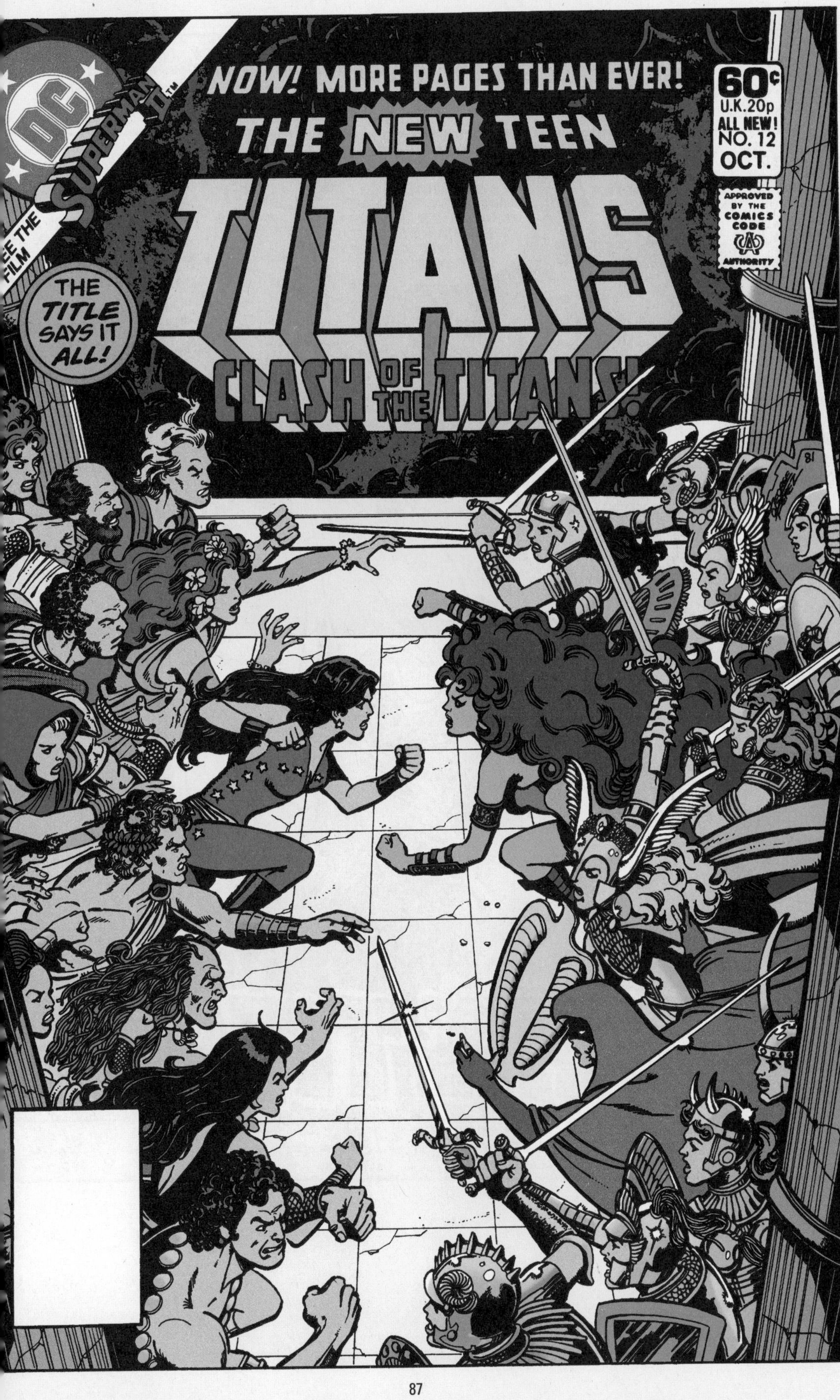
DC
SUPERMAN II™
SEE THE FILM
NOW! MORE PAGES THAN EVER!
THE NEW TEEN
TITANS
CLASH OF THE TITANS!
60¢
U.K.20p
ALL NEW!
NO. 12
OCT.
APPROVED BY THE COMICS CODE AUTHORITY
THE TITLE SAYS IT ALL!

STANDING HERE, THEY STARE BEWILDERED, DOUBTING ALL THEY SEE. RAVEN, DARK-SHROUDED MYSTIC MISTRESS; STARFIRE, ALIEN PRINCESS FROM VEGA'S EIGHTH PLANET, TAMARAN; AND HIPPOLYTA, QUEEN OF THE AMAZONS WITH HER BATTLE-READY WARRIORS. BEFORE THEM IS A SIGHT MOST IMPOSSIBLE: FOR HERE, FAR BELOW PARADISE ISLAND, IN THE HELLPITS OF MYTHIC TARTARUS, LOOMS THE SOFT-GLOWING IMAGE OF A GODDESS FROM HIGH OLYMPUS...

ATHENA! GODDESS OF WISDOM! THEN IT WAS *YOUR* POWER THAT WHISKED AWAY MY DAUGHTER AND THE ELDER GODS?

NO, FAITHFUL HIPPOLYTA, THEY HAVE *THEMSELVES* TRAVERSED THE DISTANCES 'TWEEN THIS WORLD AND GREAT OLYMPUS.

WHILE *I* HAVE COME TO *YOU*, FOR WE OLYMPIANS, CHILDREN OF THE INVADING *TITANS OF MYTH*, HAVE NEED OF YOUR VALIANT *ARMY!*

SOON THERE SHALL BE A *WAR*, A WAR THAT MIGHT NOT ONLY DESTROY THE *GODS* THEMSELVES --

-- BUT ALSO THIS PLANET YOU CALL *EARTH!*

CLASH OF THE TITANS

MARV WOLFMAN	GEORGE PÉREZ	ROMEO TANGHAL	BEN ODA	ADRIENNE ROY	LEN WEIN
WRITER -- CO-CREATORS -- ARTIST		EMBELLISHER	LETTERER	COLORIST	EDITOR

ATHENA, FOR A THOUSAND YEARS OR MORE HAVE WE LIVED BY YOUR WORD, BUT *CRONUS*, LEADER OF THOSE TITANS, SWEARS THERE CAN BE A NEW *GOLDEN AGE* ON EARTH.'

THE BEAUTY AND SERENITY THAT *ONCE* WAS COULD AGAIN BE HAD BY *ALL*!

NO, HIPPOLYTA, THERE CAN BE *NO* SECOND GOLDEN AGE...

FOR, SHOULD WELL-MEANING CRONUS EVER *SIT* ON THE THRONE OF OLYMPUS, WHAT SHALL THEN EXIST WILL MERELY BE--*CHAOS UNLEASHED!*

FOR THE SAFETY OF ALL, WE OLYMPIANS MUST *SLAY* THESE TITANS WHO ARE OUR PARENTS, AS THEY DID *THEIR* PROGENITORS!

MUST IT *ALWAYS* BE THAT WAY, ATHENA? PARENT AGAINST CHILD?

MUST *ALL* GENERATIONS EVER BE AT *WAR* WITH EACH OTHER?

MYSELF AGAINST *TRIGON*? YOU AGAINST *CRONUS* AND THE OTHERS...?

WHAT INTERESTS *ME*, ATHENA-- IS WHAT CAN *YOU* OFFER US? THEY PROMISE ETERNAL *PEACE*...

...AND EVEN WE WARRIORS OF TAMARAN PREFER EMBRACING PEACE TO BATTLE!

I CAN OFFER NOTHING THAT HAS NOT ALREADY *BEEN*. I OFFER NO PARADISE, OR PEACE OR EVERLASTING *HOPE*.

BUT *LISTEN* PLEASE BEFORE YOU TAKE SIDES AND I PROMISE THAT YOU WILL *UNDERSTAND!*

2

BUT NOW WE MUST TAKE LEAVE OF THIS DEEPEST OF ALL STYGIAN PITS AND RISE TO THE HIGHEST OF ALL SUMMITS: THE PEAK OF MOUNT OLYMPUS--

--LEGENDARY HOME OF THE GODS!

THERE, RHEA, MY WIFE -- OUR GOAL NOW STANDS BEFORE US!

AND YOU, CRONUS, SHALL AGAIN RULE AS IS YOUR RIGHT!

AHHH, MY LOVE, THE GRANDEUR OF OUR DIVINE MISSION FILLS ME WITH THE WARMTH OF THE LIVING SUN!

AS LONG AS I STAND WITH YOU, HYPERION, I SHARE YOUR WARMTH... AND YOUR LOVE...

WE STAND TOGETHER, AND TOGETHER WE SHALL TOPPLE THE GODS!

YET, IN THE FURTHEST REACHES OF WONDER GIRL'S MIND, THERE REMAIN THE SLIGHTEST VESTIGES OF NAGGING DOUBT...

...DOUBT SHARED BY ANOTHER OF THESE ELDER GODS WHO CALL THEMSELVES THE TITANS!

TETHYS, MY LOVE, WE BELONG IN OUR UNDERSEA HOMES, NOT HERE IN THESE WIND-SWEPT SKIES.

I WANT NOTHING OF THIS BATTLE!

YET, OCEANUS-- WE MUST OBEY CRONUS' COMMAND! HE IS OUR LEADER!

AT LAST--OLYMPUS! IT HAS BEEN A LONG TIME, EH, CRIUS?

BUT NOT LONG ENOUGH TO ERASE THE FOUL PAST FROM THE GODS OF MEMORY, IS IT, MNEMOSYNE?

I WILL FOREVER REMEMBER OUR HATED IMPRISONMENT IN TARTARUS!

3

AS I WILL THE *GLORIES* THAT WERE OURS WHEN LAST WE TITANS WALKED THE EARTH!

THOSE ARE *GOOD MEMORIES,* MY HUSBAND... RUINED ONLY WHEN ZEUS AND HIS OLYMPIANS DEFEATED AND *BANISHED* US.

MAN'S WORLD HAS BEEN RIFE WITH *HORRORS* FOR SO VERY LONG...TO EVEN *HOPE* FOR SOMETHING BETTER SIMPLY *STAGGERS* MY MIND.

AND THERE SHALL *BE* BETTER...

...WHEN YOU BECOME THE GODDESS YOU WERE *MEANT* TO BE.

YOUR BROW CREASES? DOES THAT THOUGHT *TROUBLE* YOU?

TO BECOME A *GODDESS?* THAT WILL BE MY *THIRD LIFE.* YOU SEE, I WASN'T AN *AMAZON* AT BIRTH. I CAN'T *REMEMBER* WHO I REALLY AM.

THEN MNEMOSYNE AND I SHALL *RESTORE* YOUR MEMORIES ONCE OUR MISSION HERE IS *DONE!*

CRONUS, YOU PAUSE. *WHY?* IS THERE A *BARRIER?*

SOON WE'LL FLY *PAST* THE CLOUDS AND SEE THE *MOON* ONCE AGAIN. I ALMOST CANNOT *WAIT,* COEUS.

BUT WE *MUST,* PHOEBE. THOUGH WE MOON GODS WANT TO ROMP AGAIN ON OUR LUNAR CHILD, WE *CANNOT--*

NO, COEUS, I PAUSE TO *REFLECT* FOR JUST A MOMENT. AHH, LET US MOVE ON NOW, AND LET *NOTHING* STOP US.

--NOT UNTIL OLYMPUS IS *OURS!*

4

CRONUS, *LOOK* BEYOND THE MISTS, GUARDING THE OLYMPIAN GATES -- *THE THREE SEASONS!*

THEN QUICKLY, WE MUST *SUBDUE* THEM!

THEY ARE MY CHILDREN AS WELL AS ZEUS'-- THEIR POWER IS *TERRIBLE!*

THEN CONSIDER THEM *STOPPED,* THEMIS.

BUT... EIRENE! EUNOMIA! IT IS AS ATHENA *PREDICTED.* THE TITANS *RETURN!*

YOU *BATTLE* THEM! I MUST WARN OUR *FATHER!*

NO, PIKE, ZEUS MAY INDEED *HEAR* OF OUR COMING, BUT HE WILL NOT LEARN OF IT FROM *YOU!*

THAT THE MOON GODS *SWEAR!*

THE *SLEEP OF NIGHT* WILL OVERTAKE YOU... YOU'LL REST *UNHARMED* AS A GIFT TO THEMIS, YOUR MOTHER.

HYPERION, WE ARE *THROUGH!* ONLY THE *GATES* STAND BETWEEN US AND THE SHATTERING OF THAT ORACLE'S *CURSE!*

WELL, WHAT DO YOU *WAIT* FOR, CRONUS?

PATIENCE, BROTHER... LET US *SAVOR* THIS MOMENT, FOR OUR *DESTINY* AWAITS BEHIND THIS FRAGILE DOOR.

DESTINY-- AND THE *POWER INFINITE!*

CRONUS BREATHES IN DEEPLY AS HE RAISES HIS SCYTHE HAND HIGH...

BUT LET US MOVE AHEAD OF CRONUS AND *BRIDGE THE GULF* THAT SEPARATES HIM FROM THE *MAGNIFICENCE* OF OLYMPUS!

OH, IT HAS BEEN SPOKEN OF IN MYTH, BUT NO MERE LEGEND CAN EXAGGERATE ITS MAGNIFICENT *REALITY.*

IT IS *GLORIOUS,* THE CENTER OF ALL THAT IS! IT IS *POWER,* AND THE POWER IS WITHOUT EQUAL!

AND, STANDING AT ITS THRESHOLD, ITS GOD SUPREME-- *ZEUS,* HE WHO WIELDS THE THUNDERBOLT COSMIC!

HEAR ME, OLYMPIANS-- WE ARE READY FOR *WAR,* AND WE ARE READY FOR *VICTORY!*

PLEASE, MY HUSBAND, DO NOT *DESTROY* THEM.

WHAT? YOU DARE BEG FOR *LENIENCY* WHEN THEY COME TO DESTROY *US?* HAVE YOU GONE *MAD,* HERA?

BUT CRONUS IS YOUR *FATHER,* DOES THAT MEAN *NOTHING* TO YOU?

IT *DOES,* AND I DO NOT FORGET THAT WHEN I WAS BUT A *CHILD* HE ORDERED *ME* DESTROYED.

ONLY MY BELOVED MOTHER, *RHEA,* PROTECTED ME UNTIL THE *ORACLE'S* PREDICTION COULD COME TRUE.

AYE, FATHER--EVEN I *REMEMBER--* HE SAID "THE SON WOULD RISE AND BANISH THE FATHER." HE SAID "THE CHILD SHALL RULE AND THE FATHER WOULD *DIE!"*

SO, YOU SEE-- IT IS MY *DESTINY,* HERA, AND, BY THE POWER OF MY THUNDERBOLT, OUR PARENTS, THESE ELDER GODS, THESE SELF-PROCLAIMED *TITANS--*

--MUST ALL *PERISH* LEST WE OLYMPIANS DIE IN THEIR STEAD!

WITH A HEAVY CRUNCH, CRONUS' SCYTHE CLEAVES THE GLIMMERING GATES AS IF THEY WERE WIND-BLOWN STRAW...

...AND OLYMPUS SUDDENLY STANDS OPEN AND UNGUARDED...

...OR SO IT WOULD SEEM TO THE NAKED EYE.

NO ARMIES AWAIT US FOR BATTLE? THIS IS *UNLIKE* OUR CHILDREN.

TAKE CARE, MY BROTHERS AND SISTERS--SOMETHING IS *WRONG.*

STEP CAREFULLY, ALL.

I FEAR THE VERY *GROUND* WE TREAD UPON MAY BE ALIVE WITH *TRAPS* SET BY THAT DEVIOUS SON OF MY BLOOD!

WHAT?

MMMMMMMMMMMMM!

BY THE CHAOS THAT SPAWNED US ALL.!!

THE FURIES! DAMN THEIR SOULLESS, SERPENTINE HIDES!

NOW THE FIGHT *BEGINS!*

TO MY *SIDE!* THE BATTLE LINE HAS BEEN DRAWN!

7

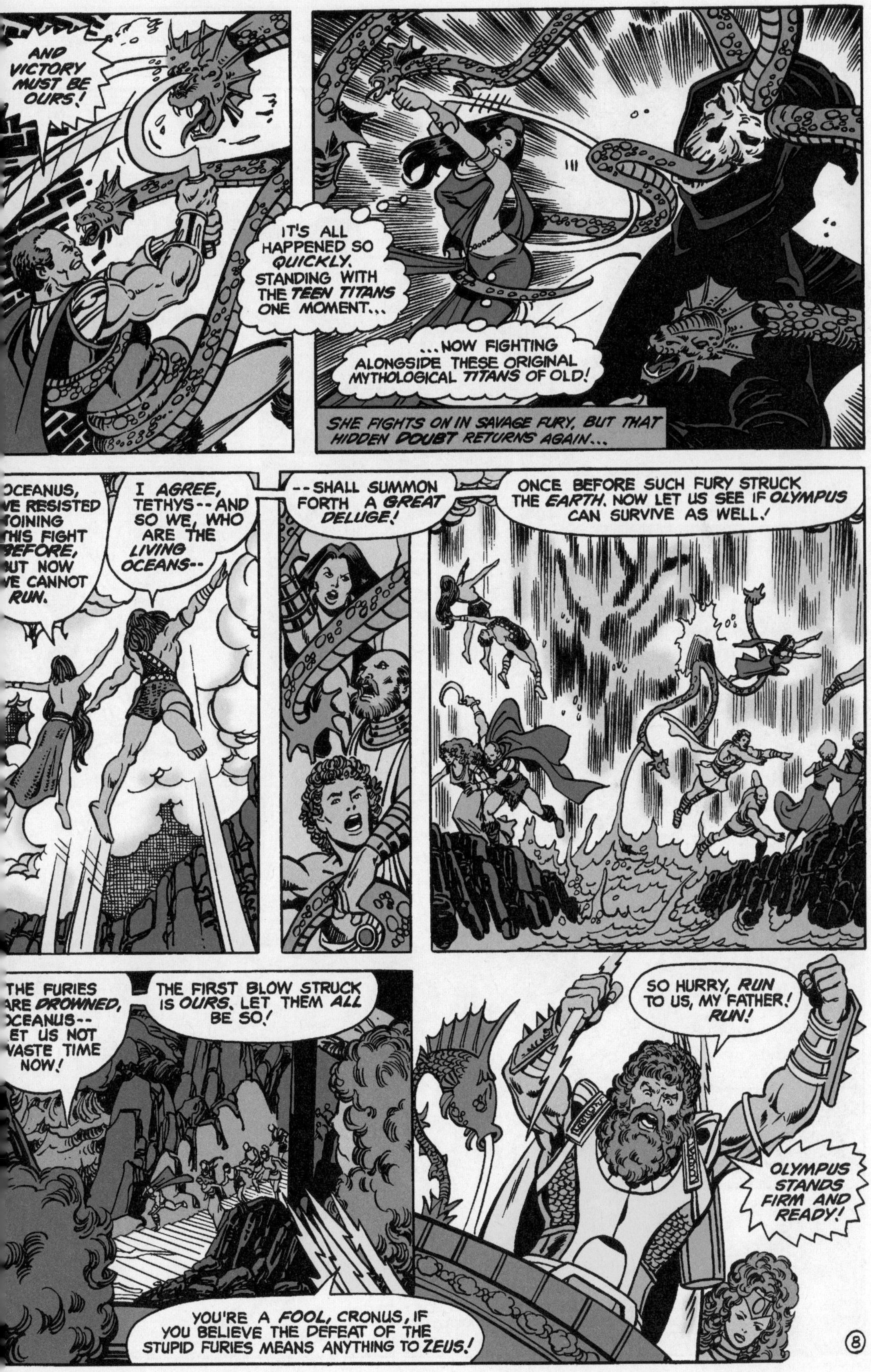
AND VICTORY MUST BE OURS!
IT'S ALL HAPPENED SO QUICKLY. STANDING WITH THE TEEN TITANS ONE MOMENT...
...NOW FIGHTING ALONGSIDE THESE ORIGINAL MYTHOLOGICAL TITANS OF OLD!
SHE FIGHTS ON IN SAVAGE FURY, BUT THAT HIDDEN DOUBT RETURNS AGAIN...
I AGREE, TETHYS--AND SO WE, WHO ARE THE LIVING OCEANS--
--SHALL SUMMON FORTH A GREAT DELUGE!
ONCE BEFORE SUCH FURY STRUCK THE EARTH. NOW LET US SEE IF OLYMPUS CAN SURVIVE AS WELL!
THE FIRST BLOW STRUCK IS OURS. LET THEM ALL BE SO!
SO HURRY, RUN TO US, MY FATHER! RUN!
OLYMPUS STANDS FIRM AND READY!
YOU'RE A FOOL, CRONUS, IF YOU BELIEVE THE DEFEAT OF THE STUPID FURIES MEANS ANYTHING TO ZEUS!
8

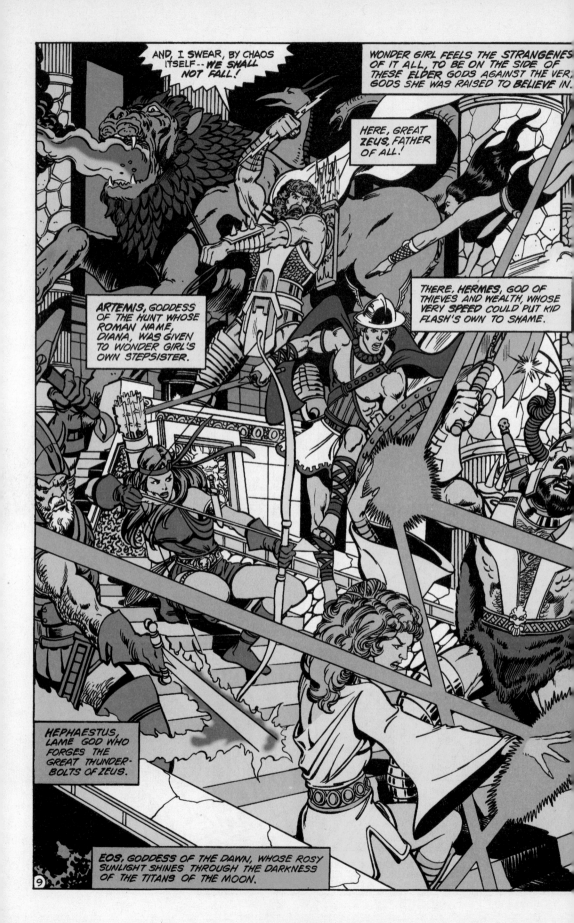

AND, I SWEAR, BY CHAOS ITSELF--*WE SHALL NOT FALL!*

WONDER GIRL FEELS THE STRANGENES OF IT ALL, TO BE ON THE SIDE OF THESE ELDER GODS AGAINST THE VER, GODS SHE WAS RAISED TO BELIEVE IN.

HERE, GREAT ZEUS, FATHER OF ALL!

ARTEMIS, GODDESS OF THE HUNT WHOSE ROMAN NAME, DIANA, WAS GIVEN TO WONDER GIRL'S OWN STEPSISTER.

THERE, HERMES, GOD OF THIEVES AND WEALTH, WHOSE VERY *SPEED* COULD PUT KID FLASH'S OWN TO SHAME.

HEPHAESTUS, LAME GOD WHO FORGES THE GREAT THUNDER- BOLTS OF ZEUS.

EOS, GODDESS OF THE DAWN, WHOSE ROSY SUNLIGHT SHINES THROUGH THE DARKNESS OF THE TITANS OF THE MOON.

9

BOREAS, WIND GOD, STORMING PROUD INTO THE PATH OF THE INVADING HORDE.

STANDING TALL IS ARES, GRIM-VISAGED GOD OF WAR!

SO MANY GODS! APOLLO! POSEIDON! HERA! SO MANY AGAINST ONLY TWELVE VALIANT TITANS.

NOW WORRY, TOO, CREASES WONDER GIRL'S BROW.

10

THE CLASH BEGINS, AND WONDER GIRL, STILL ONLY MORTAL, CAN ONLY GAZE IN AWE.

HERE, BEFORE HER, IS GREATNESS.

BUT THIS GREATNESS IS STAINED AND DIRTIED WITH BLOOD...

...AND HATE.

FATHER FIGHTS SON...

FATHER BATTLES DAUGHTER...

...AND WONDER GIRL'S STOMACH TIGHTENS AS SHE FEELS ALL TOO ILL AT EASE.

BUT STILL SHE MOVES LIKE THE SWIFT-LEGGED PANTHER, AND HER STRENGTH, WHICH RIVALS THAT OF HERACLES HIMSELF, IS SAVAGE AND MIGHTY BEYOND HUMAN BELIEF.

IN AN INSTANT, MIGHTY ARES, WAR GOD, FALLS!

WONDER GIRL GLANCES AT HER SIDE, FEELING FLESH POUNDING GODLY FLESH, AND STEEL GLANCING OFF UNSHATTERABLE STEEL...

BUT, FAR OFF, IN THE SEAS WHICH FOREVER ENCIRCLE OLYMPUS, POSEIDON, GOD OF THE OCEANS, CONFRONTS HIS PARENTS, OCEANUS AND TETHYS.

GET AWAY, BOTH OF YOU-- BEFORE I AM FORCED TO KILL!

ZEUS HAS GIVEN ME HIS COMMAND, AND EVEN I CANNOT DENY HIM.

YOU WILL NOT HAVE TO, ERRANT SON, FOR YOURS IS STILL THE POWER OF A CHILD WHEN COMPARED WITH THAT OF A TITAN BORN.

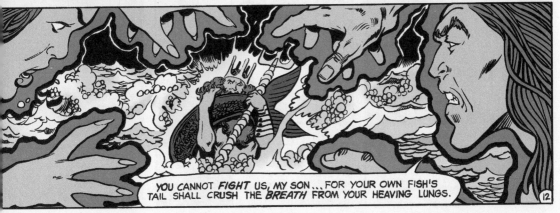

YOU CANNOT FIGHT US, MY SON... FOR YOUR OWN FISH'S TAIL SHALL CRUSH THE BREATH FROM YOUR HEAVING LUNGS.

12

BUT, EVEN AS THE HORRORS OF WAR OVERTAKE OLYMPUS, WONDER GIRL BATTLES ON 'TWEEN THE LIGHTNING AND THE THUNDER WHICH ROCK WHAT WAS ONCE A PALACE OF PEACE.

SHE BATTLES THOUGH DOUBTS PLAGUE HER. YET, WHAT CAN SHE, A MERE MORTAL, DO, WHEN EN-THRALLED BY THE GOD OF THE SUN?

EPIC STRUGGLES 'TWEEN LIGHT AND DARK BEGIN TO RIP AT HER WILL...

SHE BATTLES BECAUSE SHE MUST, FOR HYPERION'S GOLDEN GLOW STILL HOLDS HER MIND, AND MORE -- HER HEART.

WATER STORMS FALL FROM THE SKY AND SHE SEES APOLLO AND HEPHAESTUS BOTH RESIST WITH ALL THEIR GODLY POWER.

... AS ALL HER DOUBTS RUSH FORWARD LIKE THE RAGING TIDE.

AND SHE, WHO HAS SPENT MOST OF HER LIFE WITHOUT KNOWING FEAR, TREMBLES AS COLD DARKNESS GRIPS THE SKY-TOWERING SPIRES OF THIS HOME OF THE ALL-KNOWING GODS.

13

BUT THEN THE DOUBT DROWNING HER MIND IS SUDDENLY GONE-- FOR THE MOMENT, AT LEAST-- AS IAPETUS, TITAN-GOD OF JUSTICE, SCREAMS...

ZEUS SENT THIS BEAST TO SLAY YOU? WELL, BY HERA -- HE WON'T GET THE CHANCE!

...AND AS LION-HEADED, GOAT-BODIED, DRAGON-TAILED CHIMERA SLASHES FORWARD WITH RAZOR-SHARP TALONS, AND STREAMS OF FIERY BREATH...

"BY HERA"? I STILL SWEAR BY THE NAMES OF THOSE GODS I NOW FIGHT.

BY WHY? WHY AM I DOING THIS?

THIS ISN'T MY BATTLE! THIS ISN'T MY WAR! YET I FIGHT AND I CANNOT STOP!

WHY? WHY? WHY?

WHILE...

HOW MANY TIMES MUST I SLAY YOU, FATHER?

YOU CALL ME A FOOL, ZEUS-- BUT YOU ARE MORE THAN FOOLISH!

WITH YOUR POWER YOU COULD HAVE MADE A PARADISE OF THIS UNIVERSE...

WHEN WILL YOU FINALLY REALIZE YOUR DAYS ARE OVER?

...YOU COULD HAVE CREATED AN EVERLASTING PEACE THROUGHOUT ALL THE WORLDS BOTH KNOWN AND NOT.

14

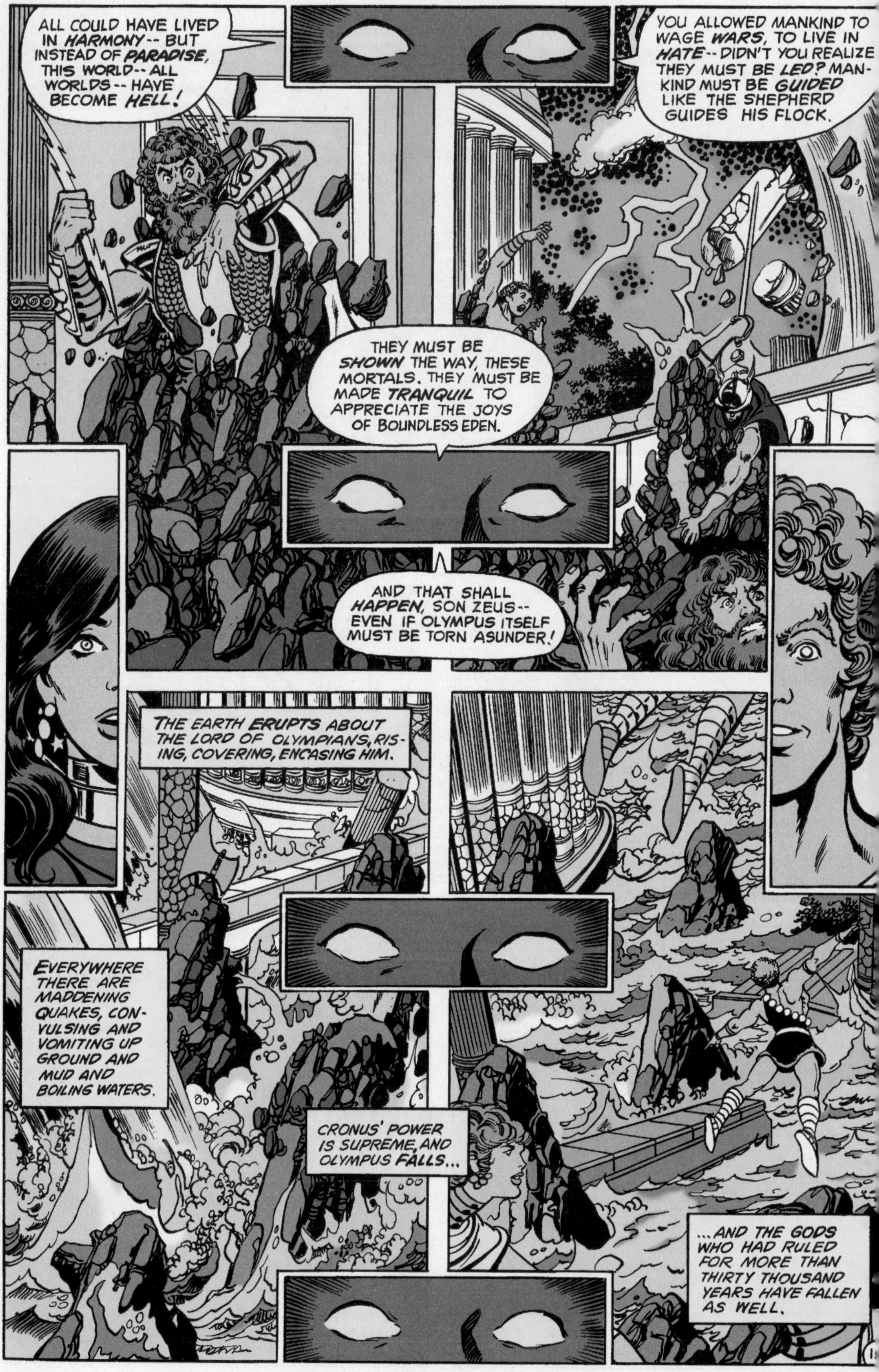
ALL COULD HAVE LIVED IN HARMONY -- BUT INSTEAD OF PARADISE, THIS WORLD -- ALL WORLDS -- HAVE BECOME HELL!
YOU ALLOWED MANKIND TO WAGE WARS, TO LIVE IN HATE -- DIDN'T YOU REALIZE THEY MUST BE LED? MANKIND MUST BE GUIDED LIKE THE SHEPHERD GUIDES HIS FLOCK.
THEY MUST BE SHOWN THE WAY, THESE MORTALS. THEY MUST BE MADE TRANQUIL TO APPRECIATE THE JOYS OF BOUNDLESS EDEN.
AND THAT SHALL HAPPEN, SON ZEUS -- EVEN IF OLYMPUS ITSELF MUST BE TORN ASUNDER!
THE EARTH ERUPTS ABOUT THE LORD OF OLYMPIANS, RISING, COVERING, ENCASING HIM.
EVERYWHERE THERE ARE MADDENING QUAKES, CONVULSING AND VOMITING UP GROUND AND MUD AND BOILING WATERS.
CRONUS' POWER IS SUPREME, AND OLYMPUS FALLS...
...AND THE GODS WHO HAD RULED FOR MORE THAN THIRTY THOUSAND YEARS HAVE FALLEN AS WELL.

IT IS *OVER*, MY LOVE.... WE HAVE *WON!*

OLYMPUS IS *OURS!!* THE GODS ARE *HELPLESS* NOW...

ENCASED IN *STONE* EVEN AS *WE* WERE FOR ALL THOSE MANY YEARS.

BUT, LET US NOT MAKE *THEIR* MISTAKE, MY BROTHERS.

THEY MERELY *BANISHED* US TO THE HELLPITS OF TARTARUS--

--LET US *DESTROY* THESE UPSTARTS WHILE WE STILL HAVE *CONTROL.*

DESTROY? NO, CRONUS, THAT'S AGAINST EVERY-THING WE WERE FIGHTING FOR.

YOU PROMISED ALL *PEACE.* HOW CAN YOU *BEGIN* BY CAUSING *DEATH?*

HOW CAN YOU SPREAD *LOVE* IF THERE IS ONLY *HATE* IN YOUR HEART?

DONNA, THAT IS *ENOUGH!* CRONUS IS OUR *LEADER!*

YOUR WORDS *STING,* MORTAL! WHAT YOU SAY HAS *MERIT,* BUT JUST CANNOT *BE.*

YOU *LIE* TO YOURSELF IF YOU BELIEVE THAT, CRONUS. YOU DO IT FOR *YOURSELF* AND NO OTHER.

YES, MY DAUGHTER... ATHENA'S WISDOM HAS *GUIDED* US ON OUR JOURNEY TO OLYMPUS.

AND IT APPEARS WE HAVE ARRIVED JUST *IN TIME.*

BECAUSE YOU CANNOT SEEM TO *REALIZE*--

I *DO* BELIEVE IN LOVE AND PEACE, BUT IF WE FAIL TO *DESTROY* THESE CHILD-GODS, THEY WILL SOME DAY RETURN TO DESTROY US! WHAT WE MUST WE DO FOR THE *WORLDS* THAT WILL REALIZE SALVATION.

YOU?!?

-- YOUR DREAMS OF THIS NEW GOLDEN AGE WOULD ONLY *DESTROY* THE VERY ONES YOU CLAIM TO WISH TO *HELP.*

16

YOU SEE THE EARTH AS IT WOULD BE IF *CRONUS'S* RULE HELD SWAY.

YOU SEE *PEACE*, YOU FEEL THE *TRANQUILITY* THAT PERVADES ALL.

THEN YOUR OWN WORDS PROVE US *RIGHT*, OLYMPIAN.

IT'S *BEAUTIFUL*, ATHENA... IT'S WHAT MANKIND'S ALWAYS *DREAMED* OF.

I WILL HAVE GIVEN THE WORLD *LOVE*...

...AND THAT IS MORE THAN *ZEUS* HAS EVER DONE!

THE VISION CONTINUES, CRONUS... *WATCH*, THEN SPEAK LATER.

"*YOUR VERY OWN WORDS BETRAY YOU, CRONUS. YOU DON'T BELIEVE MAN IS EQUAL TO THE GODS...*

"*YOU SEE THEM AS WORSHIPPING YOU.*

"*YOU SEE THEM AS SHEEP, TO PROTECT AS YOU WOULD YOUR FLOCK.*

"*YES, THERE WOULD BE PEACE AND TRANQUILITY, BUT MANKIND'S WILL WOULD BE DESTROYED.*

"*YOUR NEW GOLDEN AGE WOULD BRING BEAUTY, BUT AT WHAT COST?*

"*THE ANSWER, CRONUS-- IS MAN'S FREEDOM!*

"*THEY HAVE A DIVINE RIGHT TO BE FREE, NOT TO BEND TO YOUR THINKING, TITAN.*"

IF THEY WANT PEACE, THAT IS THEIR *RIGHT*. IF THEY ARE FOOLISH ENOUGH TO DEMAND *BLOOD*, THAT TOO SHOULD BE THEIRS TO DECIDE.

LONG AGO ZEUS *UNDERSTOOD* THAT TRUTH. MAN HAS FREE WILL TO DO AS HE WISHES...

...AND THE GODS MUST BE FOREVER RESTRICTED FROM *INTERFERING* WITH THOSE WHOM THEY HAVE CREATED.

CAN YOU *DENY* THIS, CRONUS? CAN YOU, GOD OF GODS?

PLEASE, CRONUS... ANSWER HER!

18

YOU *TELL* ME, HYPERION. IS THIS WHAT WILL *HAPPEN* IF CRONUS RECREATES HIS *GOLDEN AGE?*

DONNA, I--

DONNA, HYPERION HOLDS YOU UNDER *HIS* SWAY. HIS SUN POWERS CONTROL YOUR *HEART.*

CAN YOU BELIEVE *CRONUS* WOULD PROVE ANY *DIFFERENT?*

IS SHE *RIGHT?* HYPERION? DID YOU *MAKE* ME LOVE YOU?

FOR HEAVEN'S SAKE, HYPERION, *DID YOU DO THIS TO ME?!?*

WE ARGUE TOO LONG, AND THE TIME FOR *TALK* IS DONE!

WE TITANS HAVE *WON* OUR BATTLE WITH THE GODS OF OLYMPUS!

YOU MORTALS SHALL NOT TALK US OUT OF OUR RIGHTFUL *VICTORY!*

THEN, WE'LL TURN THAT VICTORY *AGAINST* YOU, CRONUS--

--FOR YOU'RE NO GOD OF *MINE!*

AND NOT EVEN THE LIVING *GOD,* X'HAL HERSELF DEMANDS SUCH MINDLESS SUBSERVIENCE!

THEN THIS X'HAL OF YOURS IS A *FOOL!*

WHAT *USE* IS POWER UNLESS ONE *WIELDS* IT?

THEN THE DIE HAS BEEN *CAST!*

THERE MUST BE WAR!

19

BROTHERS AND SISTERS, LET US *UNITE* OUR POWERS... LET US SHARE OUR *STRENGTHS*.

ONE FINAL BATTLE, AND THE WORLD IS OURS!

BY HERA! THEY SHATTER THE VERY *GROUND* BENEATH OUR FEET!

BUT NOT EVEN THE WILL OF THE *TITANS* SHALL STOP US!

OVER SHIFTING ROCK OR GUSHING WAVE-- WE AMAZONS FIGHT TO THE *END*!

KORIAND'R, THE AMAZONS TAKE ON THE TITANS...IT IS UP TO US TO *FREE* THE ONE WHO CAN HELP US GAIN VICTORY.

A MOMENT, RAVEN...THAT BLAST WAS *POWERFUL*.

AND AGAIN I HAVE BEEN *DEFEATED* WITH FAR TOO MUCH *EASE*.

IF WE *SURVIVE* THIS WAR, RAVEN, I MUST RETURN TO THE TRAINING OF THE *OKAARAN WARLORDS*!

DO WHAT YOU WILL IF WE *LIVE*...

...BUT FOR NOW, ZEUS MUST BE *FREED*!

HE LIVES... I CAN *SENSE* HIS SOUL....

THEN *STAND BACK*, RAVEN-- I'LL FREE HIM WITH A *STARBOLT*!

NO, GIRL, MY *HUSBAND* PLACED THE OLYMPIAN THERE ...AND THERE SHALL HE *REMAIN*!

RHEA! YOU ABOVE ALL KNOW THE *FOLLY* OF THIS FIGHT. YOU RISKED YOUR HUSBAND'S WRATH BEFORE IN *SAVING* ZEUS FROM CRONUS' RAGE.

BUT... I CANNOT *DEFY* HIM AGAIN... I CAN'T!

20

THEN I *TOO* MUST DO WHAT MUST BE DONE!

I, WHO *ABHOR* VIOLENCE, MUST LASH OUT, OR THERE WILL BE *BLOOD* STAINING THE GROUNDS OF OLYMPUS AND EARTH ALIKE!

THIS WILL NOT *HURT* YOU, RHEA...MY *SOUL-SELF* WILL MERELY *EASE* YOUR ANGER, *SUBDUE* YOUR NEED FOR WAR.

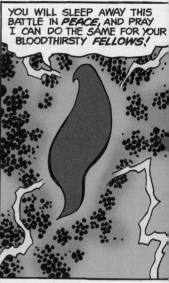

YOU WILL SLEEP AWAY THIS BATTLE IN *PEACE*, AND PRAY I CAN DO THE SAME FOR YOUR BLOODTHIRSTY *FELLOWS!*

KORIAND'R, HAVE YOU FOUND A WAY TO *FREE* THE OLYMPIAN?

I'M *TRYING*, RAVEN, BUT NOT EVEN MY *STARBOLTS* CAN SMASH CRONUS' WALL OF STONE.

DO YOU KNOW HOW *FRUSTRATING* IT IS? BEING SO *POWERLESS* WHILE POSSESSING SO MUCH *POWER?*

WHILE...

IT IS *YOUR* FAULT, WOMAN-- YOU WHO ARE MY LOVE'S *MOTHER!* YOU SET HER *AGAINST* ME.

YOU'LL *DIE* FOR THAT-- AS MY *PARENTS* HAD TO DIE THAT WE TITANS WOULD LIVE.

NO, HYPERION-- *STOP!*

WHATEVER *HATRED* EXISTS BETWEEN YOU AND YOUR ELDERS...OR YOU AND YOUR CHILDREN--

--THAT HATRED DOES NOT EXIST IN ME.

I *LOVE* MY MOTHER, AND IF YOU *HURT* HER, OR EVEN *TRY--*

--SO HELP ME, HYPERION-- GOD, OR TITAN, OR WHAT-EVER YOU ARE-- *I WILL MAKE YOU SUFFER!*

DONNA... DAUGHTER...

AT LAST, RAVEN, I'VE CREATED A *FISSURE*... THE ROCK WILL *BREAK* NOW.

STAND BACK, RAVEN, AND, BY X'HAL--

21

--THE OLYMPIAN WILL BE FREE!

BY THE CHAOS!

NO...NOT AGAIN...HOW MANY LIVES DOES THIS ZEUS POSSESS?

MORE THAN ENOUGH, MY FATHER!

AND WISDOM ENOUGH TO KNOW HOW TO USE SUCH LIVES.

AGAIN WE STAND AT EACH OTHER'S THROATS --READY TO KILL OR BE KILLED.

BUT, THERE IS NO REASON FOR THIS FOLLY. YOU MUST REMEMBER THE WORDS OF THE ORACLE.

I REMEMBER HIM, DAMN YOU! I REMEMBER HIM SAYING THE CHILD SHALL LIVE ON, THE PARENT SHALL PASS ON!

BUT THIS TIME HIS WORDS NEED NOT COME TRUE.

THERE IS NO OTHER WAY, CRONUS ...AND YOU MUST KNOW THAT NOW.

FROM PARENT TO CHILD, THE MANTLE IS ALWAYS PASSED ON.

22

I WAS BORN OF YOUR SON'S *BROW*--AND I, *ATHENA*, AM *GODDESS* OF WISDOM. I SEE CLEARLY WHAT OTHERS *CANNOT*.

...AND I KNOW THAT, AS GAEA AND URANUS PASSED THE POWER UNTO *US*, SOME DAY WE WILL PASS ON *OUR* POWER AS WELL.

THAT IS THE WAY OF THE *UNIVERSE*. NEITHER MAN NOR GOD MAY *CHANGE* THAT ONE ETERNAL *TRUTH*.

YOU DEMAND OUR *DEATHS?*

NO!

YET WE CANNOT LIVE *HERE*...SUCH IS NOT OUR *WAY*, ATHENA.

ONLY *YOU*, OCEANUS, FOUGHT OUR *WAGING* THIS WAR. WHAT SAY YOU *NOW?*

THERE IS BUT ONE PLACE WE CAN GO, CRONUS -- *TARTARUS!*

RETURN TO THAT *HELL?* HOW CAN ONE FORGET ITS *HORRORS?* THERE MUST BE *ANOTHER* PLACE, CRONUS.

THERE IS *NONE*, MNEMOSYNE, AND WE HAVE NO PLACE *HERE*.

I FEAR ATHENA'S WORDS ARE *TRUE* ...WHAT WE WISH FOR MAN, AS NOBLE AS OUR ASPIRATIONS MAY BE--

--ITS *RESULT* WOULD BE MORE THAN FOLLY--'TWOULD BE *DISASTER!*

TARTARUS *NEEDN'T* BE A HELL. YOU CAN MAKE IT *MORE*.

FIGHT TO MAKE IT THE *PARADISE* YOU SEEK.

SHE IS *CORRECT*, CRONUS.

OUR *TIME* HERE, OUR *PLACE* HERE, IS NO MORE. LET THOSE WHO HAVE COME AFTER US *INHERIT* WHAT IS NOW RIGHTFULLY THEIRS.

23

CRONUS--*NO!* WE MUST NOT ABANDON OUR *IDEALS.*

THEY ARE ALL *WRONG.* WE *CAN* REMAKE THIS WORLD AS YOU SEE IT!

WE CAN *AVOID* THE PROBLEMS THEY PREDICT.

HYPERION, IT IS *OVER*... THE OLYMPIANS, OUR CHILDREN, ARE *CORRECT.*

THEN WHAT AM I TO *DO?* I HAVE ALREADY LOST MY *FIRST* LOVE, THIA--

--MUST I LOSE THIS *SECOND* LOVE AS WELL?

THERE WASN'T *LOVE* BETWEEN US, HYPERION ... NO *TRUE* LOVE.

NO, YOU CANNOT *SAY* THAT. I *LOVED* YOU... I *DID.*

YES, I USED MY POWERS TO *MAKE* YOU LOVE ME, BUT THAT WAS FOR *US*...

AND THINK-- SOON YOU CAN BE A *GODDESS*... AN *IMMORTAL.*

NO, BROTHER, SHE CAN *NEVER* BE A GODDESS.

SHE IS A *MORTAL*...

...AND THAT IS WHAT SHE MUST FOREVER *REMAIN.*

YOU SOUGHT TO POSSESS *HER* AS I SOUGHT TO POSSESS A *WORLD.* IT IS *WRONG.*

NO... NO ...IT IS NOT *FAIR,* CRONUS ...TO HAVE SO MUCH--

--NOT FAIR TO LOSE IT ALL, AND TO *WANT* SO MUCH *MORE.*

I AM A GOD OF THE *SUN* ... I TOUCHED THE *LIGHT* ...AND NOW... NOW YOU WANT TO PLUNGE ME INTO *DARKNESS* FOREVER

IT... IT IS NOT *FAIR*... NOT FAIR *AT* ALL...

WHY... WHY MUST I *SUFFER* SO?

IN SOME WAY, TO SOME MEASURE, HYPERION, WE *ALL* SUFFER-- AND ALL WE CAN HOPE FOR IS TO *GROW.*

THAT'S *ALL* WE CAN HOPE FOR...

...THAT'S ALL...

24

THERE IS STILL ONE LAST *ITEM* TO ATTEND TO, MY HUSBAND.

THE OLYMPIANS!

OUR SON ZEUS COULD FREE THEM NOW, BUT LET THE ENMITY BETWEEN PARENT AND CHILD *END.*

WE WHO GAVE YOU LIFE AN *AGE AGONE...*

...NOW RETURN TO YOU ITS *FREEDOM* AS YOU DESERVE.

IT IS *OVER* NOW.

AND WE ARE *READY.*

TARTARUS *AWAITS* US... BUT THIS TIME WE GO NOT AS *DEFEATED* TITANS...

WE TRAVEL NOT TO SOME *PRISON...*

...BUT TO OUR *HOME.*

FOR WE *TOO* HAVE GAINED OUR FREEDOM... AND HOPEFULLY GAINED EVEN *MORE.*

ALL OF YOU BUT *I*... I HAVE *LOST*... LOST *HOPE*... LOST *LOVE...*

YOU *FOUND* LOVE, HYPERION... YOU EVEN *INSPIRED* LOVE... I CARED...

...AND EVEN *NOW*, I CARE ...FOR THE *GOODNESS* THAT IS IN YOU.

FAREWELL, MY PARENTS...YOU GO NOT TO *HELL* --

-- BUT TO *HEAVEN.*

AND ONE DAY, WE, YOUR CHILDREN, SHALL WALK *BESIDE* YOU AGAIN.

AND ON THAT *BRIGHT* DAY, WE SHALL WALK TOGETHER IN *LOVE.*

25

EPILOGUE ONE:

PARADISE ISLAND: AS A PLANE SWOOPS HIGH AND AWAY FROM THIS ISLE OF PEACE AND HOPE.

SOON, IT WILL BE GONE.

I DO NOT *UNDERSTAND.* WHY DID DONNA LEAVE WITHOUT EVEN A WORD?

I READ HER *SOUL,* KORIAND'R... AND HER *HEART.*

AND PERHAPS *I,* ABOVE ALL, KNOW WHAT HAPPENED TO HER.

FOR *LIKE* HYPERION, I TOO HAVE MANIPULATED THAT EMOTION CALLED *LOVE...*

...AND I KNOW HOW TERRIBLY *CRUSHED* DONNA NOW FEELS.

FOR EVEN THAT ARTIFICIALLY CREATED LOVE IS FELT BY BOTH MAN AND WOMAN -- AND IT IS A PAIN I HAVE YET TO *ERASE.*

MY HEART *REACHES* OUT FOR HER...

...FOR I *TOO* LOVED A GOD WITH ALL MY HEART AND ALL MY SOUL...

...AND I... I HAVE NEVER LOVED *ANOTHER* MAN SINCE.

I CAN ONLY PRAY THAT *MY* FATE AND MY *SUFFERING* IS NOT SHARED BY THE DAUGHTER I LOVE.

EPILOGUE TWO:

THE LABORATORY OF PAULA VON GUNTHER...

THE MALE RESPONDS WELL TO THE *PURPLE RAY.*

HE WILL *NOT* DIE AFTER ALL.

COME, HESTIA, PAULA AND THE OTHERS WILL WANT TO *KNOW.*

THE AMAZONS LEAVE TO SPREAD THE JOYOUS WORD THAT GARFIELD LOGAN, WHO HOVERED ON THE VERY BRINK OF DEATH, NOW LIVES...

BUT SOON, THEY WILL ALL RETURN TO DISCOVER...

...THIS IS NOT QUITE THE SAME GARFIELD LOGAN THEY HAD ONCE KNOWN.

I... I LIVE AGAIN.... AND I LIVE -- TO KILL!!

26

EPILOGUE THREE:

NEW YORK CITY STANDS TALL, PROUND, AND SEEMINGLY ETERNAL...

AND, IN THE APARTMENT OF ONE TERRY LONG, AGE 29, PROFESSOR OF HISTORY AT MANHATTAN UNIVERSITY...

HUH? WHO CAN *THAT* BE?

IF THAT'S *McREADY*... I PAID THE BLASTED *RENT* LAST--EH?

DONNA?

TERRY, PLEASE-- OPEN THE *DOOR*...

DONNA, WHA--?

DON'T, TERRY-- PLEASE DON'T *TALK* NOW...

...AND PLEASE DON'T ASK ME WHAT *HAPPENED.*

JUST *HOLD* ME...

...AND DON'T LET ME *GO*... NOT FOR A VERY LONG TIME.

BELIEVE ME, DONNA, I *WON'T*...

...I *LOVE* YOU.

I TRULY LOVE *YOU.*

AND DAY PASSES INTO NIGHT, AND NIGHT TO DAY...

...AND THE FAINT LIGHT OF HOPE BEGINS TO GLOW, AND THE DOUBTS, THOUGH NEVER GONE, RECEDE FAR, FAR AWAY...

NEXT ISSUE: WONDER GIRL IN NEW YORK! RAVEN AND STARFIRE ON PARADISE ISLAND! BUT, WHAT OF THE GUYS?

TITANS-- TOGETHER!

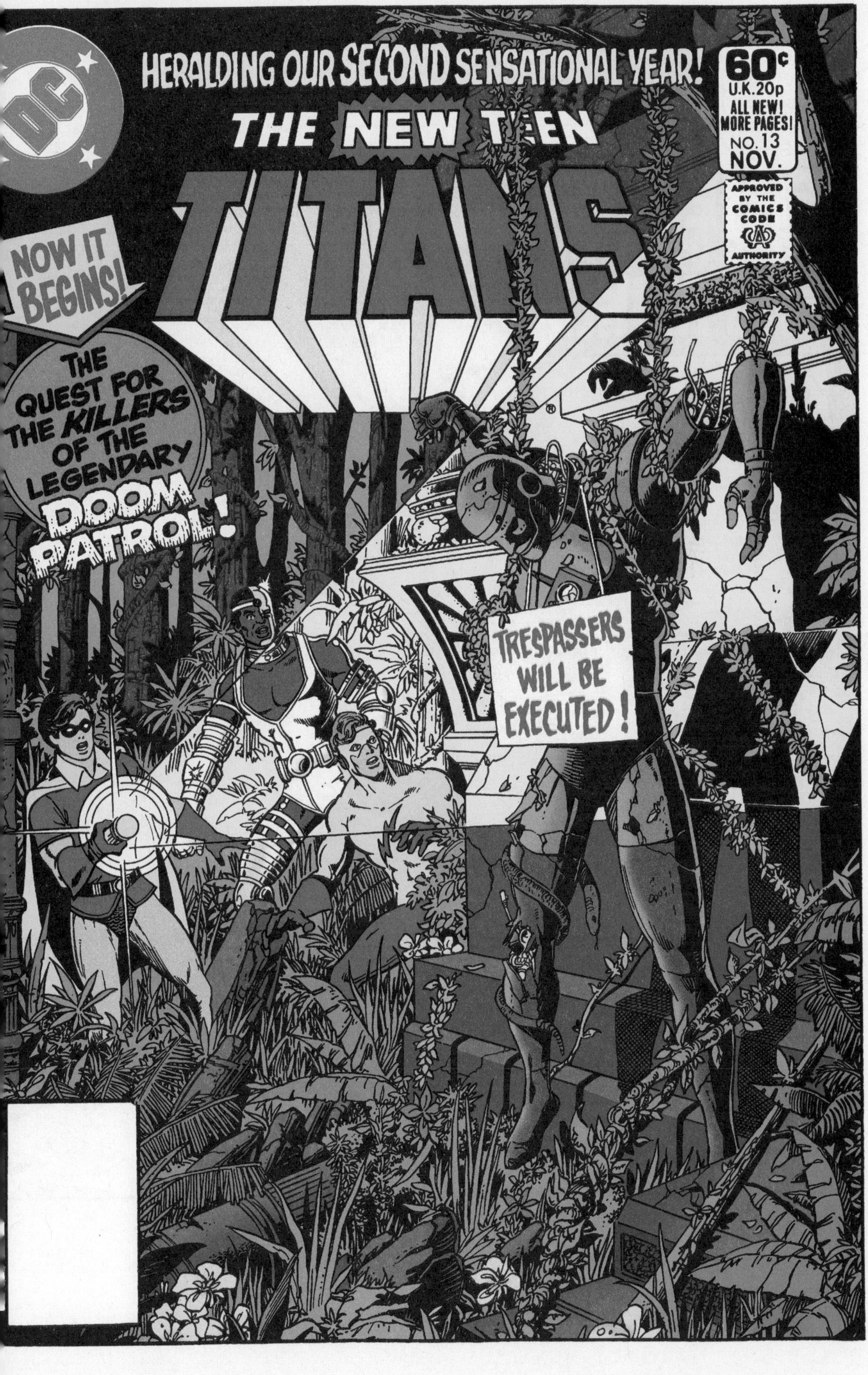
HERALDING OUR SECOND SENSATIONAL YEAR!
60¢
U.K.20p
ALL NEW! MORE PAGES!
NO. 13
NOV.
THE NEW TEEN
TITANS
APPROVED BY THE COMICS CODE AUTHORITY
NOW IT BEGINS!
THE QUEST FOR THE KILLERS OF THE LEGENDARY
DOOM PATROL!
TRESPASSERS WILL BE EXECUTED!

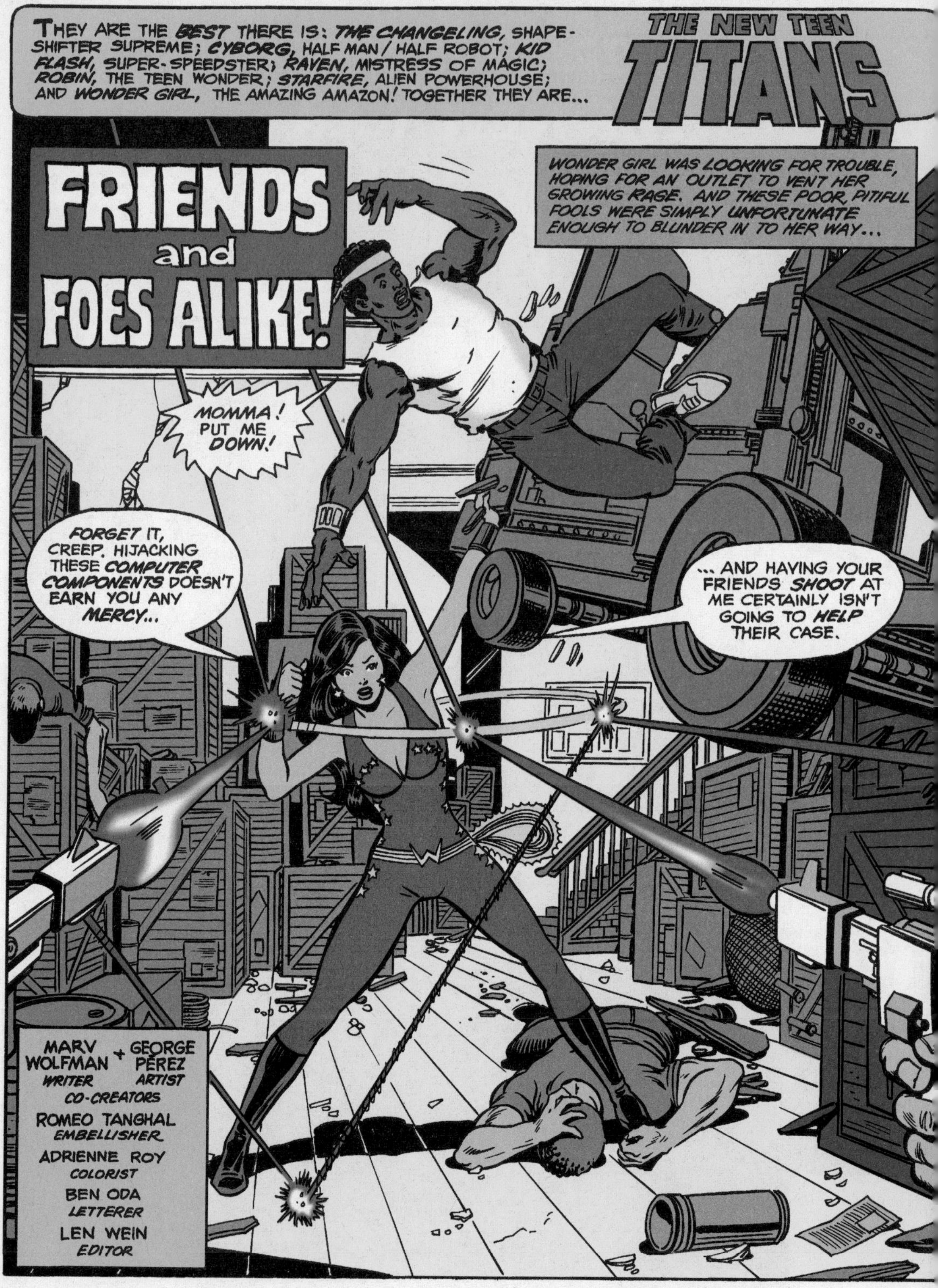
THEY ARE THE BEST THERE IS: THE CHANGELING, SHAPE-SHIFTER SUPREME; CYBORG, HALF MAN / HALF ROBOT; KID FLASH, SUPER-SPEEDSTER; RAVEN, MISTRESS OF MAGIC; ROBIN, THE TEEN WONDER; STARFIRE, ALIEN POWERHOUSE; AND WONDER GIRL, THE AMAZING AMAZON! TOGETHER THEY ARE...
THE NEW TEEN TITANS
FRIENDS and FOES ALIKE!
WONDER GIRL WAS LOOKING FOR TROUBLE, HOPING FOR AN OUTLET TO VENT HER GROWING RAGE. AND THESE POOR, PITIFUL FOOLS WERE SIMPLY UNFORTUNATE ENOUGH TO BLUNDER IN TO HER WAY...
MOMMA! PUT ME DOWN!
FORGET IT, CREEP. HIJACKING THESE COMPUTER COMPONENTS DOESN'T EARN YOU ANY MERCY...
...AND HAVING YOUR FRIENDS SHOOT AT ME CERTAINLY ISN'T GOING TO HELP THEIR CASE.
MARV WOLFMAN WRITER + GEORGE PÉREZ ARTIST
CO-CREATORS
ROMEO TANGHAL EMBELLISHER
ADRIENNE ROY COLORIST
BEN ODA LETTERER
LEN WEIN EDITOR

OH, MAN-- SHE'S PICKIN' UP THAT FORK-LIFT LIKE IT'S A *TOY.*

SPLIT, MAN-- *RUN!* I AIN'T TACKLIN' *THAT* BROAD!

WHAT ABOUT THE *BOSS?* HE'LL *KILL* US FER SCREWIN' UP.

OH, DON'T WORRY ABOUT *THAT,* PUNK. THERE WON'T BE ENOUGH *LEFT* OF YOU FOR *HIM* TO GET HIS HANDS ON.

SHOOT! I DON'T *LIKE* THIS, LEROY... NOT ONE BIG, BAD *BIT!*

SHE'S GONNA LET US HANG LIKE DEAD MEAT IN AN *ICE BOX!*

SKRASHH!

NOT *DEAD,* MISTER-- BUT YOU MIGHT *WISH* YOU WERE.

TODAY WAS DEFINITELY THE *WRONG DAY* TO PULL OFF A JOB IN MY *NEIGHBORHOOD!*

SWOK

I'M *MAD,* FELLAS... MADDER THAN I'VE EVER *BEEN...*

I WANT TO *SMASH* SOMETHING... AND I DON'T PARTICULARLY CARE *WHAT.*

NO, THAT'S NOT *TRUE!* I *DO* CARE...

...BLAST IT, I *HAVE* TO CARE.

I MAY NOT *LIKE* IT, BUT AS MUCH AS I *WANT* TO HATE YOU, I *CAN'T.*

THESE FEELINGS GO AGAINST EVERYTHING I WAS *TAUGHT.*

2

117

WONDER GIRL BREATHES IN DEEPLY, THEN EXPELS HER HATRED ALONG WITH HER BREATH. CALMLY, SHE PRESSES THE ALARM BELL AND JUST WAITS UNTIL...

LOUIE, I CAN'T THINK OF A GUY WHO'D DESERVE IT *MORE.*

HEY, MAN, GET US *AWAY* FROM THAT LOONY, SHE COULD'A TORE US *APART.*

WE'VE BEEN HUNTING FOR THIS GANG FOR *MONTHS.* YOU'VE SAVED US AN AWFUL LOT OF *WORK.*

JUST WANT TO SAY *THANKS,* WONDER GIRL.

IT'S *OKAY,* OFFICER, I WAS JUST DOING MY *JOB!*

NO, THAT'S A *LIE.* I WENT OUT LOOKING FOR SOMEONE TO *HURT.*

AND *WHY--?* BECAUSE *HYPERION* USED SOME SORT OF *SPELL* ON ME -- MADE ME *LOVE* HIM.*

I FELT LIKE A *PAWN,* NOT IN *CONTROL--*

*AS SHOWN LAST ISSUE. --Len.

SO, WHAT DO I *DO?* I GO OUT OF MY WAY TO *LOSE* THAT CONTROL ON *MY OWN.*

BRIGHT, DONNA-- REAL *BRIGHT.*

TERRY! I ALMOST *FORGOT* YOU WERE WAITING. I'M *SORRY.*

DON'T *MENTION* IT, LOVE... IT WAS... WELL... *FASCINATING* WATCHING YOU IN ACTION.

MY STRENGTH DOESN'T *INTIMIDATE* YOU?

WELL, I'M NOT ABOUT TO CHALLENGE YOU TO AN *ARM-WRESTLING* MATCH, BUT, NAH-- IT DOESN'T *BOTHER* ME.

I HAVE THREE *OLDER SISTERS.* I GREW UP BEING BEATEN UP BY *GIRLS.*

BESIDES, GORGEOUS, WITH YOU IT'S *KINKY.*

HEY, LOWER THAT ARCHED *EYEBROW,* LOVE... I'M JUST *KIDDING.*

3

I'VE GOT A GOOD GRASP OF WHO *I* AM AND YOUR SPECIAL POWERS DON'T MAKE ME LESS *IMPORTANT*.

BUT THAT'S NOT WHAT'S *TROUBLING* YOU, IS IT? IT'S *HYPERION*, RIGHT?

YOU SEE RIGHT *THROUGH* ME, TERRY. YEAH, IT'S *HYPERION*.

I KNOW ALL *ABOUT* GODS ENTHRALLING BEAUTIFUL YOUNG MORTALS.

THAT DOESN'T MAKE IT *EASIER*, TERRY. I FEEL HELPLESS KNOWING I COULD BE *CONTROLLED* SO EASILY.

WELL, YOU CAN *DWELL* ON THAT, DONNA, EVEN THOUGH IT CAN'T CHANGE THE *FACTS*.

OR YOU CAN PUT IT *ASIDE*, KNOW YOU'RE A *GOOD PERSON* INSIDE, THAT YOU ARE *LOVED* AND CAN LOVE *BACK*.

LITTLE LADY THAT I LOVE, I'M A *HISTORY PROFESSOR*, REMEMBER?

YOU'VE GOT YOUR WHOLE *FUTURE* AHEAD OF YOU, DONNA...

DON'T LET THIS CRIPPLE YOUR *BELIEF* IN YOURSELF.

I'VE GOT A FUTURE, BUT FOR HOW *LONG*, REALLY? GARFIELD'S *YOUNGER* THAN I AM--

--AND HE'S ONLY *CLINGING* TO LIFE BY A FINE *THREAD*. *

*THE TERMINATOR SHOT GAR LOGAN, A.K.A. THE CHANGELING, IN TITANS #10. -- Len.

"WE RUSHED HIM TO *PARADISE ISLAND*, PLACED HIM UNDER THE *PURPLE RAY*... HOPING ITS LIFE-RESTORING RAYS COULD SAVE HIM."

"DIDN'T YOU SAY HE WAS *RECUPERATING*?"

HE'S NOT *DYING*, TERRY... BUT THAT'S FAR FROM BEING *HEALTHY*.

WHO KNOWS WHAT THIS WILL *DO* TO HIM... OR TO ANY OF *US*...

WE SUPER-HEROES AREN'T *USED* TO HAVING OUR FACES RUBBED IN OUR OWN *MORTALITY*.

READ ALL-STAR SQUADRON

TAXI

AND THAT'S WHY YOU'RE GOING BACK... TO *PARADISE ISLAND*, RIGHT?

I *HAVE* TO, TERRY... TO MAKE CERTAIN HE'S ALL *RIGHT*.

I'LL BE *WAITING* FOR YOU, DONNA.

GOD, TERRY, I *HOPE* SO. PLEASE... *KEEP WELL*.

ALWAYS *KEEP WELL*.

YOU'RE TOO *GOOD* A MAN TO EVER HAVE ANYONE *HURT* YOU.

4

119

PARADISE ISLAND: LEGENDARY HOME OF THE AMAZONS...

THE TRUMPET CALL COMMANDS THE ARENA TO SILENCE AS ALL EYES CENTER ON THE COMBATANTS BELOW...

THIS IS A DAY OF *REJOICING*, THE AMAZONS' BATTLE WITH THE GODS IS *OVER*, AND NOT ONE OF THEM HAS *DIED*...

AND THE GREEN ONE FROM MAN'S WORLD WILL *LIVE*, ACCORDING TO ALL REPORTS...

SO, WITH CELEBRATION, COMES THE *TOURNAMENT*...

...AND JOINING THE AMAZONS IN THIS TEST OF METTLE IS THE ALIEN PRINCESS KNOWN AS *KORIAND'R*, OR *STARFIRE* OF THE NEW TEEN TITANS...

AS *HIPPOLYTA*, QUEEN OF THE AMAZONS, IT IS MY JOYOUS DUTY TO CALL THIS CONTEST TO *ORDER*.

THERE WILL BE *TWO* GRUELING TESTS OF STRENGTH AND COURAGE...

...COMBAT BY *LANCE*, AND COMBAT BY *BATTLE-STAFF!*

REMEMBER, SISTERS-- REMAIN MOUNTED ON YOUR *KANGAS!* FOR IF YOU SHOULD *FALL*, YOU LOSE THE EVENT.

TO ALL OF YOU, *GOOD LUCK* ...AND MAY ATHENA'S WISE HAND *GUIDE* YOU NOW!

...HE FLAG DROPS, AND THE TOURNEY BEGINS...

THEY'RE BETTER TRAINED IN *RIDING* THESE BEASTS, BUT THAT WON'T *STOP* ME.

THE WARLORDS OF OKAARA TAUGHT ME HOW TO TAME *ANY* CREATURE.

THE FIRST HIT IS *MINE!*

THIS EXCITES ME LIKE THE TOURNAMENTS ON *TAMARAN*...

THOK!

I FEEL SO *FREE*, SO FILLED WITH *JOY!*

BUT...

WOK!

X'HAL! I DIDN'T SEE THAT *RIDER!*

HMMM, I FEEL WARM *BLOOD* ON MY CHEEK! I'VE BEEN *CUT.*

KORIAND'R IS *HURT...* PLEASE, STOP THE GAMES.

ONCE BEGUN THEY *CANNOT* BE STOPPED, RAVEN. BUT IF SHE *FALLS*, SHE'LL BE TAKEN FROM THE ARENA AND *TREATED.*

I WRENCHED MY *ARM*, BUT I'LL NOT FALL TO DEFEAT SO *EASILY*... AND CERTAINLY NOT SO *QUICKLY.*

AGHHH... I HAVE THE BEAST BY ITS *MANE*... IF I CAN HOLD ON BUT A MOMENT *MORE*...

...REPOSITION MYSELF IN THE *SADDLE*...

I'VE DONE IT!

AND THEY WERE NOT *READY* FOR ME TO MAKE MY *MOVE.*

STARFIRE LETS LOOSE WITH AN UNBRIDLED WHOOP OF VICTORY...

...AS THE CHEERING CROWD RISES TO ITS FEET, REJOICING IN HER MAGNIFICENT TRIUMPH!

6

SHE'S *GOOD*, HIPPOLYTA--BETTER TRAINED THAN I *REALIZED*.

INDEED, RAVEN-- I'D SAY SHE'D *RIVAL* MY DAUGHTER, *DIANA*, HERSELF.

BUT LET US SEE HOW SHE HANDLES THE *BATTLE STAFFS*.

YOU KNOW HOW TO *USE* THIS WEAPON, KORIAND'R?

I *DO*, TIBYA... I *GREW UP* WIELDING SUCH A STAFF.

THE WARLORDS TRAINED ME FOR THE BETTER PART OF A *YEAR* IN ITS SUBTLETIES.

THE WARLORDS OF OKAARA -- HOW *SCARED* OF THEM I WAS WHEN *TRAINING* ON THEIR WORLD.

YET, *WITHOUT* THEIR TRAINING, I DOUBT IF I COULD HAVE *SURVIVED* THE CITADEL'S *TORTURE*.

MEMORIES:

THE STAFF MUST BECOME *PART* OF YOU, KORIAND'R...

AND THINK OF YOUR *ENEMIES* AS MERELY COMPOSED OF *ATOMS*--

--ATOMS YOU CAN PENETRATE WITHOUT *HARM*, USING THE *KNOWLEDGE* WE GIVE YOU.

BUT...

THSK

THINK OF YOURSELVES AS ONE ENTITY.

THINK FIRST BEFORE ENGAGING AN ENEMY IN *BATTLE*--

--FOR ONCE THAT COMMITMENT IS *MADE*, YOU CAN-NOT RETREAT UNTIL VICTORY IS *YOURS*.

UNHH! *TOO MANY* OF THEM... HAVE TO *CONCENTRATE*.

7

YOU CAN FEEL YOUR *ENEMY* ABOUT YOU, YOUNG ONE...

...FEEL THE *RIPPLES* IN THE AIR AS THEY *MOVE.*

THEY WILL *ALERT* YOU TO THEIR PRESENCE EVEN BEFORE THEY ARE *SEEN.*

THREE OF THEM *SURROUNDING* ME.

THEY THINK I'VE BEEN *HURT* MORE THAN I AM.

GOOD, I WILL LURE THEM *CLOSER*--

REMEMBER, LITTLE ONE, YOU CAN *DEFEAT* YOUR ENEMY NO MATTER THEIR *SIZE,* NO MATTER THEIR *POWER.*

FAK!

--THEN *STRIKE!*

AHHH, I'VE *MISSED* THESE TESTS OF *COURAGE*... THESE *TRIALS BY COMBAT.*

FOCUS ALL YOUR *STRENGTH* INTO THE MOMENT OF ACTUAL *CONTACT* WITH YOUR ENEMY...

...AND THEY WILL NOT *SURVIVE.*

WHAK

FOR TOO LONG NOW I'VE *FORSAKEN* THE OKAARAN TRAINING RITUALS, BUT *NO LONGER.*

THAKK!

I WILL NEVER AGAIN ALLOW MYSELF TO GROW *WEAK!*

8

SHE RISES NOW, EXULTANT IN HER VICTORY, A PROUD, ALMOST VAIN SMILE CROSSES HER LIPS -- THEN QUICKLY VANISHES.

SHE REMEMBERS THE WARLORD'S WARNING...

THERE IS NO *JOY* TO BE HAD IN BATTLE. YOU FIGHT ONLY BECAUSE YOU *MUST.* IT IS *DUTY.*

"DO NOT RELISH VICTORY, FOR THAT WEAKENS YOU AND OPENS YOU TO A MOST HUMBLING DEFEAT."

YET, KORIAND'R CANNOT RESIST THE *SATISFACTION* SHE FEELS IN THIS TOURNAMENT VICTORY. SHE FEELS THE JOY SPREAD WARMLY THROUGHOUT HER BODY...

...AND THE THUNDEROUS OVATION IN HER HONOR ONLY SERVES THAT PLEASURE.

YOUR ISLAND IS SO MUCH LIKE *TAMARAN*... THE TRAINING FOR *COMBAT,* THE TOURNAMENTS OF *POWER*...

NO, KORIAND'R-- THE AMAZONS *DECRY* VIOLENCE, THEY EMBRACE *PEACE.*

INDEED, THIS ISLAND WAS *FOUNDED* AS A MEANS TO *AVOID* THE WARS OF MAN.

IT IS FAR MORE LIKE MY *TEMPLE AZARATH* THAN *YOUR* WARLIKE WORLD.

RAVEN, WE *DO* BELIEVE IN PEACE AND COMPASSION AND LOVE...

... BUT WE *ALSO* BELIEVE IN FIGHTING TO *KEEP* WHAT WE-- EH--?

THE GROUND IS *SHAKING!* SOMETHING'S *WRONG!*

BTOOM!!

GREAT *HERA!* PAULA'S LABORATORY ISLAND--IT'S *EXPLODING!*

THE *LABORATORY?* THAT IS WHERE *GARFIELD* IS!

WHAT'S *HAPPENED* TO HIM?

9

SINCE I'VE BECOME THIS WALKING *MACHINE SHOP,* SHE'S THE FIRST *NORMAL* PERSON WHO DOESN'T EVEN *FLINCH* WHEN SHE LOOKS AT ME.

SO WHAT DO I *DO* TO MY ONE OUTSIDE FRIEND? FIRST I GET HER *KIDNAPPED* JUST BECAUSE SHE *KNOWS* ME--*

--THEN I SEND HER *HOME* WITHOUT EVEN *LETTIN'* HER KNOW EXACTLY *WHAT* HAPPENED OR *WHY.*

*TITANS #10--GUESS WHO.

IT'S ALMOST LIKE I WAS TRYIN' TO MAKE HER *HATE* ME... ONLY THAT DOESN'T MAKE *SENSE,* DOESN'T IT?

IF SHE'S *REALLY* YOUR FRIEND, VIC, SHE WON'T TURN *AGAINST* YOU.

GUYS, SOMETHING'S WRONG... *DREADFULLY* WRONG.

YOU FIND *ROBOTMAN?*

JUST *HURRY,* PLEASE-- RIGHT *AHEAD.* IT'S *AWFUL*...

WONDER IF WEST'S *RIGHT*--THIS ROBOTMAN WAS GAR LOGAN'S *BUDDY* BACK IN HIS *DOOM PATROL* DAYS.

MEBBE I'M JUST SCARED I'LL *LOSE* ANOTHER FRIEND.

ROBOTMAN WAS SEARCHING FOR GAR'S STEPFATHER, *STEVE DAYTON*--AND DAYTON WAS SEARCHING FOR THE DOOM PATROL'S *KILLERS*...

DID HE *FIND* THEM? WHAT *HAPPENED* TO HIM?

MAN, SEEING *STEELE* THERE... IT MADE ME *SICK*...THAT COULD'VE BEEN *ME*... OR *ANY* OF US.

AND AFTER WHAT HAPPENED TO *GAR*... MY DOUBTS ABOUT BEING A FULL-TIME SUPER-HERO HAVE *RESURFACED* AGAIN-- IN SPADES!

IT'S H-HIM... IT'S *ROBOTMAN*!

BUT--WHAT *HAPPENED* TO HIM?

THEY *STARE* AT THE TORN AND MANGLED FIGURE HOISTED BEFORE THEM, AND THEY ARE SUDDENLY VERY MUCH *FRIGHTENED.*

WARNING TRESPASSERS WILL BE EXECUTED!

THE *LEGENDS* OF *ROBOTMAN* AND HIS FABLED *STRENGTH* ECHO THROUGH THEIR *HORRIFIED* MINDS.

WHAT COULD POSSIBLY HAVE *DONE* THIS TO HIM?

VIC, IS HE--?

MY EAR AMPLIFIERS ARE PICKIN' UP HIS *INTERNAL* GENERATORS...

HIS *BODY* MAY BE FIT FER A SCRAP PILE, BUT HE'S STILL *ALIVE* IN THERE...

...SOMEWHERE.

I'M GONNA MAKE SURE HE *STAYS* ALIVE.

DO YOU NEED *HELP*?

NO WAY, I'M HANDLING THIS *ALONE*!

MY DAD TAUGHT ME ALL ABOUT *CYBERNETICS* -- SO I COULD *REPAIR* MY *OWN* BODY PARTS.

'SIDES, *LOOKIN'* AT HIM MAKES ME THINK OF THAT OLD SAYIN' ABOUT THE *GRACE OF GOD.* THIS COULD'A BEEN *ME.*

IF THERE'S ANY WAY A' BRINGIN' 'IM BACK TO *LIFE*, I'LL *FIND* IT...

...'CAUSE, IF I *FAIL*, I'LL NEVER BE ABLE TO LOOK *LOGAN* IN THE FACE *AGAIN*!

12

SILENCE...

...AND THEY WAIT FOR WHAT SEEMS AT LEAST CENTURIES...

UNTIL...

UNHHHHH...

I'M DREAMIN'... I GOTTA BE DREAMIN'!..

...OR MEBBE I'M JUST DEAD!

ROBIN... KID FLASH... YOU TWO I KNOW--

--BUT WHAT IN BLUE BLAZES ARE YOU?

I'M THE NEW 1981-STYLE SUPER-CYBORG.

IT'S A GOOD THING I'M DEAD--OTHERWISE I'D BARF.'

STEELE, WHAT HAPPENED TO YOU? WHO DID THIS?

I... I DON'T REALLY REMEMBER, KID. I WAS LOOKIN' FOR DAYTON-- FOUND THIS UNDERGROUND FORTRESS...

...THEN, SUDDENLY, WHAMMO! I WAS BLOWN APART LIKE A USED KLEENEX.

NOW I'M AWAKE AGAIN! ONLY I CAN'T MOVE.

JUST HOLD YOUR CATHODE TUBES, OLD-TIMER... I'M RECONNECTIN' YOUR LEG JOINTS NOW.

BY THE WAY, MY NAME'S VIC STONE, AND I THINK WE GOT OURSELVES A MUTUAL FRIEND.

AND THAT BRINGS US RIGHT BACK TO PARADISE ISLAND, WHERE...

PAULA'S LABORATORY-- *DESTROYED*. BUT WHAT COULD HAVE *DONE* THAT?

WAS GARFIELD *HURT?* THAT'S ALL THAT *MATTERS.*

HESTIA, WHAT *HAPPENED* HERE?

THE *PURPLE RAY*...THERE WAS TOO MUCH *POWER*...

...*FEEDBACK* CAUSED THE *EXPLOSION*...

YOU *REST*, HESTIA...YOU'LL WAKE UP WITH NO *PAINS*...

...BUT, KORIAND'R-- WE'VE GOT TO FIND *GARFIELD*...

TOO LATE, WITCH-- I'VE FOUND *YOU!* I'M *ALIVE*...

...*ALIVE* AND READY TO *KILL!*

ATHENA-- WE NEED YOUR *WISDOM* NOW, GREAT GODDESS.

THE PURPLE RAY HAS DRIVEN THE MANLING *MAD!*

14

HE WAS GARFIELD LOGAN, THE CHANGELING, A SHAPE-SHIFTER... BUT NOW HE IS ONE HUNDRED TONS OF RAGING, THICK-SKINNED BEAST... A DEADLY BRACHIOSAURUS WHOSE ONLY CRAZED THOUGHTS ARE OF DEATH...

QUEEN HIPPOLYTA-- DO WE *KILL* THE BEAST?

I...I DO NOT *KNOW*... THAT IS A *MAN*...

...AND YET--

GRAWWLLL!

BACK OFF, YOU FOOLS-- *TREMBLE*-- FOR THESE ARE YOUR *LAST MOMENTS ALIVE!*

I WANT TO KILL! I WANT TO *DESTROY!*

SISTERS, HE HAS GIVEN US NO *CHOICE*--

ATTACK!!

THE AMAZONS ARE *FEARFUL* AS THEY HURL THEIR *SHARP-POINTED* SPEARS, AND THEY HAVE EVERY REASON TO BE....

...FOR EACH STRONG SHAFT MERELY SNAPS IN *TWO* AS THEY GRAZE THE GREAT BEASTS' SCALY HIDE.

THAT RAY OF YOURS DID *MORE* THAN MERELY DRIVE HIM *INSANE*--

--HE COULD NEVER HAVE MADE SUCH A *TRANSFORMATION* BEFORE!

AGGHHHH!

COME TO ME, ALL OF YOU, LET ME *DESTROY* YOU ALL AT ONCE!

GRAWLL!

HERA HELP US! HE'S MORE A *BEAST* THAN A MAN...

I FEAR ONLY THE *GODS* CAN STOP HIM NOW.

NO, HIPPOLYTA, WE DO NOT *REQUIRE* A GOD...

...ONLY THE *EMPATH* NAMED *RAVEN!*

THE GREAT GREEN BEAST LIFTS HIS MASSIVE HEAD SKYWARD, HIS LONG TONGUE SWEEPS ACROSS HIS CRAGGY LIPS. THIS DARK ONE WILL PROVIDE A FEAST TONIGHT...

⑮

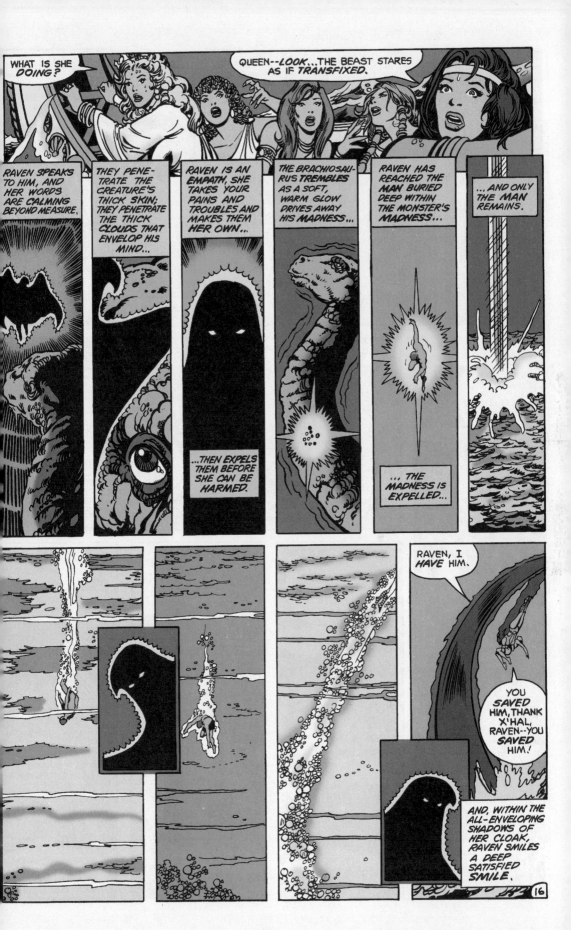

WHAT IS SHE DOING?

QUEEN--LOOK...THE BEAST STARES AS IF TRANSFIXED.

RAVEN SPEAKS TO HIM, AND HER WORDS ARE CALMING BEYOND MEASURE,

THEY PENETRATE THE CREATURE'S THICK SKIN; THEY PENETRATE THE THICK CLOUDS THAT ENVELOP HIS MIND...

RAVEN IS AN EMPATH, SHE TAKES YOUR PAINS AND TROUBLES AND MAKES THEM HER OWN...

...THEN EXPELS THEM BEFORE SHE CAN BE HARMED.

THE BRACHIOSAURUS TREMBLES AS A SOFT, WARM GLOW DRIVES AWAY HIS MADNESS...

RAVEN HAS REACHED THE MAN BURIED DEEP WITHIN THE MONSTER'S MADNESS...

... THE MADNESS IS EXPELLED...

...AND ONLY THE MAN REMAINS.

RAVEN, I HAVE HIM.

YOU SAVED HIM, THANK X'HAL, RAVEN--YOU SAVED HIM!

AND, WITHIN THE ALL-ENVELOPING SHADOWS OF HER CLOAK, RAVEN SMILES A DEEP SATISFIED SMILE.

16

FOR LONG MOMENTS THERE IS ONLY DARKNESS...

LOGAN'S MIND SORTS OUT THE REALITY FROM THE NIGHTMARE...

THEN...

OH, WOW!

I DIED! I DIED AND I'M IN HEAVEN.

'CAUSE IF THIS ISN'T THE LAND OF ANGELS, I DON'T KNOW WHAT IS!

YOU'RE ALIVE, GARFIELD. THANK GOODNESS.

KORIAND'R? YOU'RE HERE, TOO? HEY, THEN I'M NOT DEAD, AM I?

I KNOW! I WOKE UP IN A CONVENTION FOR CENTERFOLD GIRLS, RIGHT?

SO IF I'M ALIVE... LEMME AT 'EM!

NO, MY FRIEND, YOU MAY NOT SET FOOT OFF THIS TABLE.

IF ANY MAN TOUCHES THE GROUND OF PARADISE ISLAND, WE AMAZONS WILL LOSE OUR FABLED POWERS.

HUH?

YOU MEAN I'M STUCK UP HERE?

WITH ALL THOSE GORGEOUS GALS JUST OUTTA ARM'S REACH?

ARGGHHHH!

IT'S NOT FAIR! WHAT HAVE I DONE WRONG IN MY LIFE?

NOW I'M SURE I DIED... ONLY THIS ISN'T HEAVEN--

--IT'S HELL!

MY OMNI-WAVE RECEIVER!

AS AN IMAGE SHIMMERS INTO VIEW ON QUEEN HIPPOLYTA'S BRACELET...

DONNA... DAUGHTER? WHERE ARE YOU?

I'M HOVERING OVER THE MAIN ISLAND, MOTHER... WHERE ARE YOU?

COME, DAUGHTER... LAND ON PAULA'S ISLAND... WE'LL MEET YOU THERE.

BUT AS WONDER GIRL'S T-JET LANDS AMIDST THE JOYOUS THRONG, LET US ONCE MORE RETURN TO THE AFRICAN VELDT, WHERE...

...TOOK ME MORE'N *TWO WEEKS* TO STUMBLE ACROSS THIS SECRET ENTRANCEWAY ...AND THAT WAS WITH *KNOWIN'* IT WAS SOME- WHERE NEARBY.

THERE'S NO WAY YOU COULD FIND IT BY *ACCIDENT.*

AND THIS IS WHERE *MADAME ROUGE* AND *GENERAL ZAHL* ARE PLAYING HIDE-AND-SEEK?

OKAY, IT'S UP TO *ME* NOW. YOU GUYS STAY PUT WHILE I DO SOME SUPER-SPEED *SCOUTING.*

WATCH YOURSELF, HUH? IF THOSE TWO COULD TRUSS UP *ROBOTMAN* ...

...EVEN YOU'RE NOT *IMMUNE!*

DON'T I *KNOW* IT... WHICH IS WHY I'VE GOT TO DO THIS.

GOT TO *PROVE* TO MYSELF THAT MY WAFFLING ABOUT BEING EITHER ORDINARY *WALLY WEST* OR SUPER-HERO *KID FLASH*--

--IS A MATTER OF LOGICAL *CHOICE*...

...AND NOT BECAUSE I'M *AFRAID*... NOT BECAUSE I'M A *COWARD!*

18

BECAUSE, HEAVEN HELP ME, WHY ELSE AM I *AVOIDING* BEING WHAT I REALLY *AM?*

I'VE GOT MY SUPER-POWERS... I CAN'T AVOID *USING* THEM.

YET, SOMETHING KEEPS ME FROM SAYING-- YES, I'M KID FLASH, *SUPER-SPEEDSTER...*

I CAN'T BE A *NORMAL* KID ANY MORE... EVEN IF THAT'S WHAT I TRULY *WANT* TO BE.

YES, SOMEONE *SPECIAL* WITH SPECIAL *POWERS* AND SPECIAL *RESPONSIBILITES.*

I'VE GOT TO LEARN IF THAT SOMETHING IS THE FACT THAT I'M JUST *SCARE* OR--

UH-OH, *VOICES* --COMING FROM BEHIND THIS *ROCK...*

THERE MUST BE AN *ENTRANCEWAY* SOMEWHERE, BUT WHY BOTHER *LOOKING* FOR IT--

--WHEN I CAN SIMPLY *VIBRATE* MY *ATOMS...*

...AND ACTUALLY PASS THROUGH THE *WALL* ITSELF TO-- *HOLY HANNAH!*

A MAN-MADE CHAMBER ...WITH *GUARDS* OF SOME SORT.

THIS MUST BE THE WAY TO *MADAME ROUGE* AND COMPANY...

THAT IS, COMPANY SPELLED *TROUBLE* -- WITH A CAPITAL *"T"!*

OKAY, FIRST THINGS *FIRST*-- GET RID OF *THOSE* TWO, THEN CALL FOR THE OTHER *TITANS!*

AND A LITTLE *SUPER-SPEED WIND BLAST* SHOULD DO THE TRICK.

THEY DON'T *FEEL* THE WIND WHERE THEY STAND, BUT THEY HEAR THE SUDDEN, INEXPLICABLE HOWLING...

THEY GLANCE UPWARD IN AN ATTEMPT TO SEE WHAT IS *HAPPENING*...

BUT, IT IS A *VAIN* ATTEMPT AT *BEST.*

DUST STORM!

NO--THERE CAN *BE* NO DUST STORM DOWN HERE. WE ARE *UNDER ATTACK!*

SHOOT!

GREAT *ORDER* THERE, PAL. HOW DO YOU EXPECT TO *HIT* SOMETHING YOU CAN'T *SEE?*

NOT THAT I'M GOING TO GIVE YOU THE *CHANCE* ANYWAY.

KRAK!

SPAK!

HMM, MUST BE *SLOWING DOWN*... IT TOOK MORE THAN TWO SECONDS TO *SUBDUE* THEM. OH, WELL ... *NEXT* TIME.

HEY, GUYS... ALL *CLEAR.* C'MON *DOWN.*

WE'LL BE RIGHT *THERE,* BUDDY.

FOLLOW ME. I KNOW THE *WAY.*

I CHECKED IT ALL OUT BEFORE THEY *WAYLAID* ME.

AND SHORTLY...

CRIPES! YOU SAID THEY WERE HEADQUARTERED DOWN HERE, BUT I NEVER EXPECTED *THIS!*

20

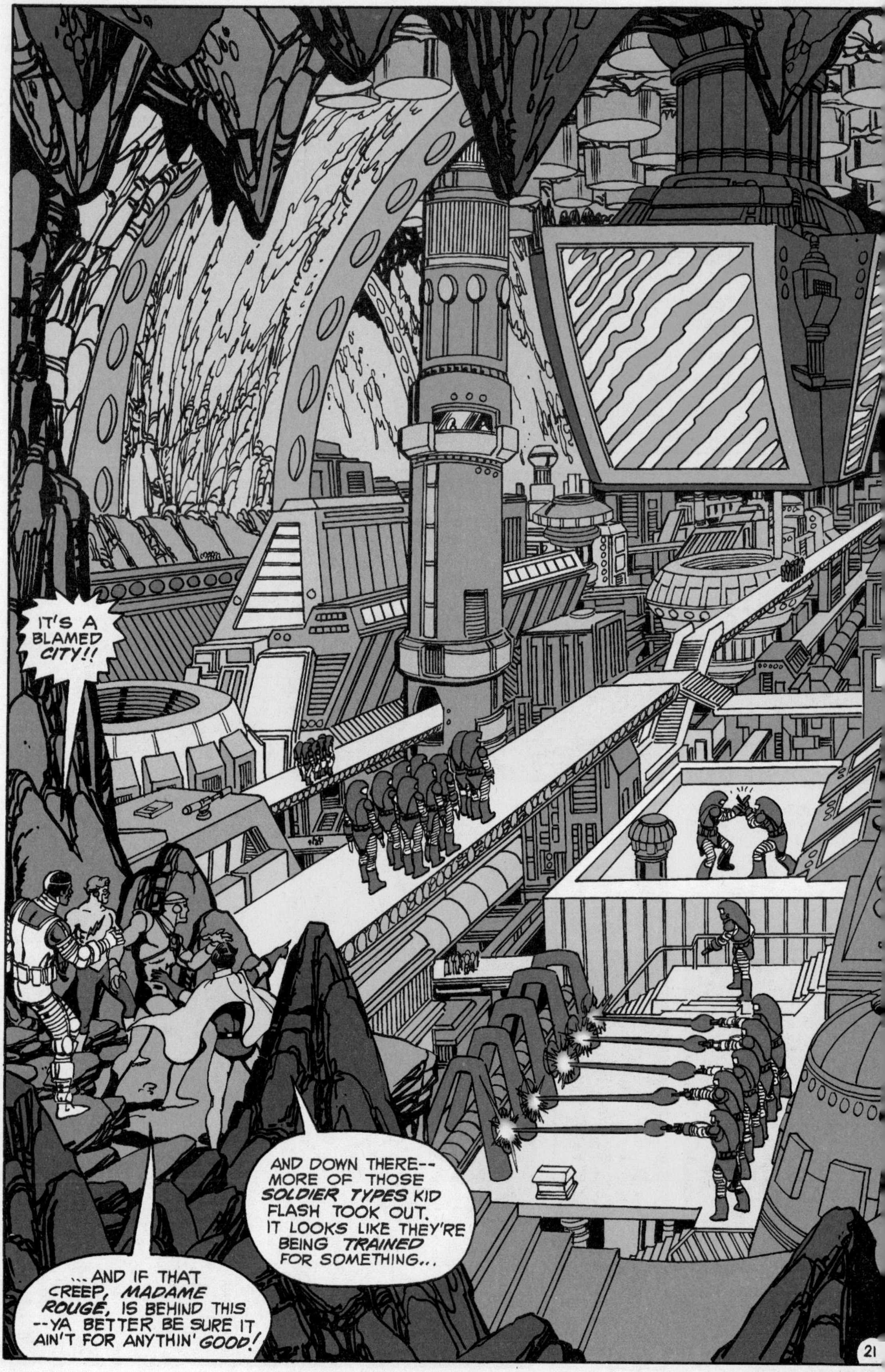
IT'S A BLAMED *CITY!!*
AND DOWN THERE-- MORE OF THOSE ***SOLDIER TYPES*** KID FLASH TOOK OUT. IT LOOKS LIKE THEY'RE BEING ***TRAINED*** FOR SOMETHING...
...AND IF THAT CREEP, ***MADAME ROUGE,*** IS BEHIND THIS --YA BETTER BE SURE IT AIN'T FOR ANYTHIN' *GOOD!*
21

IT'S ALSO OBVIOUS WE CAN'T TAKE THEM ALL ON BY OURSELVES.

LET'S JUST FIND STEVE DAYTON AND GET OUT OF HERE.

THEN WE CONTACT THE GIRLS AND MAYBE EVEN THE JUSTICE LEAGUE.

HOLD IT, GUYS-- OVER THERE, ON THAT VIEW SCREEN...

ISN'T THAT MADAME ROUGE?

SOLDIERS! ATTENTION! SECURITY HAS BEEN BREACHED!

WE HAVE INTRUDERS! FIND THEM! DESTROY THEM!

IT'S HER! THAT BLASTED KILLER!

SHE AN' ZAHL MURDERED THE DOOM PATROL!

I WANNA BREAK HER STINKIN' LITTLE NECK!

HOLD ON, STEELE... C'MON, CALM DOWN.

LET ME GO, BLAST YOU! I'VE BEEN HUNTIN' DOWN THAT WITCH FER YEARS! LEMME AT HER!

STOP IT, CLIFF... WE'RE HERE TO FREE DAYTON, NOT TO GAIN VENGEANCE...AT LEAST NOT YET.

OKAY, KID--OKAY! I'LL DO WHAT YOU SAY... FER NOW.

BUT WHEN WE COME BACK HERE, I'M TEARIN' APART ROUGE AND ZAHL MYSELF!

AN' I'M WARNIN' YA NOW-- DON'T DARE GET IN MY WAY!

22

BUT WHERE DO WE BEGIN *LOOKIN'?* DAYTON COULD BE *ANYWHERE.*

WHICH IS WHY THIS RECON JOB'S BEST SUITED TO *ME.*

I'LL HAVE EVERY *CORRIDOR* HERE CHECKED IN *SECONDS.*

AND, JUST AS PREDICTED...

YA SURE THIS IS THE *RIGHT* ONE, FLASHER?

TRUST ME, STONE. WHEN HAVE I EVER *LIED* TO YOU?

DAYTON'S IN CORRIDOR C-6.

RIGHT *THERE!*

TROUBLE IS, THE CELL'S *LOCKED.* I CAN *VIBRATE* THROUGH, BUT YOU *CAN'T.*

LEMME *SMASH* IT DOWN, WHIZ KID.

NO, WE'VE GOT TO KEEP THIS *QUIET.*

BESIDES, WE DON'T NEED *MUSCLE* WHEN I'VE GOT A WELL-STOCKED *UTILITY BELT.*

STEELE, YOU HAVEN'T YET ASKED ABOUT *LOGAN.* HOWCUM?

HE'S NOT WITH *YOU* GUYS, RIGHT? I FIGGER SOMETHING MUST'A *HAPPENED.*

SO I'D RATHER NOT *KNOW* WHAT IT IS UNTIL I GET *ONE* REAL MAD OUT OF THE WAY.

OKAY, GUYS, IT'S *OPEN.*

WOW! YOU EVER THINK OF A CAREER IN *CRIME?*

NAH! I HATE *NIGHT WORK!*

WHIZ KID, I OWE YA AN *APOLOGY* -- YOU WERE *RIGHT!*

THERE'S OUR BOY *NOW!*

23

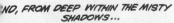

AND, FROM DEEP WITHIN THE MISTY SHADOWS...

UHH, THAT *LIGHT* ...PLEASE, *SHUT IT OFF*... IT'S *BLINDING* ME.

WHO'S *THERE?* PLEASE -- TELL ME WHO'S *THERE.*

IT'S THE *CAVALRY*, DAYTON... WE'RE HERE TA *RESCUE* YOU.

W-WHO *ARE* YOU? WHO ARE *ALL* OF YOU?

C'MON, DAYTON, QUIT FOOLIN' AROUND, IT'S *ME*, YER OLD DOOM PATROL PAL... YA GOTTA *REMEMBER...*

CLIFF, DON'T YOU *SEE* HIS EYES? THEY'RE *GLAZED OVER.* HE'S BEEN *DRUGGED.*

HEY, GUYS... SORRY TO INTERRUPT YOUR *HELLOS*, BUT--

--WE'VE GOT *BAD COMPANY* COME A-CALLING!

THEY CAN'T *SEE* ME WHILE I'M MOVING AT *SUPER-SPEED...*

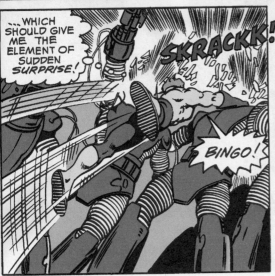

...WHICH SHOULD GIVE ME THE *ELEMENT* OF *SUDDEN SURPRISE!*

SKRACKK!

BINGO!

RED'S *GOT* 'EM! NOW LET'S MAKE SURE THEY *STAY* DOWN!

...MENTO... MENTO SUIT... I REMEMBER *MENTO* SUIT... KNOW WHERE IT'S BEEN *HIDDEN...*

24

JUST *WATCH OUT* FOR THEM, CYBORG.

THESE CREEPS ARE PRETTY *FAST!*

HE MOVES TOO *QUICKLY.*

I-I CANNOT *SHOOT* HIM!

BEHIND MY COLLAPSIBLE *SHIELD,* CYBORG... AND GET READY FOR THAT *MANEUVER* WE WORKED OUT LAST WEEK.

SHIELD? YOU GOT A *KITCHEN SINK* IN THAT BELT OF YOURS, TOO?

NAH, I DIDN'T HAVE *ROOM* AFTER I INSTALLED THE *BATHTUB.*

SPANG

KLANG

TROUBLE WITH *YOU,* SHORTY, IS I NEVER KNOW WHEN YOU'RE *JOKIN'* OR NOT.

PAL, I WAS CRACKING JOKES WHILE *YOU* WERE RUNNING HURDLES IN *HIGH SCHOOL.*

AND SPEAKING OF *CRACKING* THINGS, YOU'RE NOT EXACTLY *CHOPPED LIVER* YOURSELF.

KRAK!

YOU'VE GOT THAT *BREAKAWAY PUNCH* DOWN PAT!

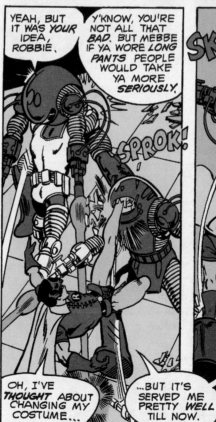

YEAH, BUT IT WAS *YOUR* IDEA, ROBBIE.

Y'KNOW, YOU'RE NOT ALL THAT *BAD.* BUT MEBBE IF YA WORE *LONG PANTS* PEOPLE WOULD TAKE YA MORE *SERIOUSLY.*

SPROK!

OH, I'VE *THOUGHT* ABOUT CHANGING MY COSTUME...

...BUT IT'S SERVED ME PRETTY *WELL* TILL NOW.

SKRINK!

STRAKK!

SEE?

25

140

THAT'S *IT?* THEY SEND LESS THAN A *DOZEN* JERKS TO FIGHT US?

AN' I WAS JUST GETTIN' *WARMED UP,* TOO.

SOMETHING'S *WRONG...* WE SAW *HUNDREDS* OF THEM OUT THERE.

UNLESS THIS IS JUST A *TRAP.*

WHICH MEANS WE'D BETTER *SPLIT--* AND *FAST!*

HE HAD HIS SCIENTISTS DESIGN A *SUPER-SUIT*... IT FOCUSES HIS *BRAIN ENERGY.*

LISSEN, IF HE KNOWS WHERE IT *IS,* WE CAN *USE* IT.

FORGET IT, STEELE! WE DON'T HAVE THE TIME TO *WASTE.*

TAKE IT *EASY,* VIC -- KID FLASH JUST *TOOK OFF* TO--

HE'S ALREADY *BACK?*

MENTO... MENTO SUIT ...MUST HAVE *MENTO* SUIT...

CAN'T YA *CLAM* HIM UP OR SOMETHIN'? WHAT'S THIS *MENTO SUIT* GARBAGE HE KEEPS MUMBLIN' ABOUT?

SORRY I TOOK SO *LONG,* BUDDY.

BUT THERE WERE A HALF DOZEN MEMBERS OF ROUGE'S GOON SQUAD *GUARDING* THIS BROOKS BROTHERS' REJECT.

BUT, FRANKLY, WHAT *GOOD* IS THE SUIT GOING TO DO HIM IN THE *DAZED* CONDITION HE'S IN?

WE'LL WORRY ABOUT THAT *LATER...*

RIGHT NOW, CONCENTRATE ON GETTING OUT OF HERE *ALIVE!*

26

THERE ARE NO GUARDS BLOCKING THEIR WAY TO FREEDOM, AND SO, JUST MINUTES LATER...

WE MADE IT.

YEAH, BUT I STILL DON'T *LIKE* IT. SOMETHING'S *WRONG*...

...AND I CAN'T SHAKE THIS QUEASY FEELING THAT ROUGE AND ZAHL HAD THIS *PLANNED* ALL ALONG.

YOU ARE *CORRECT*, MON PETITE AMI.

EVERYTHING HAS BEEN PLANNED AND EXECUTED JUST AS I *PREDICTED*.

DER WAR IS NOT YET *OVER*, ROUGE... DEY MAY YET *DEFEAT* YOU IN YOUR MOMENT OF *TRIUMPH*!

NEVER, ZAHL! NEVER!

FOR NOW WE HAVE AN *INSIDE MAN* AMONGST THEIR RANKS.

I SWEAR TO YOU, MON AMI, *THE TITANS WILL DIE!*

TAKE OFF IN TWO MINUTES, ROBIN... EVERYTHING'S *SET*.

GOOD, THE FASTER WE GET *AWAY* FROM HERE, THE BETTER I'LL LIKE IT.

AH, DON'T CREASE YER CAPE WORRYIN', KID, WE'RE *SAFE*.

NOTHIN' COULD HURT US *NOW*!

DAYTON SMILES AT ROBOTMAN'S LAST REMARK, AND HIS EYES GLEAM FOR A VERY BRIEF MOMENT. BUT THIS IS NOT THE TIME. HE WILL *WAIT*.

NEXT ISSUE: THE TITANS REUNITE AT LAST! PLUS MADAME ROUGE'S SCHEME REVEALED:

REVOLUTION!

PLUS A SURPRISE FROM THE PAST!

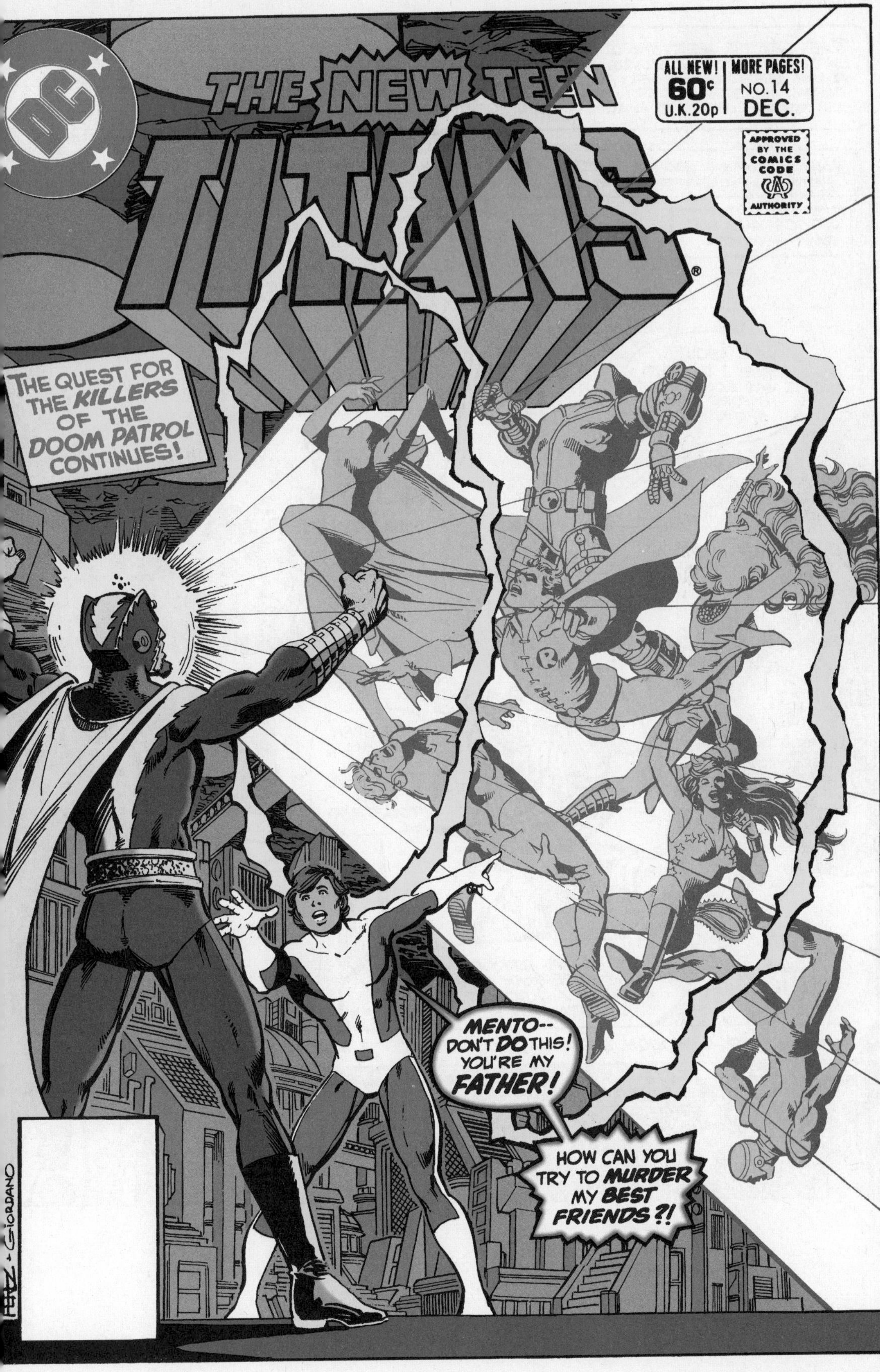
DC
THE NEW TEEN
TITANS®
ALL NEW! 60¢ U.K.20p
MORE PAGES! NO.14 DEC.
APPROVED BY THE COMICS CODE AUTHORITY
THE QUEST FOR THE KILLERS OF THE DOOM PATROL CONTINUES!
MENTO-- DON'T DO THIS! YOU'RE MY FATHER!
HOW CAN YOU TRY TO MURDER MY BEST FRIENDS?!
PÉREZ • GIORDANO

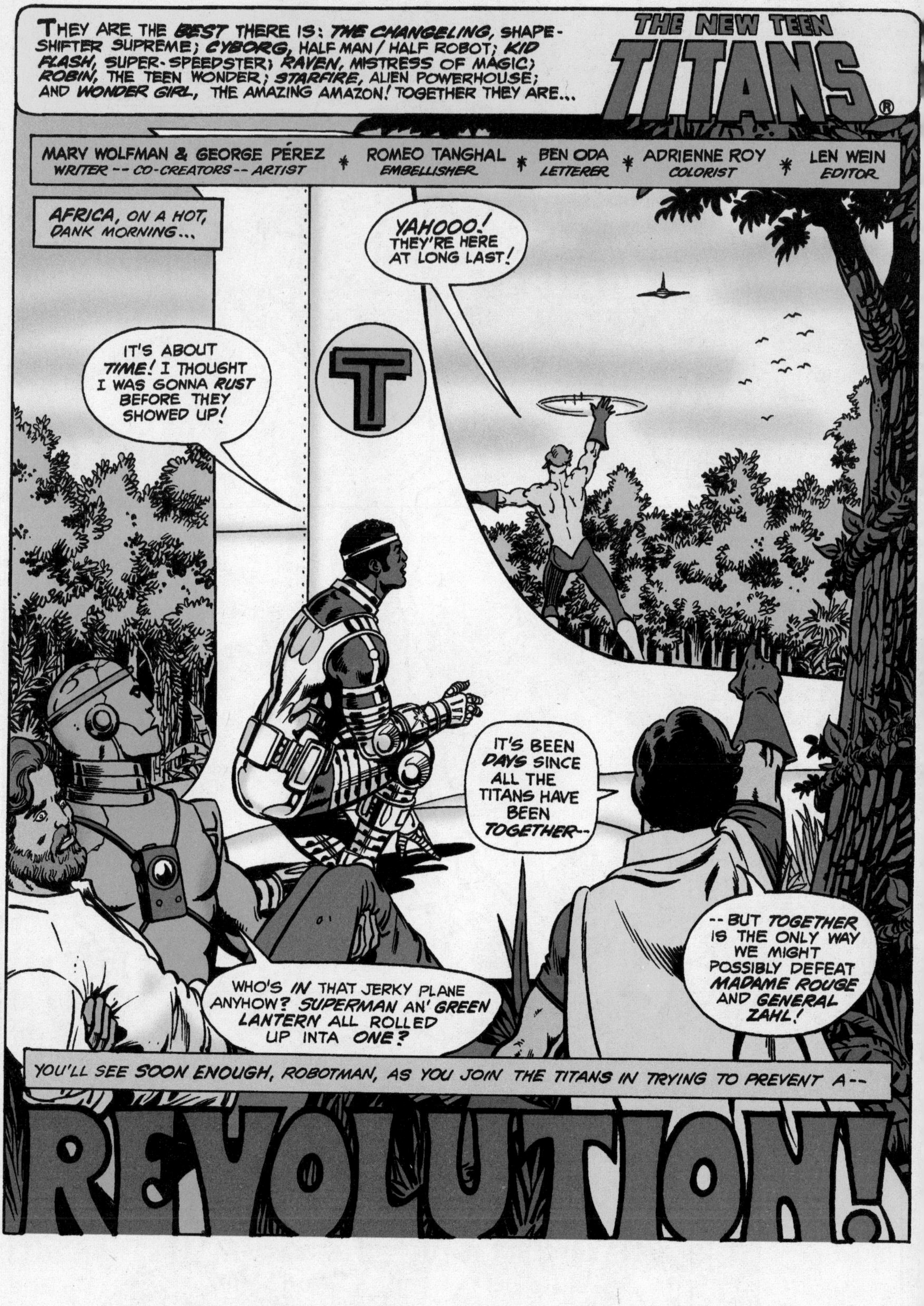
THEY ARE THE BEST THERE IS: THE CHANGELING, SHAPE-SHIFTER SUPREME; CYBORG, HALF MAN / HALF ROBOT; KID FLASH, SUPER-SPEEDSTER; RAVEN, MISTRESS OF MAGIC; ROBIN, THE TEEN WONDER; STARFIRE, ALIEN POWERHOUSE; AND WONDER GIRL, THE AMAZING AMAZON! TOGETHER THEY ARE...
THE NEW TEEN TITANS®
MARY WOLFMAN & GEORGE PÉREZ WRITER -- CO-CREATORS -- ARTIST * ROMEO TANGHAL EMBELLISHER * BEN ODA LETTERER * ADRIENNE ROY COLORIST * LEN WEIN EDITOR
AFRICA, ON A HOT, DANK MORNING...
YAHOOO! THEY'RE HERE AT LONG LAST!
IT'S ABOUT TIME! I THOUGHT I WAS GONNA RUST BEFORE THEY SHOWED UP!
IT'S BEEN DAYS SINCE ALL THE TITANS HAVE BEEN TOGETHER--
--BUT TOGETHER IS THE ONLY WAY WE MIGHT POSSIBLY DEFEAT MADAME ROUGE AND GENERAL ZAHL!
WHO'S IN THAT JERKY PLANE ANYHOW? SUPERMAN AN' GREEN LANTERN ALL ROLLED UP INTA ONE?
YOU'LL SEE SOON ENOUGH, ROBOTMAN, AS YOU JOIN THE TITANS IN TRYING TO PREVENT A--
REVOLUTION!

NO, THEY'RE WONDER GIRL, STARFIRE AND RAVEN-- OUR *OTHER* MEMBERS.

BUT BELIEVE ME, THEY ARE POWERFUL ENOUGH TO *HELP* US NOW.

I JUST WANNA SEE *LOGAN*... WANNA SEE IF THAT GREEN-HAIRED SQUIRT'S STILL UP TA CAUSIN' *TROUBLE!*

WONDER GIRL, YOU'RE CLEAR FOR *LANDING.*

GOT YOU, ROB-- CONVERTING TO *V.T.O.L.* NOW.*

*VERTICAL TAKE OFF AND LANDING--Len.

FORWARD MOMENTUM GIVES WAY TO POWERFUL VERTICAL THRUST FROM THE T-JET'S SLEEK BELLY--

--AND THE GREAT SHIP LOWERS ITSELF ONTO THE GRASSY KNOLL...

WE GOT YOUR MESSAGE ON *PARADISE ISLAND.* CONGRATULATIONS ON FINDING *DAYTON.*

TROUBLE IS, WONDER GIRL-- THAT WAS THE *EASY* PART.

HEY! YER *ALIVE!* YER *REALLY* ALIVE!

THAT'S WHAT I *LIKE* ABOUT YOU, GLITTER-BRAIN -- YOU'RE REALLY QUICK TO GRASP THE *OBVIOUS!*

Y'KNOW, I *MISSED* YOU, VIC -- *REALLY.*

SOMETHING *WRONG,* WONDER GIRL? SOMETHING *BAD* HAPPEN ON PARADISE ISLAND?

SOMETHING I'D RATHER NOT *TALK* ABOUT, ROBIN. IT WAS *PERSONAL.*

LISTEN, WE'VE BEEN *FRIENDS* PROBABLY LONGER THAN ANYONE *ELSE* HERE... AND I THINK WE'VE BEEN *GOOD* FRIENDS.

IF THERE'S ANYTHING *BOTHERING* YOU, OR ANYTHING YOU WANT TO TALK ABOUT -- I'M HERE, *REALLY.* ANYTIME.

TH-THANKS... I MAY TAKE YOU UP ON THAT... *SOMEDAY.*

2

WALLACE, CAN WE... TALK?

UHH, SURE, RAVEN... WHAT ABOUT?

US.

US? IS THERE AN US? I WASN'T SURE.

I CARE FOR YOU, WALLACE, I TRULY DO -- AND WHAT I DID TO YOU--

--EMPATHICALLY FORCING YOU TO LOVE ME -- I KNOW IT WAS TERRIBLY WRONG.

RAVEN, I--

NO, PLEASE-- LET ME FINISH. I HAVE JUST FREED MYSELF FROM AZARATH'S CONTROL--

--AND I MUST LEARN MORE ABOUT MYSELF BEFORE I CAN PLEDGE MYSELF TO ANYONE ELSE ...INCLUDING YOU.

DO YOU UNDERSTAND?

I-- THINK SO.

OH WALLACE I TRULY HOPE SO.

IT WAS INCREDIBLE-- ALL THESE GORGEOUS WOMEN ON PARADISE ISLAND, ALL WAITING JUST FOR ME.

I TELL YA, I SWEPT 'EM ALL OFF THEIR DAINTY LITTLE COMBAT SANDALS!

SURE, SALAD-HEAD... A REAL LOVER BOY, THAT'S YOU.

HUH? I... UHH...

BRONZE THIS MOMENT, GUYS -- LOGAN'S CAUGHT WITHOUT SOMETHIN' STUPID TO SAY.

MY GOD, CLIFF. THEY DIDN'T TELL ME.

AND YOU'VE GOT DAYTON? WOW! MAN, AM I GLAD TO SEE YOU!

THEY'VE GOT TWO FOOT-BALL STADIUMS FILLED WITH PAPERWORK BACK IN--

HEY-- WHAT'S WRONG WITH HIM? HE'S JUST STARING OFF INTO SPACE?

YEAH, HE DOESN'T SEEM TO REMEMBER ANYTHING, OR KNOW ANYTHING.

HE'S BEEN LIKE THIS EVER SINCE WE FOUND HIM, KID.

3

C'MON, DAYTON, YOU CAN'T *DO* THIS TO ME ... VIC--CAN'T WE *DO* ANYTHING FOR HIM?

WE GOTTA DO *SOMETHING!*

YOU KNOW, THIS LAND IS SO LUSH AND BEAUTIFUL-- WE REALLY SHOULD CONSIDER MOVING *TITANS' TOWER* HERE.

NEW YORK IS MAJESTIC, BUT THIS IS JUST SO *LOVELY.*

AHH, VIC, HOW HAVE YOU TWO *BEEN?*

AND *YOU,* DICK... I'VE *MISSED* YOU. I REALLY *DID,* YOU KNOW.

STARFIRE, PLEASE... WE'VE GOT *WORK* TO DO.

SO--?

BELIEVE ME, PAL-- WE'VE BEEN *TRYIN'!*

SHE'S ONE OF THE NEW TITANS? *NO WONDER* YOU'RE A MEMBER. HOW DO *I* JOIN?

FORGET IT, RUSTPOT-- WE DON'T TRUST *ROBOTS* OVER TWENTY!

BESIDES, I DON'T NEED ANY MORE COMPETITION.

UNHH... COSTUME ... MENTO... MUST HAVE MENTO...

WHERE *IS* IT? WHERE IS *COSTUME...?*

DAYTON'S FLIPPING OUT? I THOUGHT YOU SAID HE WAS *WIPED OUT?*

MENTO ... MUST HAVE MENTO...

HE'S GIBBERING ABOUT THAT OLD STUPID *SUPER-HERO* HE ONCE PRETENDED TO BE.

MAN, HE REALLY *HAS* FLIPPED OUT! MENTO WAS A *NOWHERE JERK!*

STEVE DAYTON... THERE IS NO NEED TO *RUN...* WE CAN *HELP* YOU.

COSTUME .... MENTO COSTUME....MUST HAVE IT...

HMMM, YES, I CAN *SENSE* SOMETHING... AN EMOTIONAL *DISTURBANCE--* AND--

--THERE IS SOME *MENTAL BLOCKAGE* IN HIS SUBCON-SCIOUS ... SOMETHING THAT FORCES HIM TO ASK FOR THIS *COSTUME,* WHATEVER IT IS.

4

I AM TRYING TO CALM HIM DOWN, BUT I *CANNOT*... THE ROOT OF HIS DISTURBANCE IS *POWERFUL*...TOO POWERFUL FOR *ME*.

JUST *GREAT!* AND I WAS NEVER TOO WILD ABOUT DAYTON *BEFORE* THIS!

I MEAN, IF IT WAS UP TO *HIM*, HE'D'A LEFT ME STANDING IN THE COLD. HE NEVER *WANTED* TO ADOPT ME.

DON'T *BELIEVE* IT, SHORT-STUFF. DAYTON ACTUALLY *LIKED* YA IN HIS OWN SCREWY WAY.

RAVEN--

LIKE HECK HE DID.

--THIS IS HIS *MENTO* COSTUME... I FOUND IT IN ROUGE'S UNDER-GROUND CITY.

DO YOU THINK MAYBE IF HE TRIED IT *ON*--?

DAYTON *BECAME* A SUPER-HERO ONLY TO WIN OVER *RITA FARR* OF THE DOOM PATROL-- TO MAKE HER HIS *WIFE*.

I DON'T THINK *STYLE* WAS ON HIS MIND.

HE STILL SEEMS TO BE SOMEWHERE ON *CLOUD NINE*.

C'MON, DAYTON--DON'T YOU REMEMBER *ANYTHING?*

...ALTHOUGH DAYTON'S EXPRESSIONLESS FACE SUDDENLY TAKES ON A DECIDEDLY ANGRY CAST...

HE WANTS THE COSTUME ...PERHAPS HE *NEEDS* IT.

ROBIN, TELL ME IF I AM *WRONG*--BUT ISN'T THAT UNIFORM ...RATHER *LUDICROUS?*

AND THAT'S AN *IMPROVEMENT* OVER HIS *OLD* FIGHTING TOGS.

C'MON, BLAST IT--*TRY!*

THERE IS NO REPLY...

...AS ROBIN'S MIND CLICKS OVER -- BATTLE WARY AFTER SO MANY YEARS OF WORKING ALONGSIDE THE BATMAN...

5

RUN! SOMETHING'S WRON--

BUT, THE TEEN WONDER'S WARNING COMES A TAD *TOO LATE*, AS STEVE DAYTON'S EYES SUDDENLY BURN WITH A HELLISH GLOW...

...AND CHAOS ENSUES...

INDEED, ONLY ONE TITAN WAS ABLE TO ACT ON ROBIN'S CRY.

ONLY ONE TITAN WHOSE INNER *VIBRATIONS* ALLOWED MENTO'S TELEKINETIC BLAST TO HARMLESSLY PASS THROUGH HIS VERY ATOMS.

ONE TITAN WHO NOT ONLY *RECOGNIZED* THE DANGER, BUT HAS BEEN ABLE TO *RESPOND* TO IT:

KID FLASH!

CAN'T BELIEVE DAYTON WAS PLAYING *POSSUM*. DEEP DOWN HE'S A *GOOD GUY*-- ONE OF *US*!

SO MAYBE THAT EXPLAINS WHY ROUGE AND ZAHL SENT SO *FEW* OF THEIR WAR-RIORS AFTER US WHEN WE ESCAPED HER CITY.

SHE *WANTED* US TO TAKE DAYTON TO FREEDOM--BECAUSE SOMEHOW SHE *CONTROLLED* HIM!

TROUBLE IS, HOW DO WE TAKE ON DAYTON WITHOUT *HARMING* HIM?

IF I REMEMBER, HIS TELEKINETIC POWERS CAN BE *DEADLY!*

6

SOMETHING'S GOTTA BE *WRONG* WITH DAYTON. HE'D NEVER ACT LIKE THIS *OTHERWISE.*

THAT'S A *RELIEF,* PAL. SO WHEN HE MANAGES TO *KILL* ME, I'LL KNOW IT WAS ONLY A *MISTAKE!*

SHEESH!

CYBORG'S *WHITE-SOUND* BLASTERS *SHATTER* THE FALLING TREES INTO A MILLION USELESS *SPLINTERS...*

...WHILE WONDER GIRL ATTACKS THE PROBLEM IN HER OWN INIMITABLE FASHION.

CAN'T YOU GET *CLOSER* TO HIM, RAVEN... DIG *DEEPER* INTO HIS *MIND?*

I HAVE *TRIED...* BUT I AM *BLOCKED* IN EVERY *ATTEMPT!*

I CAN SENSE THE *HORROR* HE FEELS AT HIS OWN DEEDS, BUT NOT THE *REASON* BEHIND HIS ATTACK.

I TELL YOU, DONNA--STEVEN DAYTON IS BEING *CONTROLLED* BY FORCES BEYOND HIS *WILL*--

--AND IF WE CANNOT *SAVE* HIM, THOSE VERY FORCES WILL TEAR HIS MIND *ASUNDER!*

NO MAN CAN WITHSTAND THAT *MENTAL PRESSURE* ON HIM FOR LONG.

IF THAT'S *TRUE,* RAVEN --IF HE *IS* BEING CONTROLLED, THEN I CAN'T USE ALL THE POWER OF MY *STARBOLTS* ON HIM.

BUT I *CAN* CONTROL THE *INTENSITY* OF MY BLAST...

...TRY TO *STUN* HIM UNTIL YOU CAN MOVE *CLOSER*--

SKRE

X'HAL!! IT'S NO USE!

HE CAN *REPEL* MY STARBOLTS-- SEND THEM *BACK* AT ME!

UNLESS I USE MY FULL POWER AND *KILL* HIM-- I'LL NEVER GET THROUGH HIS *DEFENSES!*

C'MON, STEVE--QUIT *STARING* AT ME THAT WAY, HUH?

OKAY, SO MAYBE WE WERE NEVER THE WAY A KID AND HIS DAD *SHOULD* BE, BUT THAT DOESN'T MEAN...

NO--I'M NOT GETTING *THROUGH* TO HIM--! HE'S *GLARING* AT ME-- OUT FOR *BLOOD*--

7

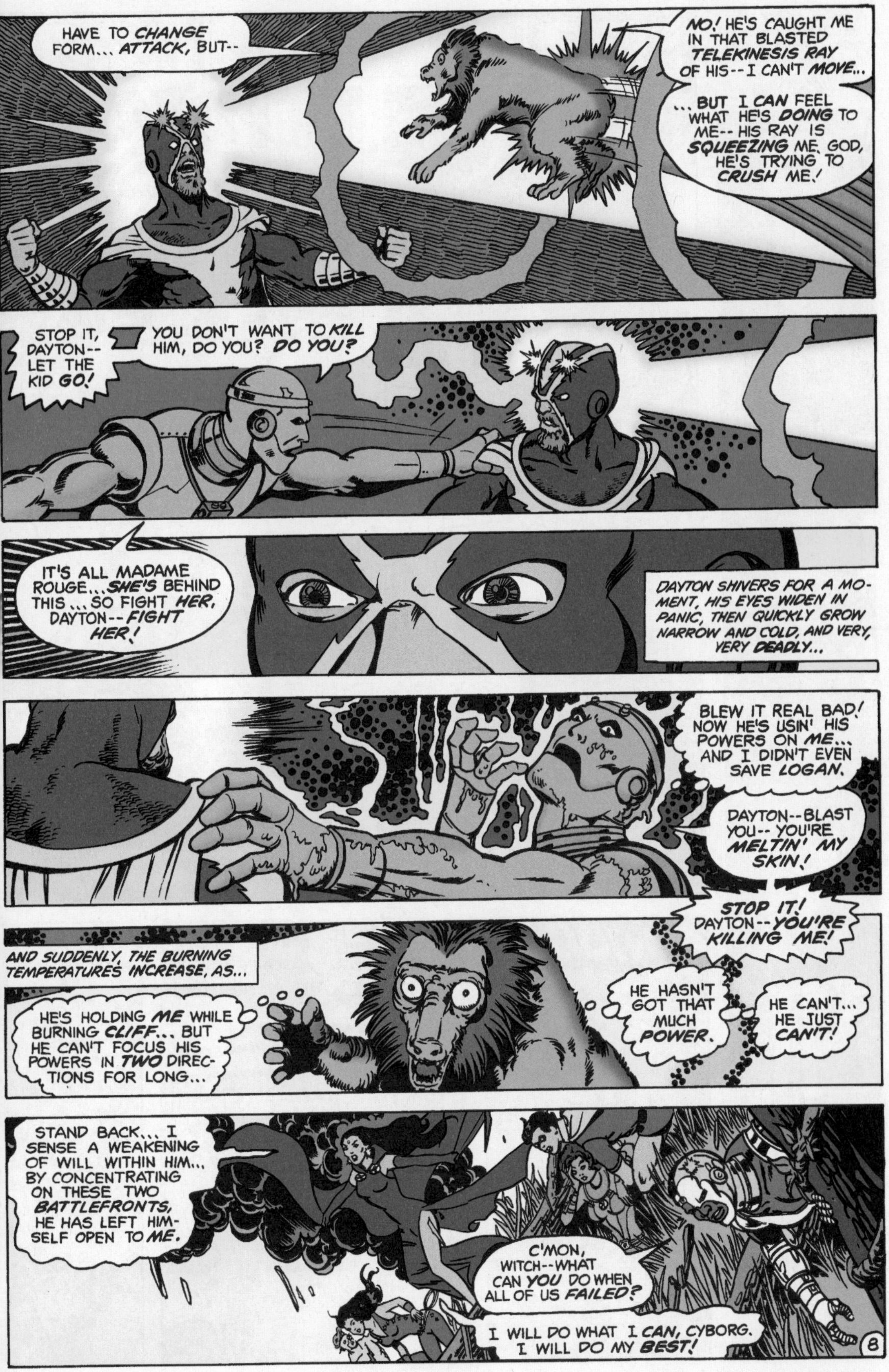

HAVE TO CHANGE FORM... ATTACK, BUT--
NO! HE'S CAUGHT ME IN THAT BLASTED TELEKINESIS RAY OF HIS--I CAN'T MOVE...
...BUT I CAN FEEL WHAT HE'S DOING TO ME--HIS RAY IS SQUEEZING ME. GOD, HE'S TRYING TO CRUSH ME!
STOP IT, DAYTON--LET THE KID GO!
YOU DON'T WANT TO KILL HIM, DO YOU? DO YOU?
IT'S ALL MADAME ROUGE...SHE'S BEHIND THIS...SO FIGHT HER, DAYTON--FIGHT HER!
DAYTON SHIVERS FOR A MOMENT, HIS EYES WIDEN IN PANIC, THEN QUICKLY GROW NARROW AND COLD, AND VERY, VERY DEADLY...
BLEW IT REAL BAD! NOW HE'S USIN' HIS POWERS ON ME... AND I DIDN'T EVEN SAVE LOGAN.
DAYTON--BLAST YOU--YOU'RE MELTIN' MY SKIN!
STOP IT! DAYTON--YOU'RE KILLING ME!
AND SUDDENLY, THE BURNING TEMPERATURES INCREASE, AS...
HE'S HOLDING ME WHILE BURNING CLIFF... BUT HE CAN'T FOCUS HIS POWERS IN TWO DIRECTIONS FOR LONG...
HE HASN'T GOT THAT MUCH POWER.
HE CAN'T... HE JUST CAN'T!
STAND BACK... I SENSE A WEAKENING OF WILL WITHIN HIM... BY CONCENTRATING ON THESE TWO BATTLEFRONTS, HE HAS LEFT HIMSELF OPEN TO ME.
C'MON, WITCH--WHAT CAN YOU DO WHEN ALL OF US FAILED?
I WILL DO WHAT I CAN, CYBORG. I WILL DO MY BEST!
8

RAVEN, BORN IN THE OTHER-DIMENSIONAL TEMPLE OF AZARATH, IS AN EMPATH...A HEALER OF SOULS...

SHE CAN REACH INTO YOUR MIND AND IMPERCEPTIBLY ALTER IT.

STEVE! PLEASE... YOU'RE HURTING ME, STEVE, DON'T YOU SEE WHO I AM?

...AND--

MY GOD, STEVE, I'M RITA-- I'M YOUR WIFE.

SHE CAN SENSE YOUR DEEPEST FEARS, AND EXPLOIT THEM, SHE CAN LEARN OF YOUR TRUEST LOVE...

WHY ARE YOU HURTING ME THIS WAY, STEVE? DON'T YOU KNOW YOU'RE KILLING ME?

PLEASE... DON'T DO THIS... PLEASE...

...DON'T HURT ME...DON'T HURT...SO MUCH PAIN--

--SO TERRIBLE...SO VERY TERRIBLE...

RI... RIT...

OH, LORD... LORD... I'M BURNING UP, STEVE... I CAN'T LAST MUCH LONGER...

RITA--?

SHE CAN DIG INTO YOUR DEEPEST SUBCONSCIOUS, SHE CAN TAKE YOUR MOST TERRIBLE PAINS...

RITA! WOOOO!

YOU DID IT, RAVEN -- HE STOPPED.

JUST NEXT TIME, GAL, DON'T WAIT SO LONG, EH?

...AND MAKE THEM HER OWN.

9

YOU WERE *INCREDIBLE*, RAVEN--YOU REALLY *WERE*.

I JUST DID MY *JOB*, WALLACE.

WHO'S SHE *KIDDING*? SHE'S IN *PAIN*.

USING HER POWERS LIKE THAT *HURT* HER AS MUCH AS IT HELPED ROBOTMAN.

ONLY SHE *HIDES* THE PAIN... PRETENDS SHE'S *COLD*. LORD, WHY DO I FEEL THAT ONE DAY SHE'S GOING TO *BREAK*?

BLAST!

I HADN'T *PREDICTED* THIS--THEY FREED THAT *LUDICROUS FOOL* FROM THE *MIND-CONTROL* I PLACED HIM UNDER.

ZAHL, THIS COULD *DELAY* EVERYTHING I HAVE WORKED SO HARD FOR.

IT VILL DELAY *NOTHING*, MADAME ROUGE. I *SWEAR* IT!

MY ARMIES HAVE TRAINED *WELL* FOR THIS COUP!

ZANDIA WILL BE OURS BY *DAWN*!

IT HAD *BETTER* BE, ZAHL. I DO NOT LIKE HAVING TO PLACE MY HOPES IN THE HANDS OF *OTHERS*. I PREFER CONTROLLING ALL THE EVENTS *MYSELF*.

WE *ALL* DO, MADAME, BUT THERE ARE TIMES WHEN ONE *MUST* WORK WITH OTHERS FOR *MUTUAL GOALS*, EH?

BE CERTAIN WE WORK *TOGETHER*, ZAHL. I HAVE NOT FORGOTTEN THAT YOU *DISOBEYED* ME AND DESTROYED THE *DOOM PATROL*.

YOU MURDERED THEIR *LEADER*-- THE MAN I HAD ONCE *LOVED*.

DISOBEY ME *AGAIN*, AND THIS TIME IT SHALL BE *YOU* WHO SUFFERS THE BLOODY *CONSEQUENCES*.

10

BUT WE HAVE WORKED TOGETHER FOR *YEARS*, WHY DO YOU QUESTION ME *NOW*?

I QUESTION *YOU*, I QUESTION *MYSELF*. WE ARE TOO CLOSE TO SUCCESS *NOT* TO QUESTION OURSELVES.

THE MAN I LOVE IS *DEAD* ... THE WORLD HAS TURNED AGAINST ME FOR *PARTICIPATING* IN HIS DEATH.

I HAVE *NOTHING ELSE* TO LIVE FOR BUT THE SUCCESS OF MY PLAN.

ZANDIA WILL BE *OURS* -- I WILL BE *ZANDIA*. I WILL BE THE *STATE* -- AS MY OWN *COUNTRYMAN* ONCE SAID.

ZANDIA: A SEEMINGLY CONTENTED RURAL COUNTRY. ITS PEOPLE APPEAR *HAPPY*, THOUGH SUCH IS NOT THE *CASE*.

YET, THAT IS A MATTER FOR *ANOTHER DAY*. NOW, HOWEVER, WE FOCUS ONLY ON A SMALL FLAT OVERLOOKING THE *PLAZA DEGRAN*...

OUI, MADAME, ALL IS READY.

THE GENERALS WILL LEAD THEIR SOLDIERS AGAINST THE *CURRENT REGIME* WHEN YOU ORDER THEM TO.

NO, *NO, MADAME!* I PROMISE YOU, THE COUP WILL NOT *FAIL*.

NOW I MUST--

AH, MONSIEUR, IT HAS TAKEN ME QUITE A WHILE TO *TRACK YOU DOWN.*

BUT, NOW THAT I *HAVE*--

MON DIEU!

THIS IS HENRI DUCHAMP, ONE OF MADAME ROUGE'S MOST LOYAL SYCOPHANTS...

SHE WILL SHED A TEAR WHEN SHE LEARNS OF HIS PASSING.

11

...IT'S LIKE WAKING UP FROM A *NIGHTMARE!*

I--I DON'T THINK I CAN THANK YOU *ENOUGH.*

AND I CAN'T POSSIBLY BELIEVE IT'S BEEN A *YEAR* SINCE I VANISHED. I CAN'T *REMEMBER* A THING THAT HAPPENED.

YOU'RE SURE OF THAT, SIR? NOTHING THAT COULD *HELP* US?

HE *SAID* HE CAN'T REMEMBER, SHORT-PANTS. ISN'T THAT *ENOUGH?*

CALM DOWN, GAR-- ROBIN'S ONLY DOING HIS *JOB.*

I KNOW THIS IS *DIFFICULT,* SIR, BUT PLEASE *TRY* TO REMEMBER.

FUNNY, I REMEMBER *YEARS* AGO --WHEN IT ACTUALLY *BEGAN*... BUT *YESTERDAY,* I DON'T REMEMBER A *THING!*

IT BEGAN, I GUESS, WITH THE FORMATION OF THE *DOOM PATROL.*

NOW, I WASN'T *THERE*--THAT DAY BELONGED TO SOMEONE *ELSE*... A CRIPPLE NAMED *NILES CAULDER!* ONLY HE CALLED HIMSELF-- *THE CHIEF!*

I SUMMONED YOU THREE HERE BECAUSE, IN ONE FASHION OR ANOTHER, THE OUTSIDE WORLD CONSIDERS YOU *FREAKS!*

YOU'RE SHUNNED AS SOMETHING *DIFFERENT,* SOMETHING NOT TO BE DESIRED -- BUT I--

--I CAN OFFER YOU A *WORLD!*

"HE BROUGHT THESE THREE TOGETHER.

FIRST, LARRY TRAINOR, A TEST PILOT.

"TRAINOR WAS FLYING AN EXPERIMENTAL PLANE THROUGH A RADIOACTIVE BELT IN THE UPPER IONOSPHERE.

"THE RADIOACTIVITY CHANGED HIM -- HE BECAME -- NEGATIVE MAN!

"CLIFF STEELE WAS THE BEST RACECAR DRIVER ON THE CIRCUIT--

"--UNTIL HIS CAR SMASHED INTO A WALL, DESTROYING STEELE'S BODY IN THE PROCESS.

"ONLY THE CHIEF'S SURGICAL SKILL SAVED HIM... BY TRANSFERRING STEELE'S STILL-LIVING BRAIN INTO THE METAL BODY OF--ROBOTMAN!

"AND RITA... MY GOD, RITA FARR-- THE MOST BEAUTIFUL ACTRESS WHO EVER LIVED.

"SHE FELL INTO A RIVER POLLUTED BY STRANGE, UNKNOWN CHEMICALS.

"AND THEY CHANGED HER... ALTERED HER BODY CHEMISTRY UNTIL SHE BECAME--ELASTI-GIRL!

12

"NEGATIVE MAN! ROBOTMAN! ELASTI-GIRL! THEY THOUGHT OF THEMSELVES AS FREAKS, BUT THEY WERE REALLY HEROES IN THE TRUEST SENSE OF THE WORD."

"FROM AFAR I FELL IN LOVE WITH RITA. I HAD MY SCIENTISTS DEVELOP MY MENTO COSTUME-- WHICH BOOSTED MY NATURAL PSYCHIC ABILITIES."

"AND I SET OUT TO MAKE HER FALL IN LOVE WITH ME. SHE DID, YOU KNOW-- DESPITE MY POWERS AND DESPITE THE FACT THAT, AS STEVE DAYTON, I WAS THE FIFTH RICHEST MAN IN THE WORLD."

"WE WERE MARRIED AND WE LOOKED FORWARD TO A LONG, HAPPY LIFE TOGETHER--"

"--BUT, BLAST IT ALL, THAT LIFE WAS CUT SHORT!"

"SHE AND THE REST OF THE PATROL WERE KILLED BY THEN-CAPTAIN ZAHL, WHO FORCED THE PATROL TO SACRIFICE THEMSELVES TO SAVE THE LIVES OF 14 INNOCENT PEOPLE IN THE FISHING VILLAGE OF CODSVILLE, MAINE."

ALL OF THEM -- THE CHIEF, CLIFF, LARRY, AND MY DARLING RITA.... ALL DEAD.

NOT ALL DEAD, BUT YOU DIDN'T KNOW I'D SURVIVED, THOUGH I WAS PROBABLY MORE READY FER THE JUNK HEAP THAN I WAS FER SUPER-HEROING.

I WAS REBUILT, BUT I DIDN'T LIKE THAT NEW ROBOT-SHAPE I WAS GIVEN, SO I CONVINCED DAYTON'S LAB BOYS TO REBUILD MY ORIGINAL TIN-CAN BODY. I'M AS GOOD AS OLD AGAIN!

14

THEN YOU'RE *NOT* LIKE ME? YOU'RE TOTALLY A *MACHINE*.

AND I COME WITH A *FIVE-YEAR WARRANTY*, TOO!

LORD, AND I USED TO FEEL *SORRY* FOR MYSELF! AT LEAST I'M STILL *HALF-HUMAN*!

OKAY, OKAY, DO WE HAVE TO LIVE *THROUGH* THOSE DAYS AGAIN?

WE ALL KNOW THE GORY PARTS AND I DON'T WANNA *HEAR* 'EM ANYMORE.

BUT THE *QUESTION* IS-- DID ALL THAT HELP YOU *REMEMBER* ANYTHIN'?

I-I REMEMBER THE *GRIEF* I FELT AT RITA'S *DEATH*, AND THE UNENDING *ANGER*.

"I HAD MY *SCIENTISTS* BOOST MY *SUPER-SUIT* FOR ME--

"--AND I REMEMBER *BEGINNING* THE *HUNT*, SEARCHING FOR THOSE *KILLERS* IN COUNTRY *AFTER* BACKWATER *COUNTRY*.

"I *CAN'T* TELL YOU HOW MANY *MONTHS* IT TOOK BEFORE I GOT A *CLUE* THAT LED ME TO *AFRICA*.

"AND *THAT-- THAT* WAS WHEN I *SAW*--

--*RITA!*

WELL, IT'S CERTAINLY TAKEN A WHILE, *DARLING*, I WAS WONDERING WHEN YOU'D *SHOW UP*.

RITA? BUT, IT'S *IMPOSSIBLE--?!?*

OH, YOU *REALLY* THOUGHT I WAS *DEAD*, DID YOU? *GOOD*.

THAT'S WHAT I *WANTED* EVERYONE TO BELIEVE WHILE I HUNTED DOWN *MADAME ROUGE* AND *CAPTAIN ZAHL*.

WH-WHAT ABOUT THE *OTHERS*? THE *CHIEF*... NEGATIVE MAN-- WHAT ABOUT *CLIFF*?

THEY ALL *DIED*-- BUT SOMEHOW *I* WAS BLOWN *FREE*.

BUT WHY ARE WE *TALKING*? WE'VE FOUND EACH OTHER AT LAST.

"*SOMETHING* WAS TERRIBLY *WRONG*. RITA'S LIPS WERE LIKE *ICE*.

(15)

"I KNEW THIS WASN'T MY WIFE... IT COULDN'T BE."

"I TRIED TO SQUIRM FREE, BUT IT WAS ALREADY TOO LATE."

YOU MORONIC SIMPLETON! HOW EASY IT WAS TO FOOL YOU BY SIMPLY ALTERING MY BODY SHAPE.

"I HAD TOTALLY FORGOTTEN HER CURSED POWER. I FELT LIKE A STUPID FOOL!"

SHE DIDN'T KILL ME... SHE SIMPLY BROUGHT ME TO HER UNDERGROUND CITY...

AND, I GUESS, FOR A YEAR SHE FED ME DRUGS... NUMBED MY WILL... UNTIL YOU FREED ME.

BUT NOW YOUR SOUL IS YOUR OWN YOU ARE A FREE MAN.

SO, WHAT NOW?

WE COULD GO BACK TO THAT JOINT AND SMASH ZAHL AND ROUGE.

YEAH, GUESS WE COULD. BUT YOU THINK WE GOT THE POWER?

I MEAN THOSE DUDES ARE PRETTY TOUGH.

MEBBE WE OUGHTTA--

SHUT UP! ALL OF YOU-- SHUT THE HECK UP!

YOU'RE GABBING AWAY LIKE THIS WAS JUST SOME SUPER-HERO GET-TOGETHER.

THOSE TWO ARE KILLERS, AND I WANT THEM TO PAY!

PAY FOR WHAT THEY DID TO ME... WHAT THEY DID TO THE PATROL!

GARFIELD, PLEASE -- BE CALM --

GET AWAY FROM ME, RAVEN ... DON'T USE YOUR BLASTED CALMING POWERS ON ME.

I WANT TO STAY ANGRY... I WANT TO BE MAD!

I DESERVE THE RIGHT TO BE MAD FOR A CHANGE!

16

WE CAN ALL *FEEL* FOR THE DOOM PATROL, WHAT HAPPENED TO *THEM*, GAR, COULD HAPPEN TO *ANY* OF US... OR *ALL* OF US.

WE'RE *ALL* ANGRY WHEN SOMETHING LIKE THIS GOES ON. BELIEVE ME--THE *RAGE* YOU'RE FEELING ISN'T FELT BY YOU *ALONE*.

WE ALL WANT TO SEE THOSE KILLERS *CAUGHT*.

WE WILL *STOP* THEM, GAR -- YOU CAN *BELIEVE* ME!

I WILL NOT LET THEM SQUIRM THROUGH MY GRASP -- NO MATTER *WHAT* I MUST DO.

YOU THINK YOU *UNDERSTAND* THIS, BUT YOU REALLY *DON'T*.

FOR YEARS I'VE BEEN SUFFERING BECAUSE I'VE VIRTUALLY SEEN *TWO* SETS OF PARENTS *KILLED*.

OH, I'VE *GONE ON*, HAVEN'T I? LAUGHING LIKE A LUNATIC -- SPOUTING STUPID *JOKES*--

--HOPING THEY'D EASE THE *PAIN*. BUT YOU KNOW, EVERY JOKE ONLY MADE THE PAIN HURT *MORE*.

NOW YOU WANT TO GUIDE ME ALONG AND SOLVE MY PROBLEMS FOR ME LIKE SOME *SURROGATE* PARENTS ...

...BUT, BLAST IT--I HAVE TO DO THIS BY *MYSELF* OR I'LL NEVER FEEL LIKE I'VE AMOUNTED TO MUCH OF *ANYTHING!*

HE'S *CRAZY!* HE DOESN'T KNOW WHAT HE'S GETTING INTO.

I'LL *STOP* HIM--

NO, *DON'T*. LET HIM GO. MAYBE HE'S *RIGHT*.

EVERYONE HAS THE RIGHT TO *PROVE* HIMSELF SOMETIME,

DOES THAT MEAN WE GOTTA SIT BACK AN' WATCH THAT LITTLE WITCH AN' HER GOOSE-STEPPIN' PAL *SKRAG* LOGAN FER KICKS?

LISSEN--THAT KID'S CONFUSED AND LOST--HE'S TRYIN' TA *PROVE* HIMSELF BECAUSE NONE OF US TAKES HIM *SERIOUSLY*.

WE LISSEN TO HIS *CORNY JOKES* AN' THINK HE'S A FLAKE AN' ORDER 'IM AROUND WITH A "DO THIS," OR "DO THAT"!

BUT HE'S A KID WHO'S DEEP DOWN *GOOD*...AN' HE'S REAL *TROUBLED*...AND WHY THE HECK AM I STANDIN' HERE *GABBIN'* WHEN I SHOULD BE *TRAILIN'* HIM?

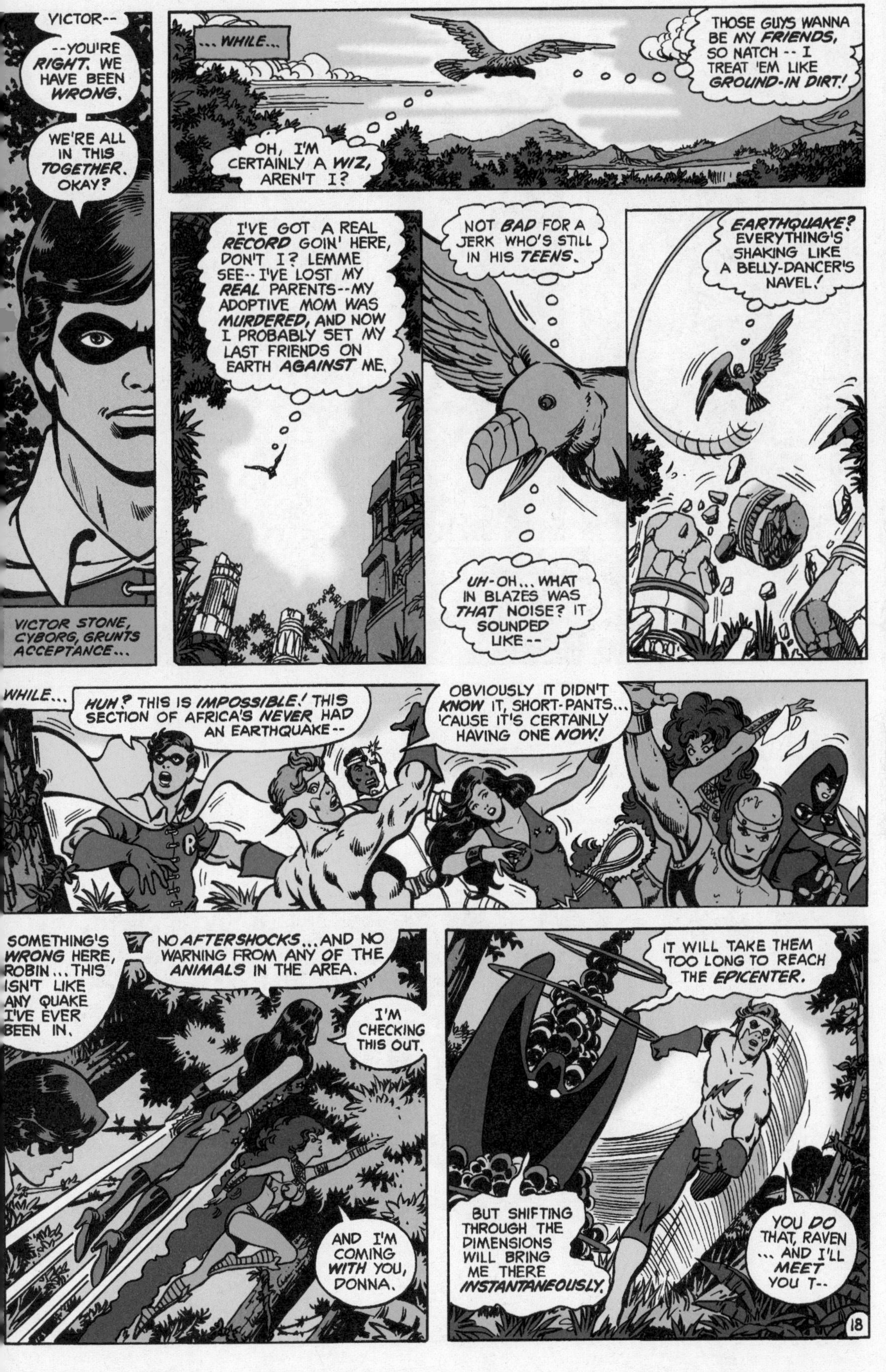
VICTOR--
--YOU'RE RIGHT. WE HAVE BEEN WRONG.
WE'RE ALL IN THIS TOGETHER. OKAY?
VICTOR STONE, CYBORG, GRUNTS ACCEPTANCE...
...WHILE...
THOSE GUYS WANNA BE MY FRIENDS, SO NATCH -- I TREAT 'EM LIKE GROUND-IN DIRT!
OH, I'M CERTAINLY A WIZ, AREN'T I?
I'VE GOT A REAL RECORD GOIN' HERE, DON'T I? LEMME SEE-- I'VE LOST MY REAL PARENTS--MY ADOPTIVE MOM WAS MURDERED, AND NOW I PROBABLY SET MY LAST FRIENDS ON EARTH AGAINST ME.
NOT BAD FOR A JERK WHO'S STILL IN HIS TEENS.
UH-OH... WHAT IN BLAZES WAS THAT NOISE? IT SOUNDED LIKE--
EARTHQUAKE? EVERYTHING'S SHAKING LIKE A BELLY-DANCER'S NAVEL!
WHILE...
HUH? THIS IS IMPOSSIBLE! THIS SECTION OF AFRICA'S NEVER HAD AN EARTHQUAKE--
OBVIOUSLY IT DIDN'T KNOW IT, SHORT-PANTS... 'CAUSE IT'S CERTAINLY HAVING ONE NOW!
SOMETHING'S WRONG HERE, ROBIN... THIS ISN'T LIKE ANY QUAKE I'VE EVER BEEN IN.
NO AFTERSHOCKS... AND NO WARNING FROM ANY OF THE ANIMALS IN THE AREA.
I'M CHECKING THIS OUT.
AND I'M COMING WITH YOU, DONNA.
IT WILL TAKE THEM TOO LONG TO REACH THE EPICENTER.
BUT SHIFTING THROUGH THE DIMENSIONS WILL BRING ME THERE INSTANTANEOUSLY.
YOU DO THAT, RAVEN ... AND I'LL MEET YOU T--
18

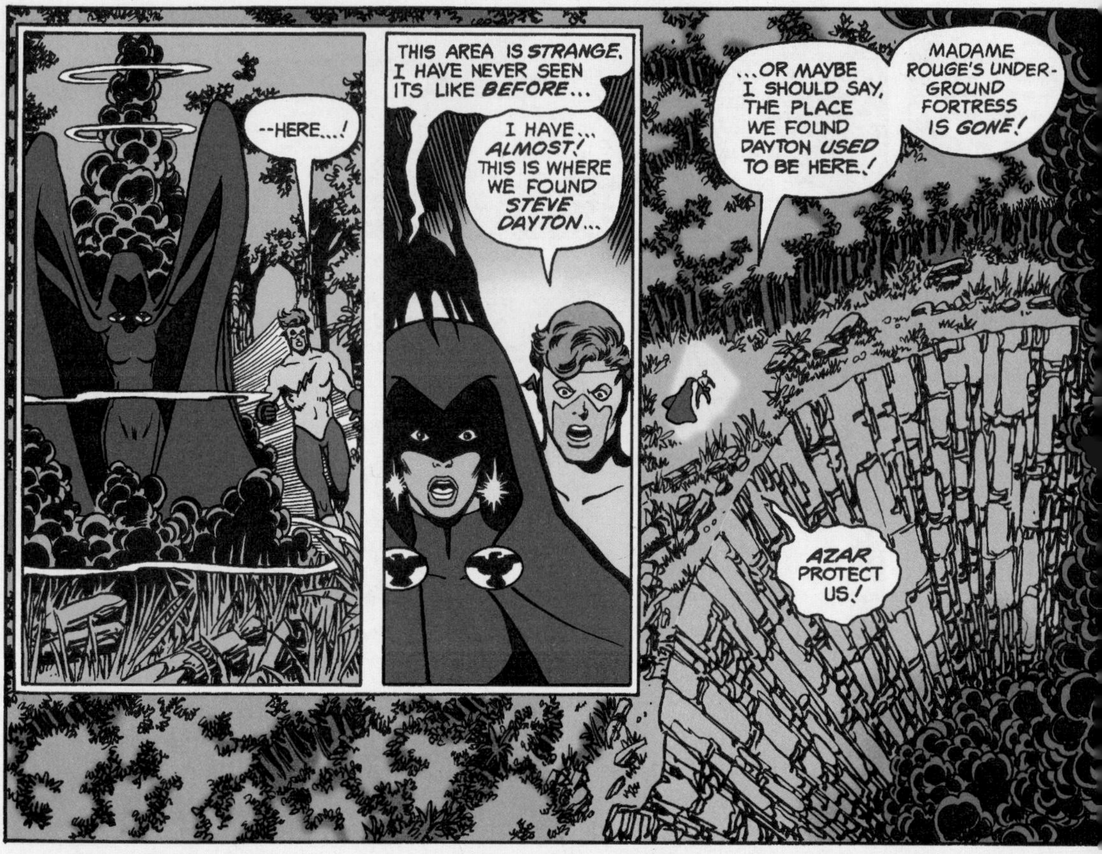
--HERE...!
THIS AREA IS STRANGE. I HAVE NEVER SEEN ITS LIKE BEFORE...
I HAVE... ALMOST! THIS IS WHERE WE FOUND STEVE DAYTON...
...OR MAYBE I SHOULD SAY, THE PLACE WE FOUND DAYTON USED TO BE HERE!
MADAME ROUGE'S UNDER-GROUND FORTRESS IS GONE!
AZAR PROTECT US!

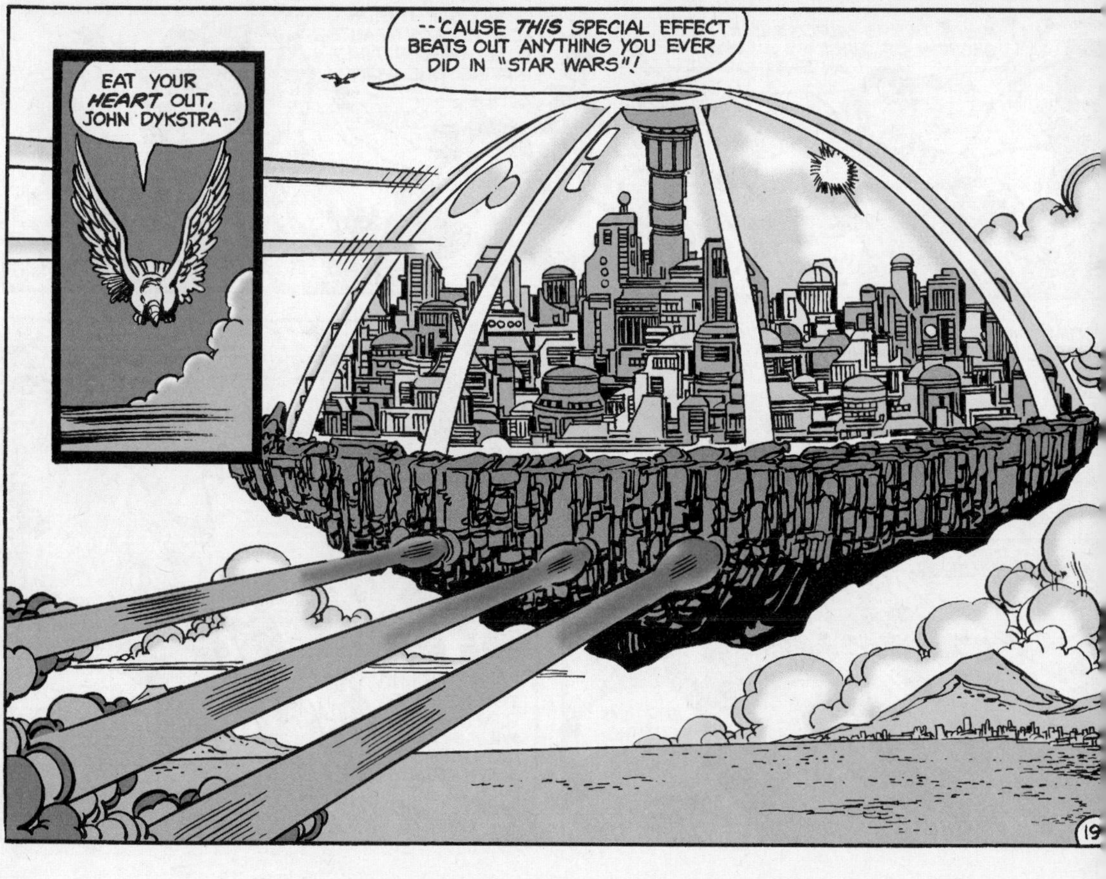
EAT YOUR HEART OUT, JOHN DYKSTRA--
--'CAUSE THIS SPECIAL EFFECT BEATS OUT ANYTHING YOU EVER DID IN "STAR WARS"!
19

I DON'T HAVE TO BE A BRAIN LIKE ROBIN TO GUESS *MADAME ROUGE* IS BEHIND THIS FLYING CITY!

SO THAT MAKES IT REAL *EASY* ON LITTLE GAR LOGAN!

WHEREVER THIS REFUGEE FROM A FLASH GORDON MOVIE GOES, I GO *WITH IT!*

PROVIDING I *LIVE* LONG ENOUGH!

THE WINDS UP HERE ARE *TERRIBLE* ...THEY'RE CUTTING RIGHT THROUGH ME LIKE A SURGEON'S *SCALPEL!*

GOTTA KEEP MY EYES *CLOSED*...SO I CAN BARELY *SEE*...

...WHICH MAY BE THE ONLY *GOOD* THING ABOUT THIS CATASTROPHE!

IF I *SAW* WHAT I WAS DOING, I'D BE *SICK* OVER HALF OF AFRICA!

GAR LOGAN HOLDS FIRM... NOTHING ON EARTH WILL MAKE HIM RELEASE HIS IRON-TIGHT GRIP. MEANWHILE...

ALL RIGHT, I'VE RE-LEARNED *LESSON ONE*-- NEVER *UNDERESTIMATE* YOUR ENEMY!

I NEVER SUSPECTED ROUGE'S FORTRESS WAS *MOVABLE!*

MOVABLE AND MOVING FAST...LOOK AT THEIR SPEED ON THE RADAR.

AT THE RATE THEY'RE TRAVELING, THEY'LL BE OUT OF AFRICA IN MINUTES.

YOU GOT A BEAM ON WHERE SHE'S *HEADING?*

YOU CAN ACTUALLY GUESS THEIR *PATH,* VICTOR?

SURE *CAN,* GOLDIE...A LITTLE TRIANGULATION, AND *WHAMMO!*

LOOK THERE AT THAT LITTLE HICKEY OF AN *ISLAND.*

GRID CO-ORDINATES SAYS IT'S *ZANDIA*...DEAD CENTER IN THE BALTIC SEA.

20

ZANDIA: POPULATION APPROX. --3,769, NO MAJOR INDUSTRY, NO IMPORTS, AND NO EXPORTS.

THOUGH THE SECRET OF HOW ZANDIA SURVIVES WILL NOT BE TOLD THIS DAY...

...TRUST US WHEN WE SAY ZANDIA DOES INDEED SURVIVE, AND QUITE WELL UNDER THE RULE OF THIS MAN...

...PRESIDENT FREDERICK GRAVES...

A NAME QUITE APROPOS CONSIDERING A GRAVE IS ALL HE WILL BE FIT FOR IN EXACTLY 3.7 SEC--

ZWITT!

MY, HOW TIME FLIES!

LORD, LOOK UP THERE!

WE'RE UNDER ATTACK!

YAGGHH

ZANDIA'S EXPATRIATE CITIZENS FALL LIKE WHEAT BEFORE A VERY DEADLY SCYTHE...

...WIELDED BY CRUEL AND VICIOUS FLYING FORCES UNDER THE ORDERS OF A VERY SINISTER GENERAL ZAHL.

LIKE LOCUSTS, THEY SWEEP PAST ZANDIA'S CENTRAL MICROFILM COMPLEX, DESTROYING INVALUABLE RECORDS WITH INSIDIOUS EASE.

THEN THEY SOAR ON, LEAVING IN THEIR JET-STREAM WAKE THE MINGLED TEARS AND RUNNING BLOOD OF USELESS DESTRUCTION...

OH, LORD! THIS IS ROUGE'S SCHEME? DESTROYING A COUNTRY FOR NO REASON?

GOD, SHE'S MORE TWISTED THAN I THOUGHT!

WELL, WHATEVER SHE IS, I'VE REALLY GOT TO STOP HER NOW.

BUT HOW--? I CAN BARELY HOLD ON... AND I CAN'T RISK SHAPE-SHIFTING UP HERE--THE WIND MOVING AT THIS SPEED COULD TEAR ME--

NOOOOO

I CAN HARDLY BELIEVE THIS--IT'S MADNESS!

WE'RE IN THE MIDDLE OF A FULL-SCALE WAR!

WELL, I DON'T SEE GAR ANYWHERE, AND I'M NOT SITTING THIS OUT JUST SO HE CAN PROVE HIS MANHOOD.

THE TITANS ARE GETTING INVOLVED WITH THIS -- NOW!

C'MON, WE THREE CAN MOVE THE FASTEST--

--TO STOP ZAHL'S KILLERS WHILE ROBIN LANDS THE T-JET!

BELIEVE ME, WONDER GIRL-- THIS WILL BE MY PLEASURE!

22

I FIND THIS BUTCHERY IMPOSSIBLE TO *BELIEVE.* THESE PEOPLE ARE *INNOCENTS,* BUT ZAHL IS HAVING THEM *SLAIN!*

SOLDIER 4-X... ENEMY TO YOUR *RIGHT!*

THEY'RE TURNING TOWARD *ME*--?

BUT IT WON'T DO THEM ANY *GOOD!*

I WASN'T ABOUT TO MISS OUT ON *THIS* FIGHT!

I CAN SET UP A SUPER-SPEED *UPDRAFT* TO LOWER ME TO THE GROUND AND TAKE OUT SOME OF ZAHL'S *GOON SQUAD* AT THE SAME TIME!

YOU SURE YOU DON'T SEE *GAR* DOWN THERE?

NOT A *SIGN,* CLIFF. YOU THINK HE DIDN'T *FOLLOW* ROUGE?

IF HE *DIDN'T,* BAT-BOY, THEN HE'S NOT THE GAR LOGAN I *KNOW!*

C'MON, *LAND* THIS HEAP--HE'S GOTTA BE DOWN THERE *SOMEWHERE.*

AT LAST I'M *FREE*-- IN MY *ELEMENT!*

SKREEE

SKREEE

I MAY HAVE BEEN FORCED TO *REIN IN* MY FULL POWER IN THE PAST--

--BUT NOW I STRIKE OUT *UNFETTERED!*

BUT HOW MANY OF THEM *ARE* THERE?

FOR EACH *ONE* I BLAST, *FIVE* MORE APPEAR!

MY POWER ISN'T *INFINITE!*

THERE'S NO WAY I CAN *CONTINUE* TO--

GREAT HERA! THEY'VE GOT KORIAND'R!

THEN THEY WERE *READY* FOR US... THEY KNEW WE WERE COMING!

BAM

BLAM

BANG

DOES THAT MEAN THIS WAS A *TRAP* TO--

KREEE

NO! THAT *WALL*--

SK RASHH!

BOTH MY FRIENDS ARE *DOWNED*--THE OTHERS HAVEN'T *LANDED* YET-- I'M *ALONE*--

-- I HAVE NO *CHOICE* NOW, I CANNOT *HOLD BACK,* OR--

24

BUT RAVEN'S NEXT WORDS ARE SUDDENLY STOPPED SHORT. FOR, AS HER ASTRAL SOUL-SELF LOWERS TOWARD THE SOLITARY SOLDIER --

--A MIND-NUMBING BEAM OF PLASMIC LIGHT STRIKES HER FROM BEHIND.

RAVEN'S SHADOW-FORM CRUMPLES WHILE ANOTHER TITAN BLAZES INTO BATTLE...

LASER BLASTS STRAFING ME FROM ALL SIDES...

--ESPECIALLY WHEN LIGHT BEAMS MOVE JUST AS FAST AS I--

...AND WITH ALL THE DISTRACTIONS HERE, IT'S HARD TO KEEP TRACK OF THEM ALL--

ONE WRONG STEP IS ALL IT TAKES--

A TURN TO THE LEFT WHEN KID FLASH SHOULD HAVE SPED RIGHT.

LESS THAN ONE SECOND LATER, THE CRIMSON COMET FALLS.

IT'S NO USE... WE'LL NEVER FIND LOGAN FROM UP HERE.

LET ME OUT NOW!

THERE ISN'T TIME FOR THAT, VIC--JUST DO YOUR BEST UNTIL I CAN FIND A PLACE TO LAND THE T-JET!

I'M TRYIN' BAT-BOY--

I GOT ONE MILLION DECIBELS OF PURE SOUND BLASTIN' DOWN THERE--

--BUT THEY MUST HAVE SOME KINDA SHIELD PROTECTIN' 'EM--MY BLASTS AIN'T GETTIN' THROUGH!

HOLD IT, STONE--STOP! LOOK, OVER THERE, ON THE RIGHT TIP OF ROUGE'S FLYING CITY--

YOU SEE HIM?

HUH? WHERE'D HE POP UP FROM? HE WASN'T THERE A SECOND AGO, I'M SURE OF THAT!

THANK GOODNESS --YOU FOUND ME, GUYS--DROP LOWER ...LET ME REACH YOU.

25

V...VICTOR...MY SOUL-SELF IS IN *DANGER*... SOMEHOW I HAVE TO *REJOIN* WITH IT... *FREE* IT!

JUST HOLD ONTA YER *COWL*, LADY-- WE'LL GET TO IT AFTER WE PICK UP THAT WALKIN' *GARDEN*!

H-HOLD IT... SOMETHING'S *SCREWY*.

LOOK!

GOOD GRIEF. WE'VE GOT TO GET *OUT* OF HERE -- *FAST!*

GOT TO *MOVE.*

RAISE THIS BIRD, AND--

BWAOMM

BRACE YOUR-SELVES!!

CRASH!!!

SIMPLETONS ...ALL OF THEM!

THESE SO-CALLED *SUPER-HEROES* -- THEY ARE ALL MINDLESS *BUFFOONS!*

HA! HA! HA! HA! HA!

SKRAGG

BRACE YOUR-SELVES!

ROUGE TO ZAHL! THE TITANS IN THE PLANE ARE STILL *ALIVE*, BUT TOTALLY *UNCONSCIOUS.*

I SHALL BRING THEM *IN.*

VERY GOOD, MADAME ROUGE. WE HAVE ALREADY CAPTURED THE *OTHERS.*

YOU SEE, AS I PREDICTED -- WE HAVE *WON!*

WE'RE *HIT!*

26

--The BROTHERHOOD of EVIL LIVES AGAIN!

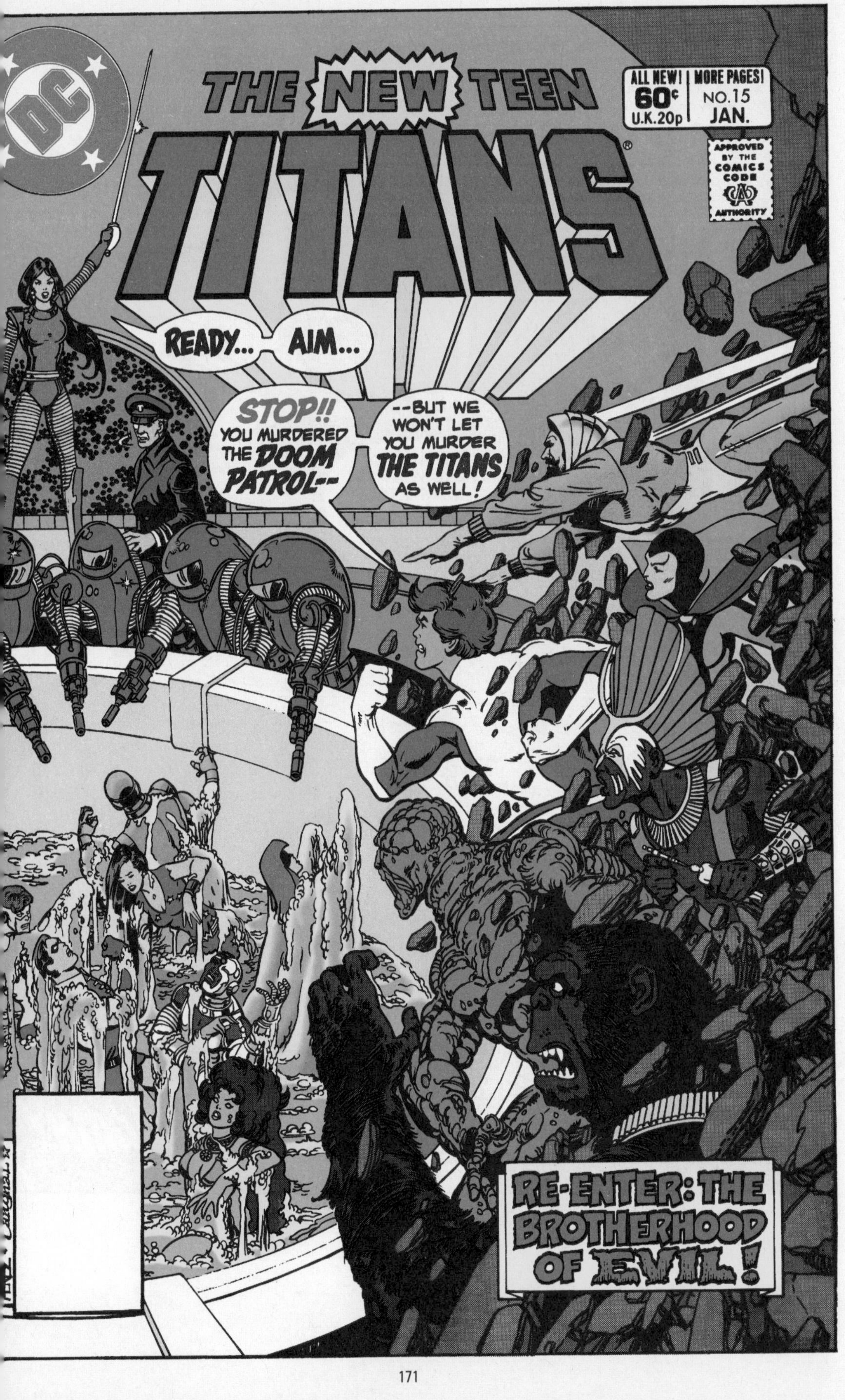
THE NEW TEEN TITANS
ALL NEW! 60¢ U.K.20p
MORE PAGES! NO.15 JAN.
APPROVED BY THE COMICS CODE AUTHORITY
READY...
AIM...
STOP!! YOU MURDERED THE DOOM PATROL--
--BUT WE WON'T LET YOU MURDER THE TITANS AS WELL!
RE-ENTER: THE BROTHERHOOD OF EVIL!

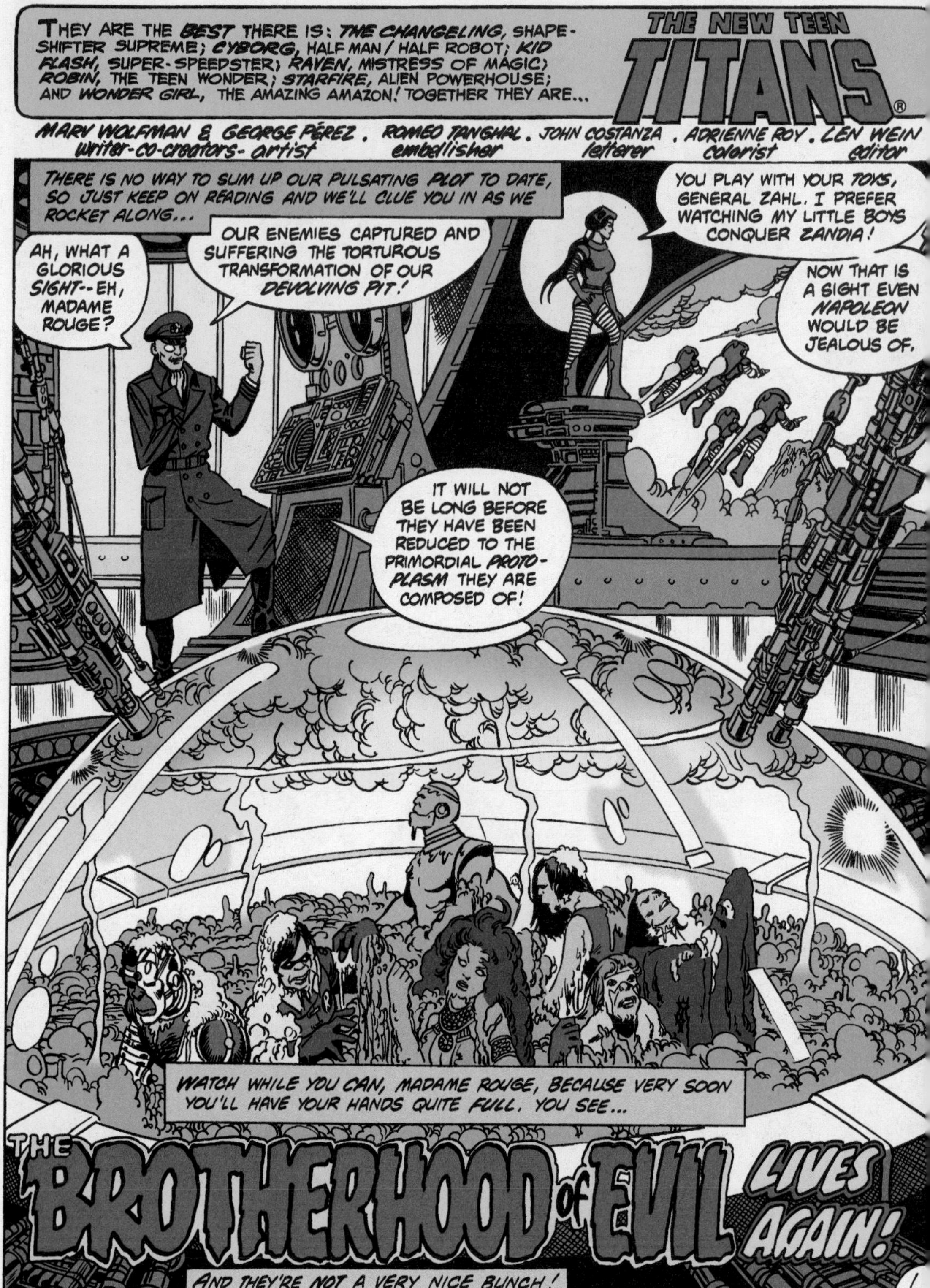
THEY ARE THE BEST THERE IS: THE CHANGELING, SHAPE-SHIFTER SUPREME; CYBORG, HALF MAN / HALF ROBOT; KID FLASH, SUPER-SPEEDSTER; RAVEN, MISTRESS OF MAGIC; ROBIN, THE TEEN WONDER; STARFIRE, ALIEN POWERHOUSE; AND WONDER GIRL, THE AMAZING AMAZON! TOGETHER THEY ARE...
THE NEW TEEN TITANS®
MARV WOLFMAN & GEORGE PÉREZ . writer-co-creators- artist
ROMEO TANGHAL . embellisher
JOHN COSTANZA . letterer
ADRIENNE ROY . colorist
LEN WEIN editor
THERE IS NO WAY TO SUM UP OUR PULSATING PLOT TO DATE, SO JUST KEEP ON READING AND WE'LL CLUE YOU IN AS WE ROCKET ALONG...
AH, WHAT A GLORIOUS SIGHT--EH, MADAME ROUGE?
OUR ENEMIES CAPTURED AND SUFFERING THE TORTUROUS TRANSFORMATION OF OUR DEVOLVING PIT!
YOU PLAY WITH YOUR TOYS, GENERAL ZAHL. I PREFER WATCHING MY LITTLE BOYS CONQUER ZANDIA!
NOW THAT IS A SIGHT EVEN NAPOLEON WOULD BE JEALOUS OF.
IT WILL NOT BE LONG BEFORE THEY HAVE BEEN REDUCED TO THE PRIMORDIAL PROTO-PLASM THEY ARE COMPOSED OF!
WATCH WHILE YOU CAN, MADAME ROUGE, BECAUSE VERY SOON YOU'LL HAVE YOUR HANDS QUITE FULL. YOU SEE...
THE BROTHERHOOD of EVIL LIVES AGAIN!
AND THEY'RE NOT A VERY NICE BUNCH!
1

JA, YOU PREFER THE MERE *CONQUERING* OF THE RABBLE WHILE I ENJOY WATCHING THEM *SUFFER!*

MMM? THIS *ROBOTMAN*... HE IS NOT *DEVOLVING.*

OF COURSE-- OUR PIT WOULD NOT AFFECT HIS *METAL BODY.* BUT THIS IS NOT TO *WORRY*, NEIN?

HIS FRIENDS ARE QUICKLY SINKING THROUGH THE *EVOLUTIONARY CHAIN*--

--VERY SOON THEIR *NEANDERTHAL* MADNESS WILL *OVERWHELM* THEM-- AND THEY WILL *CRUSH* THE METAL ONE FOR US.

ZAHL'S EVIL FRIGHTENS EVEN *ME* SOMETIMES. THERE IS NO *SOUL* IN THAT MADMAN.

BUT I WILL *PERMIT* HIM HIS PETTY PLEASURES, AT LEAST FOR *NOW.*

BUT, WHEN ZANDIA IS TOTALLY *MINE*... WELL, *C'EST LA GUERRE!* THAT IS *WAR*, NON?

FOR EVERYONE IS THE ARCHITECT OF HIS *OWN FORTUNE!*

2

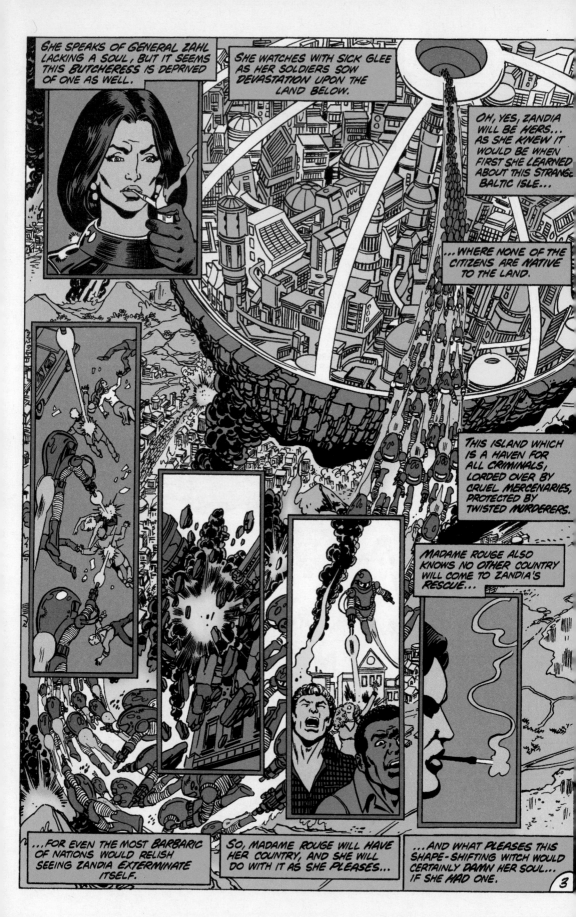

SHE SPEAKS OF GENERAL ZAHL LACKING A SOUL, BUT IT SEEMS THIS BUTCHERESS IS DEPRIVED OF ONE AS WELL.

SHE WATCHES WITH SICK GLEE AS HER SOLDIERS SOW DEVASTATION UPON THE LAND BELOW.

OH, YES, ZANDIA WILL BE HERS... AS SHE KNEW IT WOULD BE WHEN FIRST SHE LEARNED ABOUT THIS STRANGE BALTIC ISLE...

...WHERE NONE OF THE CITIZENS ARE NATIVE TO THE LAND.

THIS ISLAND WHICH IS A HAVEN FOR ALL CRIMINALS, LORDED OVER BY CRUEL MERCENARIES, PROTECTED BY TWISTED MURDERERS.

MADAME ROUGE ALSO KNOWS NO OTHER COUNTRY WILL COME TO ZANDIA'S RESCUE...

...FOR EVEN THE MOST BARBARIC OF NATIONS WOULD RELISH SEEING ZANDIA EXTERMINATE ITSELF.

SO, MADAME ROUGE WILL HAVE HER COUNTRY, AND SHE WILL DO WITH IT AS SHE PLEASES...

...AND WHAT PLEASES THIS SHAPE-SHIFTING WITCH WOULD CERTAINLY DAMN HER SOUL... IF SHE HAD ONE.

3

MAN-O-MAN, ONE MINUTE I'M STRUGGLING FOR DEAR LIFE ON MADAME ROUGE'S *FLYING ISLAND*--

--NOW SUDDENLY I'M BACKSTAGE AT THE *FREAK SHOW!*

SOMETHING TELLS ME I SHOULDA STOOD IN *BED!*

MONSIEUR LOGAN, YOU ARE A PRISONER OF THE *NEW BROTHERHOOD OF EVIL*--

--BUT YOU NEED NOT BE A PRISONER FOR *LONG.*

BLIP! BLIP BLOOP

OBEY MY COMMANDS AND YOU WILL STILL HAVE YOUR *VENGEANCE* ON THE KILLERS OF THE *DOOM PATROL!*

WHAT DO YOU SAY, YOUNG GARFIELD LOGAN?

YOU'RE THE *BRAIN*, RIGHT?

UGLY, YER GONNA HAVE YOUR *GRAY MATTER* SCRAMBLED BEFORE I'M GONNA *TEAM UP* WITH KILLERS LIKE *YOU!*

PLASMUS! STOP HIM-- BUT DO NOT *KILL* HIM!

JA, I DO SO MIT *PLEASURE*, HERR BRAIN!

B BLIP BLOOP BLIP!

HUH? I HIT 'IM --AN' HE *OOZED* RIGHT OUTTA MY WAY!

OUI, MONSIEUR-- AND CONSIDER YOURSELF *LUCKY.* TO TOUCH PLASMUS COULD MEAN *DEATH*--

--WHEREAS *WARP*... WILL NOT KILL YOU...

4

HE WILL MERELY *SHIFT* YOU TO WHERE YOU CAN DO NO *HARM*.

HOLY COW! I *LEAP* AT HIM-- AND SUDDENLY I'M ON THE OTHER SIDE OF THE *ROOM!*

I GOT A HUNCH I COULD BE IN *TROUBLE* HERE!

BE *PLEASED*, MY LITTLE ONE-- WARP *COULD* HAVE SENT YOU PLUNGING INTO AN ACTIVE *VOLCANO!*

AH, NOW THINGS ARE LOOKING *BRIGHTER*. HEY, GORGEOUS, WHY DON'T WE *BLOW* THIS JOINT-- AND *MAKE OUT* OR SOMETHING?

I THINK I'M IN *LOVE!*

LOVE? PHOBIA KNOWS NOTHING OF *LOVE*.

PHOBIA KNOWS ONLY *FEAR!!*

YOU WHO PROFESS TO LOVE WOMEN WILL NOW ONLY *FEAR* THEM!

GYNOPHOBIA GRIPS YOU IN TIGHT TALONS OF TERROR!

PLEASE-- *STOP* HER... SHE'S GONNA *HURT* ME...

I *BEG* YOU-- PLEASE TAKE HER *AWAY* FROM ME.

ENOUGH, PHOBIA! LET *HOUNGAN* HAVE HIS TURN!

I HAVE TAKEN MY COUNTRY'S *ANCIENT RITUALS* AND NOW USE THEM *SCIENTIFICALLY!*

THIS *COMPUTER FETISH* HOLDS A LOCK OF YOUR EMERALD HAIR.

IT HAS CYBERNETICALLY SORTED OUT YOUR BODY'S *CELLULAR STRUCTURE!*

A STRUCTURE I CAN AFFECT BY USING THIS *ELECTRONIC NEEDLE!*

BEHOLD! I MERELY *GRAZE* THE DOLL'S *APPEND-AGE*, AND--

OH, WOW! STOP IT! WHAT ARE YOU DOING TO MY LEG?

YOU'RE KILLING IT-- STOP!

5

HAVE YOU SEEN ENOUGH, LOGAN?

UHH, LET'S JUST SAY I'M *CONVINCED*, OKAY?

FACT IS, I THOUGHT *YOU* DIED, TOO.

THAT IS WHAT WE *WISHED* EVERYONE TO BELIEVE.

SO, BRAIN, *TELL ME*-- WHAT HAVE YOU BEEN *UP TO* LATELY?

I MEAN, YOU AND YOUR BIG APE PAL, *MALLAH*, VANISHED THE SAME TIME THE *PATROL* WAS KILLED.

"INDEED, MERE MOMENTS BEFORE MADAME ROUGE AND CAPTAIN ZAHL ATTACKED THE BROTHERHOOD'S HEADQUARTERS..."

MADAME ROUGE KNOWS THAT *I* CREATED THE FURNACE OF EVIL THAT BURNS WITHIN HER. SHE WILL DO ANYTHING TO DES--

WAIT! MALLAH, MY COMPUTER SENSORS REVEAL SHE IS *NEAR US*--READY TO *ATTACK.*

ACTIVATE *DECOY* PROCEDURE NOW!

OUI, MONSIEUR BRAIN!

"IT WAS THIS SIMPLE, LOGAN-- OUR FLOOR REVOLVED...

...WE WERE SAFE IN OUR *UNDERGROUND CHAMBER*--

-- AND WHAT ROUGE AND ZAHL *THOUGHT* THEY HAD *DESTROYED*...

...WAS *MERELY TWO LIFELIKE REPLICAS!*

MONSIEUR MALLAH AND I REMAINED IN HIDING, SEARCHING TO FORM A *NEW BROTHER-HOOD OF EVIL!*

A BROTHERHOOD YOU HAVE JUST NOW *MET!*

OUI, MONSIEUR BRAIN. I AM CALLED *WARP*-- WITH ZEE PROPER COORDINATES I CAN CREATE ZEE *WARP*-- BETWEEN ANY TWO LOCATIONS.

YOU HAVE *TASTED* THE FEAR-CREATING POWERS OF *PHOBIA*--PRAY I DO NOT DECIDE TO LET YOU *FEAST* ON THEM!

AND I, *HOUNGAN,* HAVE SHOWN YOU HOW SUPER-STITION AND SCIENCE CAN BE *MERGED*-- WITH VERY DEADLY RESULTS!

SCIENCE-- BAH! DIS SCIENCE CREATED *PLASMUS*... GENERAL ZAHL USED ME AS HIS GUINEA PIG AND IT ALMOST COST ME MY *LIFE!*

ZAHL AND HIS *WITCH* COMPAN-ION MUST *PAY* FOR WHAT THEY DID TO ME!

6

WE ALL HAVE REASONS, MONSIEUR LOGAN, TO SEEK *VENGEANCE* ON ZAHL AND ROUGE.

BLIP BLOP

BLIP BLOP

JOIN WITH US AND PERHAPS WE SHALL ALL *SUCCEED*, NO?

YOU PEOPLE ARE *SCUM*... YOU, BRAIN, WERE ONE OF THE DOOM PATROL'S GREATEST *ENEMIES*... WHICH MAKES YOU *MY* ENEMY AS WELL.

BUT ZAHL AND ROUGE *DESTROYED* THE DOOM PATROL! THEY *KILLED* MY ADOPTIVE MOTHER... RITA FARR-- *ELASTI-GIRL!*

SO, FOR *NOW* I'LL PUT ASIDE THE CONTEMPTUOUS *HATRED* I FEEL FOR YOU, BRAIN, AND I'LL FIGHT *ALONGSIDE* YOU.

BUT WHEN ALL THIS IS *OVER*... AFTER WE'VE GONE OUR SEPARATE WAYS --THE *TRUCE* WILL BE OVER--

--AND I'LL FIND A WAY TO HUNT *YOU* DOWN FOR ALL YOUR FILTHY CRIMES!

MEANWHILE... ZANDIA HAS JUST *FALLEN.* IT IS NOW *MINE!*

THERE WILL BE NO STOPPING ME *NOW!*

STOPPING *US*, MY DEAR-- *US!*

OF COURSE, ZAHL... OF *COURSE!*

ZANDIA FALLS, AND OUR ENEMIES HAVE REVERTED TO A PRIMITIVE STATE.

I FEAR THEY WILL PROBABLY RIP *EACH OTHER* APART *LONG* BEFORE THEY DEVOLVE INTO *ONE-CELLED AMOEBAS!*

IT SHOULD BE QUITE *ENJOYABLE* TO WATCH, NEIN, MADAME?

AHH, THE *FÜHRER* WOULD HAVE BEEN SO *PROUD.*

7

MADAME ROUGE STIFFENS AT THE NAME. THAT LITTLE MAN HAD SENT HIS BLOODTHIRSTY STORM TROOPERS INTO HER VILLAGE WHEN SHE WAS A CHILD -- THEY HAD KILLED HER PARENTS...

YES, SHE THINKS, ZAHL WILL HAVE TO BE DEALT WITH. BUT...

ZAHL! WHAT IS HAPPENING THERE? THAT BRIGHT LIGHT?

WELL, WELL, WARP-- RIGHT ON TARGET WITH THE FIRST TRY!

AND LOOK WHO'S HERE -- TALL, DARK AND SLIMY -- JUST WAITING FOR US TO MOW HIM DOWN!

LOGAN? DO NOT TAKE ONE STEP CLOSER, MON AMI--

--LEST I PRESS THIS DETONATOR WHICH SHALL DESTROY YOUR NEANDERTHAL FRIENDS.

LORD, WHAT'S SHE DONE TO THEM? WHAT DO I DO? TRY TO JUMP HER?

MAN, IF I WERE ROBIN, I WOULDN'T HESITATE, I'D--

BUT WHILE THE SHAPE-CHANGER MULLS OVER THE ALTERNATIVES...

YOU HESITATE. GOOD, LOGAN-- PERHAPS YOU ARE NOT QUITE SO STUPID AFTER ALL.

NOW, MY LITTLE ONE -- DO AS I SAY, OR--

--OR NOTHING, KILLER!

YOU NO LONGER HOLD THE CARDS!

SKRASH!

BLAM

INDEED, THE GAME PLAY IS MINE!

MON DIEU! MONSIEUR MALLAH! Y-YOU ARE ALIVE...

THEN-- ALL OF YOU HERE--

CORRECT, MADAME, WE WORK FOR ZEE BRAIN... AND WE WORK TOGETHER TO DEFEAT YOU!

8

ZEE BROTHERHOOD OF EVIL SHALL BE TRIUMPHA--

AGHHH!

YOU SHALL *DIE,* SWINE-- AS YOU SHOULD HAVE DIED YEARS AGO!

THE BROTHERHOOD SHALL PERISH EVEN AS IT IS *BORN* ANEW!

ZAHL'S ARMIES, AUGMENTED BY VIRTUALLY INDESTRUCTIBLE BIO-SUITS, SURGE FORWARD GLEEFUL AT THIS CHANCE TO WREAK DEVASTATION...

BUT...

ZAHL, I OWE *YOU* FOR WHAT YOU HAF DONE TO ME!

MY PROTOPLASMIC BODY, THIS *HORROR* I HAF BECOME--

--IT SHALL BE DER *WEAPON OF YOUR DESTRUCTION!*

SSSSS

HOLY HANNAH! P-PLASMUS-- WHAT DID YOU *DO* TO HIM?

GOD!

DER FOOL HAS BEEN REDUCED TO A PROTOPLASMIC *BLOB!* HE DESERVED NOTHING MORE!

AHH, *THREE* OF THEM ATTACK AT *ONCE.* THEN THIS SHALL BE A *TEST* OF PHOBIA'S POWERS!

A MOMENT TO CONCENTRATE--

9

--AND THE *SAME* FEAR SHALL GNAW AT YOU *ALL!*

OPHIDIOPHOBIA! THE FEAR OF *REPTILES--*

YOU SEE *EACH OTHER* AS THE SLITHERING SNAKES YOU *ARE!*

SKREEE   SKREEEE

SKREEE

SO *EASY...*

...AND RATHER QUITE *AMUSING,* DO YOU NOT *THINK?*

OUI, MADAME, A *LAUGH!*

BUT A *SICK* ONE, NO?

SHE IS *WITHOUT HUMOR*-- SHE *FRIGHTENS* ME.

AHHH, A *WARP* FOR MY *FRIENDS* HERE--

THE *FURTHER* I SEND MY ENEMIES, THE MORE *STRAIN* I FEEL--

--BUT THIS WARP IS SURELY *WORTH* IT, NO?

"OH, ONE WORD OF *CAUTION--*

"*IN SPACE* IT IS VERY *DIFFICULT* TO *BREATHE!*"

10

ZAHL IS A *FOOL!* HE STANDS *BEHIND* AND FIGHTS! BUT *I* SHALL NOT BE SO *STUPID!*

IF MONSIEUR MALLAH AND THE OTHERS ACTUALLY *DEFEAT* OUR SOLDIERS, I WISH TO BE *SAFE*--

--TO PLAN STILL *GREATER PLANS!*

THOUGH THIS CONSTANT BATTLING BEGINS TO *GNAW* AT ME, THERE IS *NO TURNING BACK* NOW.

CURSE THE BRAIN FOR TAKING AN ORDINARY FRENCH SCHOOL TEACHER--

--AND TWISTING HER INTO THE INFAMOUS *MADAME ROUGE!*

HOW *DIFFERENT* MY LIFE MIGHT HAVE BEEN IF--

AND WHERE DO YOU THINK *YOU'RE* GOING, LITTLE *LETHAL LADY?*

LOGAN? IS THAT *YOU?*

RIGHT ON THE FIRST GUESS, GRUE-SOME...

... A *LIGHTNING BUG* TO LIGHT UP YOUR LIFE...

AND NOW THAT I HAVE YOUR CRUMMY ATTENTION-- *WHAMMO!*

MY, MY, WHAT GREAT BIG *TEETH* I HAVE, GRANNY--

--THE BETTER TO PLAY *"JAWS"* ON YOU, EH?

MON DIEU! IT IS *IMPOSSIBLE!*

MEANWHILE... IT'S *NO GOOD!* THEIR *MINDS* HAVE REGRESSED LIKE THEIR *BODIES!*

THEY'VE BECOME *PRIMITIVE SAVAGES*-- READY TO FEAST ON A *STEEL-SKIN SUPPER!*

TROUBLE IS, THEY MAY *SUCCEED*-- EVEN IN *THIS* STATE THEY STILL HAVE THEIR *POWERS.*

CAN'T *FIGHT* THEM OFF, SO USE THE *ONLY* THING YOU'VE GOT *WORKING* FOR YOU, STEELE--

NEXT TO *THEM,* THE LITTLE SUPER-STRENGTH I'VE GOT IS--

ARGHH!

--YOUR *BRAIN,* MAN-- USE YOUR BRAIN!!

11

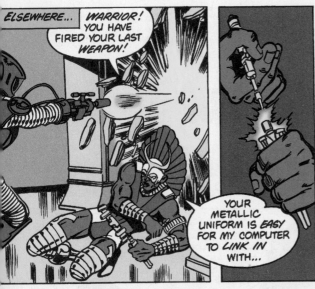

ELSEWHERE... WARRIOR! YOU HAVE FIRED YOUR LAST WEAPON!

YOUR METALLIC UNIFORM IS EASY FOR MY COMPUTER TO LINK IN WITH...

...EASY FOR ME TO TAMPER WITH...

...EASY FOR MY COMPUTER FETISH TO DESTROY!

SPTRAKK

THE POWERS OF HOUNGAN ARE NOT TO BE TOYED WITH!

THIS BETTER WORK, OR ALL MY BRAIN IS GONNA BE GOOD FOR--

--IS TO MAKE ME THE SMARTEST CORPSE IN THE JUNKYARD!

IT'S CYBORG I WANT, MY METALLIC COMRADE-IN-CYBERNETIC-ARMS!

I'VE SEEN STONE USE HIS WEAPONS, KNOW WHAT HE CAN DO--

HEY! QUIT STRUGGLING, GUY-- I'M DOING THIS FOR ALL OF US!

THERE. I'VE GOT HIS WHITE SOUND BLASTER ATTACHED...

...SET IT FOR FIFTY THOUSAND DECIBELS--

12

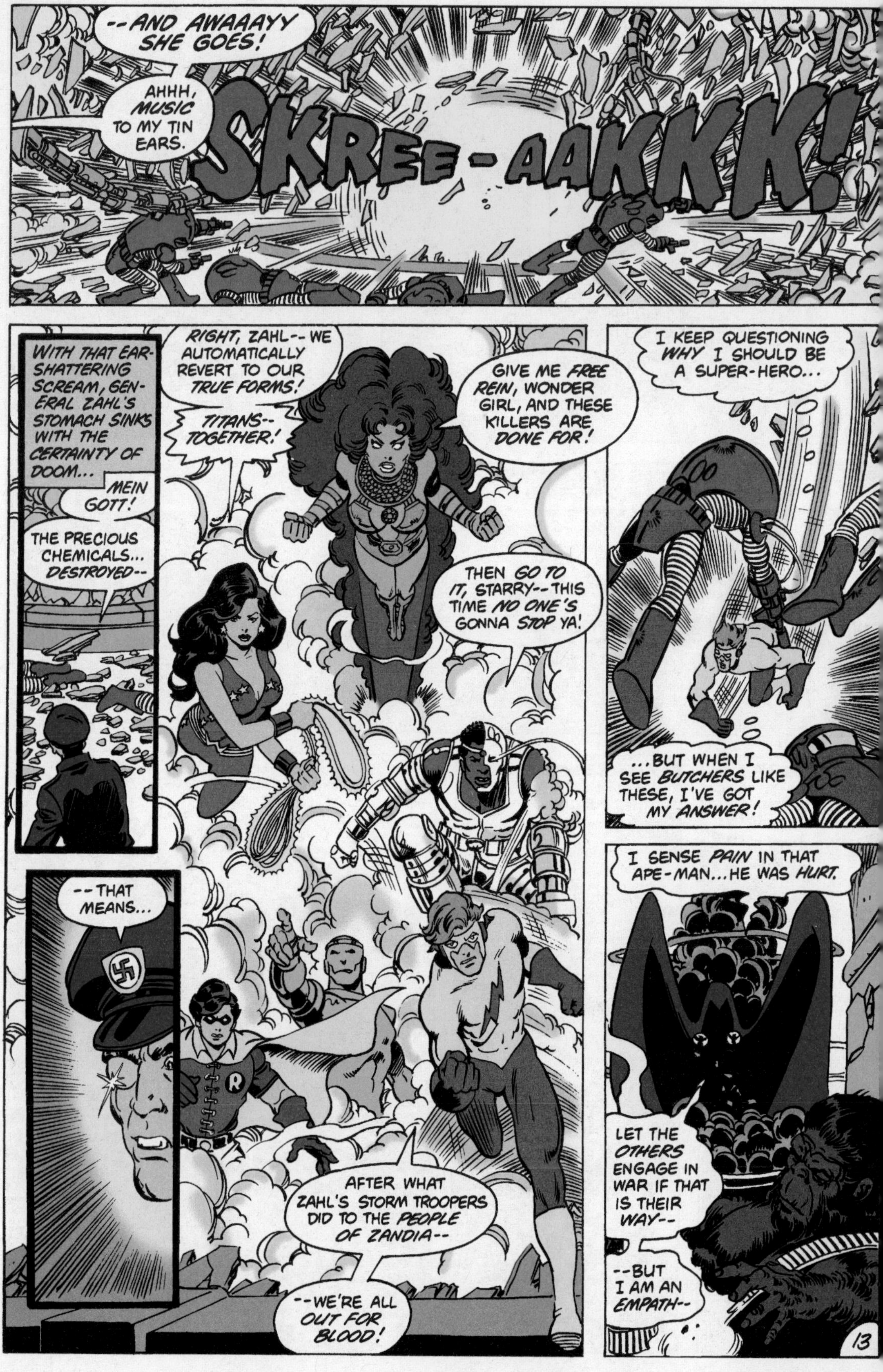
--AND AWAAAYY SHE GOES!
AHHH, MUSIC TO MY TIN EARS.
SKREE-AAKKKK!
WITH THAT EAR-SHATTERING SCREAM, GENERAL ZAHL'S STOMACH SINKS WITH THE CERTAINTY OF DOOM...
MEIN GOTT!
THE PRECIOUS CHEMICALS... DESTROYED--
--THAT MEANS...
RIGHT, ZAHL--WE AUTOMATICALLY REVERT TO OUR TRUE FORMS!
TITANS--TOGETHER!
GIVE ME FREE REIN, WONDER GIRL, AND THESE KILLERS ARE DONE FOR!
THEN GO TO IT, STARRY--THIS TIME NO ONE'S GONNA STOP YA!
AFTER WHAT ZAHL'S STORM TROOPERS DID TO THE PEOPLE OF ZANDIA--
--WE'RE ALL OUT FOR BLOOD!
I KEEP QUESTIONING WHY I SHOULD BE A SUPER-HERO...
...BUT WHEN I SEE BUTCHERS LIKE THESE, I'VE GOT MY ANSWER!
I SENSE PAIN IN THAT APE-MAN...HE WAS HURT.
LET THE OTHERS ENGAGE IN WAR IF THAT IS THEIR WAY--
--BUT I AM AN EMPATH--
13

--MY VERY LIFE IS TO *HEAL!*

TO TAKE AWAY THE *PAIN* OF THE HELPLESS...

AZAR HELP ME! EACH TIME I EMPATHICALLY HEAL *ANOTHER...*

...MY PAINS GROW MORE *TERRIBLE!*

I HURT, GREAT *AZAR--I HURT...* YET I *CANNOT STOP!*

T-TO BE AN *EMPATH MEANS* TO HEAL OTHERS AT THE EXPENSE OF *YOURSELF.*

BEHIND ME, MA'MSELLE! ZIS ONE, HE TRIES TO *KILL* YOU WHILE YOU HELP ME.

BUT *MONSIEUR MALLAH* WILL NOT *LET* HIS BENEFACTOR COME TO HARM.

NO, PLEASE-- *DON'T KILL HIM!* DON'T MAKE A *MOCKERY* OF MY LIFE!

THESE CREEPS ARE ALL OVER THE PLACE. I SMASH A COUPLE WITH MY *FISTS--*

--TAKE A FEW *MORE* OUT WITH MY *SOUND BLASTER...*

...BUT THEY KEEP CRAWLING OUTTA THE *PLASTIC* HERE!

BUT WHAT *BOTHERS* ME IS THAT I'M *GETTIN' OFF* ON *SMASHIN'* THEM!

I WANNA *HURT* 'EM EVEN THOUGH I KNOW THAT'S *WRONG!*

DOES THE *SAVAGE* THEY BROUGHT OUT IN ME STILL *CONTROL* MY THOUGHTS?

OR, IS THIS THE WAY WE *ALL* ARE, DEEP DOWN IN OUR *HEARTS?*

14

BUT...

OOF! REAL ALERT, STONE! QUIT MAKIN' LIKE SOME PHILOSOPHER WHILE THEY SNEAK RIGHT UP ON YA!

SPAMM!

UH-OH--WATCH THAT FIRST STEP--

--IT'S A REAL DOOZY!

GRABBED HOLD, BUT SOMEHOW I DON'T FEEL ALL THAT SAFE.

PULLED MY ARM OUT TO ITS FURTHEST...

TALK ABOUT YOUR LIFE HANGING BY A THREAD!

STEEL THREADS, MEBBE, BUT EVEN THEY WON'T LAST FOREVER!

OBOY!

FEEL LIKE I'M IN "RAIDERS OF THE LOST ARK"...

...ONE CLIFF-HANGER AFTER ANOTHER!

"CLIFF-HANGER"? BAD JOKE, STONE!

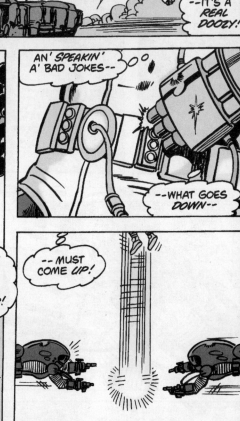

AN' SPEAKIN' A' BAD JOKES--

--WHAT GOES DOWN--

-- MUST COME UP!

HEY, GUYS, EVER HAVE ONE OF THOSE DAYS WHEN YOU SHOULD'A STOOD IN BED?

SKROOM

15

I CAN *JOKE* ABOUT THIS *SUPER*-HEROING, BUT IT *STILL* MAKES ME *SHUDDER* AT TIMES.

WE'RE FIGHTING FOR IDEALS I NEVER EVEN *DREAMED* ABOUT IN SCHOOL!

SOMETIMES WHAT WE DO SCARES THE *DAYLIGHTS* OUTTA ME, BUT MOST OF THE TIME, I STILL FEEL *GOOD*. AHH, KNOCKED HIM OUT!

DO NOT *KILL?* MADAME, I KILL ONLY *THE KILLERS!*

PLEASE, *DON'T*... IT IS *WRONG* TO DO THIS.

I *FEEL* AND *ABSORB* ALL PAINS... WHAT YOU ARE *DOING* HURTS ME BEYOND ALL YOUR *IMAGINING.*

YOU PLEAD FOR ME TO *STOP? THAT* IS INSANE, NO?

I WAS *BORN* A BEAST OF PREY! EVEN WITH MY BRAIN *ENLARGED*--

--I AM *STILL* A *CREATURE* OF INSTINCT! I CANNOT STOP *KILLING* ANY MORE THAN *YOU HUMANS* CAN!

A *HUMAN* WITH A *SOUL* CAN *CONTROL* HIS BASER INSTINCTS.

BUT I CANNOT *ARGUE* ANY LONGER... FOR MY *OWN* SANITY AND SAFETY, I CAN STAY HERE NOT A *MOMENT* MORE!

STARFIRE--?

NO, I'M *NOT KILLING* THEM, IF *THAT* IS WHAT YOU WANT TO KNOW!

BUT THEY *DESERVE* DEATH, WONDER GIRL-- THEY *TRULY* DESERVE TO--

DIE, YOU SCUM!

ARGHHH!

IF YOU *HEAR* ME, BRAIN-- I HAVE *OVEREXTENDED* MY POWER!

I--I MUST *REST* BEFORE I CAN PROJECT ANOTHER SPATIAL WARP!

THOUGH THAT FACTOR IS OF LITTLE COMFORT TO THOSE WHO SUDDENLY FIND THEMSELVES AT THE BOTTOM OF THE BALTIC SEA...

16

THERE IS A SHARP CONTRAST IN *STYLES* HERE. THE *BROTHERHOOD OF EVIL KILL* THEIR FOES! THE *TITANS* SEEK MERELY TO *STOP* THEM, TO RENDER THEM *INOPERATIVE.*

A DIFFERENCE THAT *RAVEN* NOTES WITH *APPRECIATION.*

EVEN IN BATTLE, EVEN IN THE MIDST OF WAR, THERE IS A DIFFERENCE BETWEEN GOOD AND EVIL.

BUT *WONDER GIRL* IS WORRIED AS *STARFIRE* NEARLY *BURSTS* WITH AN EVER-INCREASING NEED FOR VIOLENCE.

SKREEEE

KORIAND'R'S STARBOLTS HAVE NOT *KILLED* THE ENEMY, BUT THEY HAVE COME AWFULLY *CLOSE.*

WHAT WILL *HAPPEN,* WONDER GIRL SHUDDERS, IF THE FURY OF THIS ALIEN WARRIOR IS EVER TRULY *UNLEASHED--*?

FAR BELOW HIM, *GENERAL ZAHL* SEES THE CASUALTIES MOUNT WITH *HORRIFYING* SPEED.

HE SEES HIS SOLDIERS *CUT DOWN* WITH *TERRIFYING* EASE.

AND THIS SOLDIER DECIDES THE TIME HAS COME TO *FLEE,* TO RUN AS HE RAN FROM ANOTHER *LOSING* BATTLE SO MANY YEARS *BEFORE...*

17

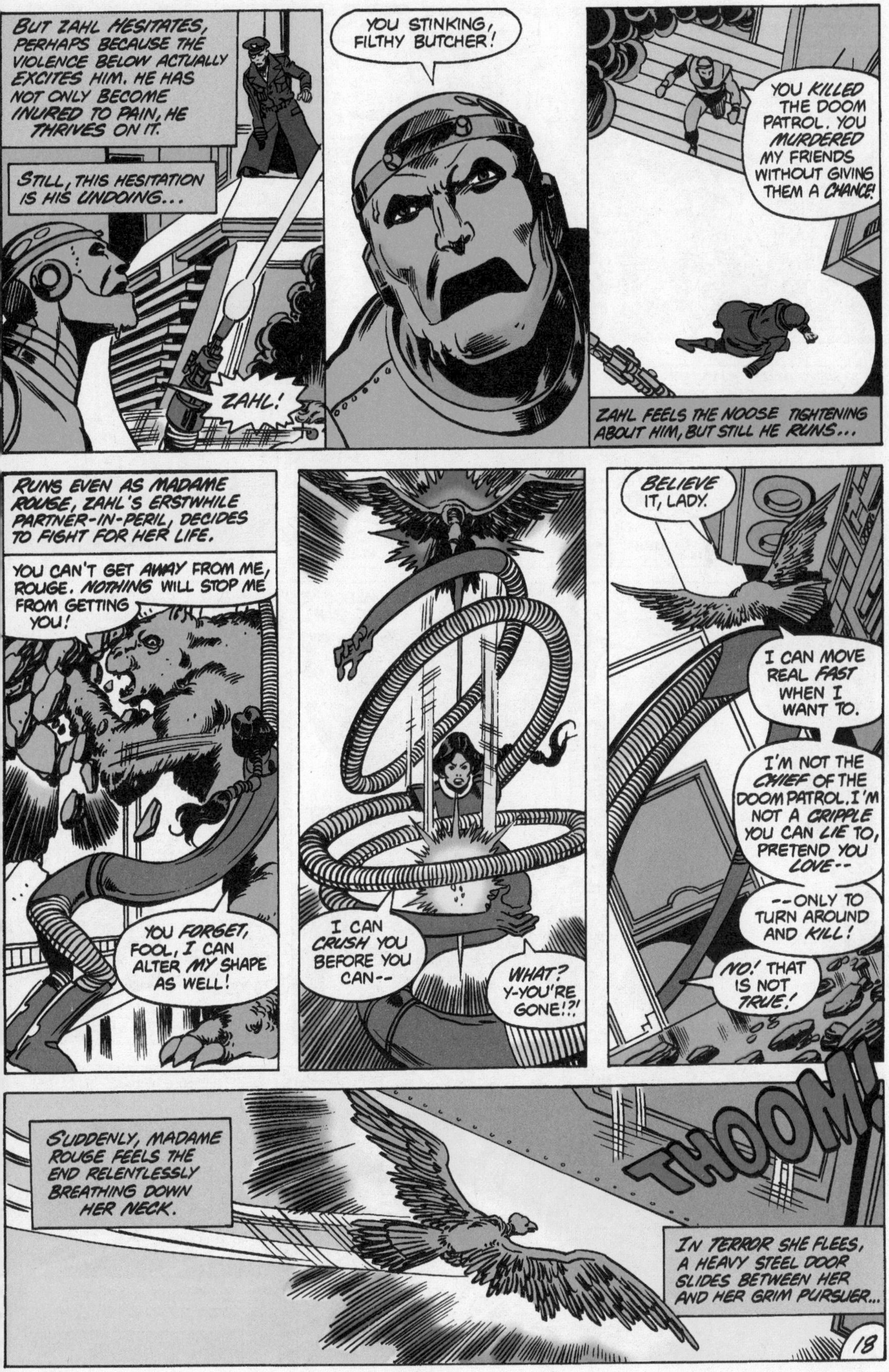
BUT ZAHL HESITATES, PERHAPS BECAUSE THE VIOLENCE BELOW ACTUALLY EXCITES HIM. HE HAS NOT ONLY BECOME INURED TO PAIN, HE THRIVES ON IT.
STILL, THIS HESITATION IS HIS UNDOING...
ZAHL!
YOU STINKING, FILTHY BUTCHER!
YOU KILLED THE DOOM PATROL. YOU MURDERED MY FRIENDS WITHOUT GIVING THEM A CHANCE!
ZAHL FEELS THE NOOSE TIGHTENING ABOUT HIM, BUT STILL HE RUNS...
RUNS EVEN AS MADAME ROUGE, ZAHL'S ERSTWHILE PARTNER-IN-PERIL, DECIDES TO FIGHT FOR HER LIFE.
YOU CAN'T GET AWAY FROM ME, ROUGE. NOTHING WILL STOP ME FROM GETTING YOU!
YOU FORGET, FOOL, I CAN ALTER MY SHAPE AS WELL!
I CAN CRUSH YOU BEFORE YOU CAN--
WHAT? Y-YOU'RE GONE!?!
BELIEVE IT, LADY.
I CAN MOVE REAL FAST WHEN I WANT TO.
I'M NOT THE CHIEF OF THE DOOM PATROL. I'M NOT A CRIPPLE YOU CAN LIE TO, PRETEND YOU LOVE--
--ONLY TO TURN AROUND AND KILL!
NO! THAT IS NOT TRUE!
SUDDENLY, MADAME ROUGE FEELS THE END RELENTLESSLY BREATHING DOWN HER NECK.
THOOM!
IN TERROR SHE FLEES, A HEAVY STEEL DOOR SLIDES BETWEEN HER AND HER GRIM PURSUER...
18

BUT TO GARFIELD LOGAN, THAT DOOR MIGHT WELL HAVE BEEN MADE FROM PAPIER-MÂCHÉ...

YOU KILLED THE CHIEF, YOU KILLED LARRY... AND, BLAST YOU, ROUGE -- YOU KILLED MY MOTHER!

AND HE WILL KILL ME. NOTHING WILL STOP HIM.

NOTHING, UNLESS--

SKRASH!

GUESS WHAT, GOOSE-STEPPER, A DEAD END!

SORTA APPROPRIATE, CONSIDERING!

LET ME OUT! DERE MUST BE A WAY OUT!

ONLY ONE WAY, ZAHL.

BAH! YOU VILL NOT KILL ME. YOU ARE WEAK!

YOU COULD NOT KILL.

ZAHL...

YEAH, MEBBE YOU'RE RIGHT, ZAHL!

BUT I CAN SURE MAKE LIVING ONE HELLUVA NIGHTMARE!

NEIN! NEIN! YOU VILL NOT TOUCH ME, YOU STEEL SWINE!

I HAVE NOT LIVED SO LONG TO BE IMPRISONED LIKE SOME PETTY THUG!

YOU VILL DIE BEFORE I--

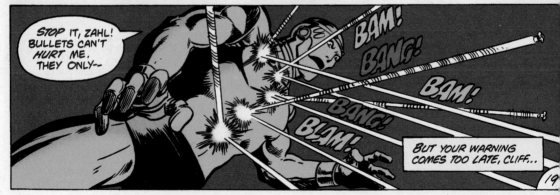

STOP IT, ZAHL! BULLETS CAN'T HURT ME. THEY ONLY--

BAM! BANG!

BAM!

BANG!

BLAM!

BUT YOUR WARNING COMES TOO LATE, CLIFF...

19

THE DEED IS DONE...

ZAHL'S OWN HAND HAS BROUGHT DOWN RETRIBUTION.

I *TOLD* YOU, ROBOTMAN, YOU VOULD *NOT* TAKE ME.

I *DIE*, BUT DAT IS ALL *RIGHT*.

I HAF THE *LAST LAUGH*, ROBOTMAN!

DER FÜHRER WOULD HAF *WANTED* IT THIS WAY... THE LAST LAUGH...

H-HEI--

HEIL HITL--

UNHHH...

THE LAST LAUGH, ZAHL?

NOBODY GETS THE LAST LAUGH, ZAHL.

YOU DON'T GET IT. THE THOUSANDS YOU'VE *KILLED* DON'T GET IT... THE CHIEF, LARRY, RITA-- *THEY* DON'T GET IT. *I* DON'T GET IT.

NOT EVEN *GOD* ALLOWS HIMSELF THE LAST LAUGH, ZAHL.

HE ONLY *WEEPS* FOR HIS CHILDREN GONE ASTRAY!

C'MON, ROUGE, THERE'S NO *ESCAPE* FROM ME.

THIS HAS BEEN BUILDING IN ME FOR *TOO LONG!*

THIS HAS BEEN *DESTROYING* ME FOR TOO MANY YEARS TO LET YOU *GET AWAY!*

HE'S *INSANE!* HE'S EVEN *METAMORPHOSING* INTO CREATURES THAT DO NOT *EXIST!* CREATURES OF HIS OWN IRRATIONAL *MIND!*

AND THE NET TIGHTENS IRREVERSIBLY...

20

HE WON'T LET ME GET *AWAY*. THERE'S *NOTHING* I CAN TURN MYSELF INTO THAT WOULD *SAVE* ME.

IF *I* *HAVE* TO DIE, THEN *I* WILL TAKE THEM ALL *WITH* ME!

WHAT ARE *YOU* *DOING*, ROUGE? GET *AWAY* FROM THERE!

FORGET IT, MON PETITE-- WE WILL ALL GO TO A MORE GLORIOUS FOREVER *TOGETHER*!

NO.' I SAID GET AWAY!

SWAK!

GAR LOGAN LASHES OUT WITH FEROCITY, AND ROUGE'S BODY IS LIMP AS IT SPILLS ACROSS THIS ELECTRONIC TOWER OF BABEL...

FOR A MOMENT, HER EYES BETRAY HER DEEPEST FEAR AS SHE REALIZES AT LAST THE END HAS COME.

MY GOD!

SKRAKK!

IT IS *HARD* FOR THE CHANGELING TO ALTER HIS FORM BACK TO HUMAN. IT IS ALMOST AS IF HE *PREFERS* DISPLAYING THIS BEAST FROM WITHIN. BUT THEN, *FINALLY*...

ROUGE--? MADAME ROUGE?

D-DID I *KILL* HER?

I DIDN'T MEAN TO.

NO. THAT'S NOT TRUE, I *DID* MEAN TO... BUT I *WOULDN'T* HAVE...

...L-LOGAN...

Y-YOU'RE ALIVE?

THANK GOD, I DIDN'T *KILL* YOU... THANK *HEAVEN*...

:COUGH: WE'RE ALL *DEAD*, LOGAN ...ALL OF US...

 ...I--I DIED *LONG AGO*--WHEN THE BRAIN ALTERED MY MIND AND TURNED ME *EVIL*...

THE SHOCK, LOGAN--IT SEEMED TO CLEAR MY MIND... PLEASE, ALL OF YOU RUN-- THIS ISLAND ⸫COUGH⸫ WILL BE THE *DEATH* OF YOU ALL...

...LOGAN,... TH-THANK YOU FOR *FREEING* ME, LOGAN--THANK YOU...

OH, GOD, NILES...I *COME* TO YOU... I *COME*... TO... YOU...

NO! NO! I--I KILLED HER... *I KILLED HER!!* HER DEATH'S NOW ON MY CONSCIENCE, TOO.

 I AM GLAD THE *REST* OF ME DIES NOW...

I--I HATED HER, I WANTED HER *DEAD*, I WANTED TO *DESTROY* HER, AND I DID... I DID!

I *HIT* HER... INTO THAT MACHINE... I CAUSED HER DEATH AS IF I HAD PULLED A *TRIGGER*...

BUT... I *WON'T* LET ANYONE *ELSE* DIE BECAUSE OF ME.

 HE RUNS BECAUSE HE HAS EXHAUSTED HIMSELF...THE LARGER THE MASS OF THE CREATURE HE BECOMES, THE MORE IT TAKES OUT OF HIM...

IF THIS BLASTED ISLAND IS GOING UP IN FLAMES, NO ONE *ELSE* IS GOING TO SUFFER.

HE RUNS, BECAUSE, FOR NOW AT LEAST, GARFIELD LOGAN IS *INCAPABLE* OF SHIFTING SHAPES...

HE RUNS FOR HIS FRIENDS STILL IN THE MIDST OF BATTLE, AND AS HE RUNS, SO MANY THOUGHTS ENTER HIS TORTURED YOUNG MIND...

22

PERHAPS RAVEN SENSES THE CONFLICTING EMOTIONS THAT ASSAIL GAR LOGAN. PERHAPS THAT IS WHY SUDDENLY SHE CRIES OUT...

STOP! PLEASE LET THE FIGHTING *END!*

THE BATTLE IS *OVER...* THOSE WE CAME TO DEFEAT... ARE LOST.

ROUGE AND ZAHL *DEAD?*

I AM *DISAPPOINTED* I WISHED TO BE THE *INSTRUMENT* OF THEIR DESTRUCTION!

WHAT *GOOD* DOES IT DO, HAVING ROUGE DIE? MY *MOM* IS STILL DEAD. AND THE *REST* OF THE PATROL *WITH* HER.

ALL THESE YEARS THE *VENGEANCE* I WAS HOPING FOR-- IT MEANS *NOTHING* TO ME NOW THAT IT'S BEEN HAD!

I--I DON'T EVER WANT TO *HURT* ANYONE AGAIN... ALL I WANT IS TO *HELP*--

LOGAN!

THE *BRAIN?* WHAT ARE *YOU* DOING HERE?

SHIFTING THIS FLOATING ISLAND, LOGAN-- I WANT ZANDIA *SAFE*-- FOR REASONS OF MY *OWN!*

AND *YOU,* LITTLE ONE, YOU HAVE DONE *TRES BIEN...* I *LAUGHED* AS I HEARD ROUGE BREATHE HER LAST!

BUT WE MUST SAVE OUR *ALLIES,* NON? *ALERT* THEM NOW!

AND... EVERYONE, THIS JOINT'S GONNA MAKE A *BOOM!* THAT MOUNT ST. HELENS WOULD *ENVY.* GET OUT OF HERE--*FAST!*

BUT HOW DO WE TAKE EVERYONE WITH US?

FOLLOW *ME,* MES AMIS--

YOU? HOW CAN WE TRUST *YOU?*

IT VOULD BE *WISE,* STEEL MAN. HERR WARP IS YOUR ONLY SALVATION!

HURRY! I SHALL BRING US ALL TO *SAFETY* THROUGH MY SPATIAL WARP.

ZE WARP *STILL* MAKES MALLAH NERVOUS.

YOU WANT TO BE *NERVOUS* --OR *DEAD,* MONSIEUR?

23

24

GONE... ALONG WITH THEIR INSANE PLANS OF CONQUEST.

THERE IS SOMETHING OF *POETIC JUSTICE* IN THIS, I THINK.

"JUSTICE"? *BAH!* THE VERY WORD *SICKENS* ME!

HOLD IT RIGHT *THERE*, LADY. ZAHL AND MADAM ROUGE MAY BE GONE BUT *YOU* CREEPS ARE JUST AS BAD AS *THEY* ARE.

OUR FIGHT AIN'T *OVER* YET.

CLIFF... DON'T *DO* ANYTHING!

I--I MADE A *DEAL* WITH THEM TO HELP SAVE THE TITANS.

THIS TIME, AT LEAST, THEY'RE *FREE* TO GO.

FREE, HUH?

SURE, WHY *NOT?* WHO WANTS *ANOTHER* FIGHT AFTER THIS, RIGHT?

LOGAN, YOU HAVE SERVED THE BROTHERHOOD *WELL*. WE SHALL LONG *REMEMBER* ROUGE AND ZAHL'S DEATH.

SO GLORIOUS... SO GLORIOUS.

YOU ACTUALLY *BELIEVE* KILLING ACCOMPLISHES SOMETHING POSITIVE.

WE KNOW THERE'S *NOTHING* POSITIVE ABOUT MURDER... IT'S NOT ONLY WRONG...IT'S *SAD!* AWFULLY, *AWFULLY* SAD.

GLORIOUS? Y'KNOW, BRAIN, I GUESS THAT'S WHAT SEPARATES THE *GOOD* GUYS FROM THE *BAD* GUYS.

25

GARFIELD HAS LEARNED *WELL*, WALLACE. BEFORE THIS HE WAS A BOY STRUGGLING WITH HIS OWN FEARS.

NOW HE IS A *MAN* COME TO GRIPS WITH HIS OWN *MORTALITY.*

HE HAS SEEN HOW WASTEFUL IT IS TO *HATE*. HOW *IMPOVERISHED* THE SOUL BECOMES WHEN *VENGEANCE* CONSUMES THE *HEART.*

OH, WE TITANS FIGHT *BATTLES*, AND I ALONG WITH YOU, BECAUSE I FEEL WE TRULY BELIEVE THAT SOMEDAY EVIL WILL BE *DESTROYED.*

I LIVE FOR *THAT DAY*, WALLACE, WHEN THE ONLY TEARS AN EMPATH SHEDS ARE THOSE *TEARS OF JOY.*

CLIFF, YOU KNOW, I USED TO FEEL SO *EMPTY.* BUT NOW--

GAR, MY GOD-- *GAR!*

HUH?

DAYTON?

I WAS SO *SCARED* FOR YOU, GAR... SO VERY SCARED. I *CARE* FOR YOU. I KNOW I HAVEN'T *TOLD* YOU THAT BEFORE, BUT I *LOVE* YOU, SON.

OH, STEVE...ST--

--DAD!

IT IS ALL *OVER?* JUST LIKE *THAT?*

YEAH. YOU WANT *EVERYTHING* TO END WITH A BANG, GOLDIE?

OVER... *NEVER* THOUGHT I'D SEE THE DAY.

I'VE BEEN LIVING WITH THIS EVER SINCE *RITA* DIED.

AND I'M *GLAD* IT'S OVER. I...NO LONGER FEEL THE *HATE.*

YOU KNOW, DAD, I ONCE THOUGHT WHEN THIS ENDED, IT WOULD END ALL MY MEMORIES OF THE DOOM PATROL.

BUT IT *DOESN'T*, YOU KNOW. I THINK *WITHOUT* THE HATE CLOUDING MY MIND --THAT THEY'RE *BRIGHTER* IN MY HEART THAN *EVER.*

26

THE DOOM PATROL: HEROES FROM THE PAST WHO SACRIFICED THEIR LIVES THAT OTHERS MIGHT LIVE. HEROES THESE YOUNG TITANS HOPE AND PRAY THEY CAN SOMEDAY GROW TO BE LIKE.

THE DOOM PATROL: SELFLESS AND DEDICATED, THEY CARED IN A WORLD WHERE CARING WAS DANGEROUS. THEY CARED WHEN IT SEEMED THAT NO ONE ELSE COULD.

THE DOOM PATROL: THEIR MEMORY WILL NOT DIE. INDEED, SO LONG AS THERE IS HOPE FOR THINGS BETTER, THEIR MEMORY CANNOT DIE.

AS LONG AS THERE IS HOPE-- THE GOOD MEMORIES NEVER DIE!

RESPECTFULLY DEDICATED TO THOSE CREATORS OF THE DOOM PATROL: ARNOLD DRAKE! BOB HANEY! BRUNO PREMIANI! BOB BROWN! MURRAY BOLTINOFF!

NEXT ISSUE \ IT HAD TO HAPPEN-- STARFIRE UNLEASHED!

27

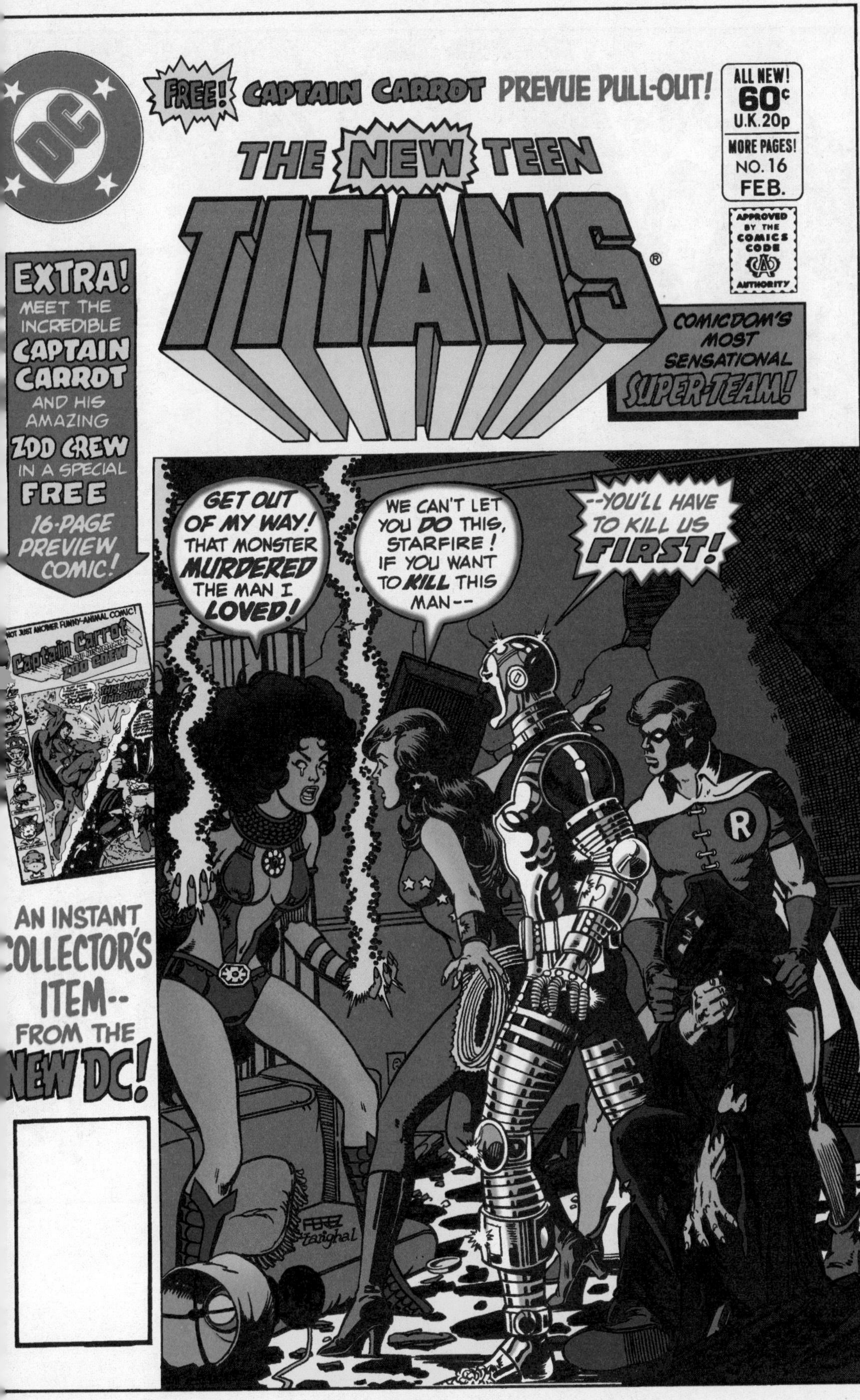

FREE! CAPTAIN CARROT PREVUE PULL-OUT!
ALL NEW! 60¢ U.K.20p
MORE PAGES! NO.16 FEB.
APPROVED BY THE COMICS CODE AUTHORITY
THE NEW TEEN TITANS
COMICDOM'S MOST SENSATIONAL SUPER-TEAM!
EXTRA! MEET THE INCREDIBLE CAPTAIN CARROT AND HIS AMAZING ZOO CREW IN A SPECIAL FREE 16-PAGE PREVIEW COMIC!
AN INSTANT COLLECTOR'S ITEM-- FROM THE NEW DC!
GET OUT OF MY WAY! THAT MONSTER MURDERED THE MAN I LOVED!
WE CAN'T LET YOU DO THIS, STARFIRE! IF YOU WANT TO KILL THIS MAN--
--YOU'LL HAVE TO KILL US FIRST!

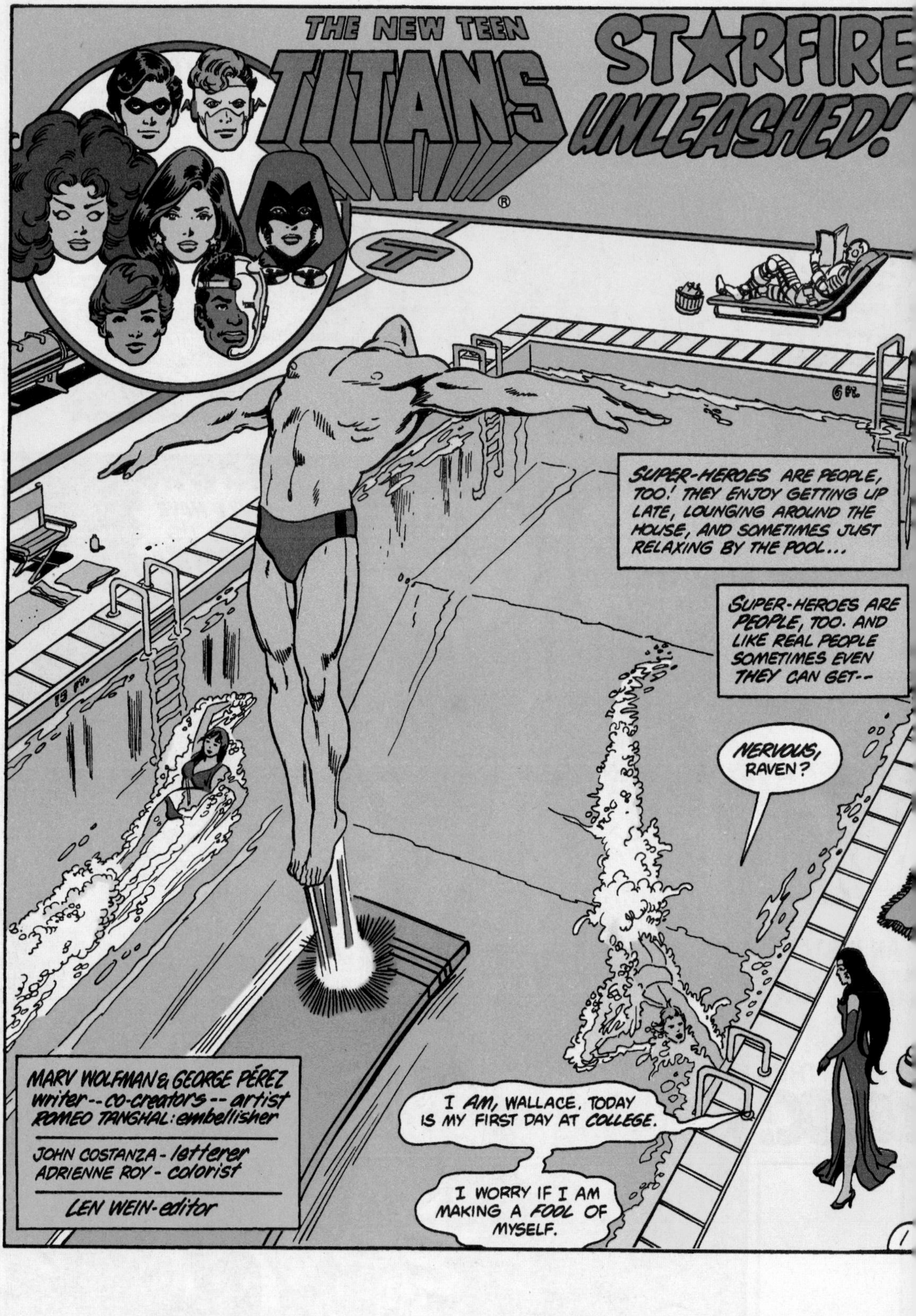
THE NEW TEEN TITANS
STARFIRE UNLEASHED!
6 FT.
SUPER-HEROES ARE PEOPLE, TOO! THEY ENJOY GETTING UP LATE, LOUNGING AROUND THE HOUSE, AND SOMETIMES JUST RELAXING BY THE POOL...
SUPER-HEROES ARE PEOPLE, TOO. AND LIKE REAL PEOPLE SOMETIMES EVEN THEY CAN GET--
13 FT.
NERVOUS, RAVEN?
I AM, WALLACE. TODAY IS MY FIRST DAY AT COLLEGE.
I WORRY IF I AM MAKING A FOOL OF MYSELF.
MARV WOLFMAN & GEORGE PÉREZ writer--co-creators--artist
ROMEO TANGHAL: embellisher
JOHN COSTANZA - letterer
ADRIENNE ROY - colorist
LEN WEIN - editor

I HAVE NO REAL *KNOWLEDGE* OF YOUR WORLD. I SPENT ALL MY LIFE HIDDEN AWAY IN THE *TEMPLE AZARATH!*

DON'T SWEAT IT. EARTH IS JUST LIKE YOUR *HOME TOWN*--

-- ONLY WE *SMILE* A HECKUVA LOT MORE!

♫ OH, I FLY THROUGH THE AIR WITH THE GREATEST OF EASE... ♪

...THE *DARING YOUNG MAN* ON THE FLYING *TRAPEZE!* ♫

IMPRESSED, DONNA? A *QUADRUPLE SOMER- SAULT?*

EARTH TO *DONNA!* EARTH TO *DONNA!*

OH, DICK, DID YOU SAY SOME- THING? I WASN'T PAYING *ATTENTION.*

SO I NOTICED. IS IT *ME,* OR DO YOU HAVE *TROUBLES?*

NAH! JUST CONCERNED ABOUT *KORIAND'R,* THAT'S ALL.

HER NEW *BOYFRIEND?*

YEAH. EVER SINCE THEY MET I'VE HARDLY *SEEN* HER.

SHE'S SUCH AN *INNOCENT* IN MANY WAYS, DICK, I *WORRY* ABOUT HER.

I DON'T WANT TO SEE HER *HURT.*

"WELL I'M GLAD SHE FOUND SOME- ONE. I STILL RE- MEMBER *OUR CONFRONTATION.*"

KORY, WE CAN'T KEEP *SEEING* EACH OTHER LIKE THIS. IT'S BAD FOR OUR *TEAMWORK.*

BUT, DICK, I THOUGHT YOU *LIKED* ME.

I *DO,* KORY... REALLY, BUT NOT THE WAY YOU *THINK.*

OH, DICK, I THOUGHT I WASN'T *ALONE* HERE ON THIS PLANET. I THOUGHT I HAD SOMEONE WHO *LOVED* ME.

THAT'S ALL, KORY-- AS A *VERY GOOD FRIEND!*

I *DO...* AS A *FRIEND.*

I KNEW SHE'D FIND SOME- ONE *ELSE*-- JUST DIDN'T EXPECT IT WOULD BE SO *SOON.*

AND NOW THAT SHE HAS, I'M A LITTLE *JEALOUS* OF THE GUY. WHAT'S HIS *NAME*--?

FRANKLIN CRANDALL, SHORT-PANTS... AN' YOU *KNEW* IT.

MEBBE YOU LIKED GOLDIE MORE 'N YOU *LET ON,* EH?

2

ACROSS THE EAST RIVER FROM TITANS' TOWER AND NORTH TO THE EAST EIGHTIES...

A SHADOW CREEPS ACROSS THE NARROW HALLWAY LEADING TO A CERTAIN PENT-HOUSE APARTMENT...

A SHADOW THAT PAUSES EVER-SO-BRIEFLY BEFORE TWO VERY FAMILIAR NAMES...

A SHADOW THAT MOVES SWIFTLY, ENTERING THE APARTMENT WITH AMAZING EASE...

WHILE BACK IN TITANS' TOWER...

YEAH, SHE MET HIM *LAST MONTH,* AFTER WE RETURNED FROM *ZANDIA...*

DONNA, DICK...RAVEN AND I HAVE TO GO.

IT'S YOUR FIRST DAY IN *COLLEGE,* ISN'T IT?

AND I AM LOOKING *FORWARD* TO IT, DONNA.

I HAVE BEEN A *STRANGER* HERE ALL TOO LONG.

WELL, GOOD LUCK, HOPE IT'S WHAT YOU REALLY *WANT.*

SEE YOU *TONIGHT,* OKAY? WE STILL HAVE THAT *DINNER DATE,* DON'T WE?

WE *DO,* DONNA. I WILL *BE* THERE.

WHEW, SHE'S *GONE.* Y'KNOW, SOMETIMES SHE *SPOOKS* ME. SHE PUTS ON THAT COLD ACT SO CONSISTENTLY, IT REALLY *BOTHERS* ME.

WE DO HAVE AN AMAZING *GROUP,* DON'T WE?

RAVEN'S SO INTRO-SPECTIVE, KORIAND'R'S SO *OUTGOING...*AND ME--

-- SOMETIMES I FEEL LIKE I'M THE *MARY TYLER MOORE* OF THE SUPER-HEROINE SET!

ANYWAY, *WHAT* WAS I SAYING--? OH YES, HOW KORY MET *FRANKLIN...*

③

"I WAS TAKING *PHOTOS* FOR CARL AT THE 'SILVER FOX ADVERTISING AGENCY--THEY'RE ONE OF MY FREELANCE CLIENTS..."

"KORY'S BEEN DOING SOME MODELING WORK THERE FOR ME-- SHE'S THE 'GOLDEN GIRL' FOR SERGIO DE LEVI'S JEANS.

SHE'S A *'BEAUT,* I TELL YOU, WE'RE'A GONNA SELL A *BILLION* JEANS WITH 'A MY GOLDEN GIRL!

AN' *YOU,* LADY PICTURE-TAKER-- WHERE YOU *GET* THIS WONDERFUL IDEA--

--PUTTIN' MY GOLDEN LADY IN 'A SPACE *?* IT'S 'A *WONDERFUL!*

OH, I DON'T KNOW, MR. DE LEVI--IT JUST SEEMED *NATURAL,* I GUESS.

"WE WERE SHOOTING MOST OF THE DAY BEFORE I NOTICED HE HAD BEEN WATCHING KORY.

"WATCHING--? HECK! HIS EYES WERE BUGGING OUT LIKE *DAFFY DUCK* IN THOSE OLD CARTOONS!

"ANYWAY, HE STOOD THERE FOR ANOTHER HOUR UNTIL I FINALLY CALLED IT A *WRAP!*

"SERGIO TRIED TO MAKE A *MOVE* ON KORY. SHE BRUSHED HIM ASIDE LIKE A PRO. THE GIRL'S NOT AS NAIVE AS WE THINK.

"FRANKLIN KEPT STARING. I THINK KORY *NOTICED* HIM THEN. SHE SEEMED TO SMILE BACK...

"AND AS CARL AND THE OTHERS PACKED UP TO LEAVE..."

THAT WAS *WONDERFUL,* KORY. WE'LL SEE YOU IN A WEEK FOR ANOTHER *SHOOT,* OKAY?

I GUESS SO, CARL. AND *THANK YOU!* THIS WAS *FUN!*

SHE THANKS *ME--?* GORGEOUS AND *HUMBLE,* TOO. WOW!

EXCUSE ME--?

"HE MOVED CLOSER TO KORY, FOR SOME REASON MY NECK HAIRS BRISTLED." 4

MISS, I HAD TO TELL YOU-- YOU'RE JUST *BEAUTIFUL*.

I FEEL *SILLY*, BUT I CAME IN HERE BY *ACCIDENT*. AND WHEN I SAW YOU POSING THERE, I COULDN'T *LEAVE*.

I FEEL I HAVE TO *TALK* TO YOU, MISS--

KORY ANDERS. I THINK *YOU'RE* RATHER HANDSOME, TOO.

C'MON, PLEASE DON'T *EMBARRASS* ME, GOSH, PLEASE, I'D REALLY LIKE TO TAKE YOU *OUT*. COFFEE? LUNCH? DINNER? YOU *NAME* IT?

JUST PLEASE DON'T SAY *NO!*

KORY, DID YOU REMEMBER, WE HAVE A *LUNCH*--

OH, DONNA, I'D LIKE YOU TO *MEET* THIS NICE MAN-- OH, I DON'T KNOW YOUR *NAME*...

FRANKLIN CRANDALL. PLEASED TO *MEET* YOU, MISS--?

TROY! DONNA TROY.

DONNA, HE ASKED ME *OUT*...

IS THAT *IMPORTANT*? HE SEEMS LIKE SUCH A *NICE* MAN.

KORY, YOU DON'T EVEN *KNOW* HIM.

GEE, KORY, I DON'T *KNOW*... DONNA, EVER SINCE I *CAME* TO YOUR WORLD I'VE SPENT *ALL* MY TIME WITH YOU AND THE OTHERS...

I HAVEN'T *MET* ANYONE, AND NOW--

OH, GAWD! I'M TALKING LIKE I'M YOUR *MOTHER* AND THIS IS YOUR *FIRST DATE*...

"OF COURSE, *GO OUT*, HAVE FUN. JUST PLEASE, KORY-- DON'T TELL HIM WHERE YOU'RE FROM.

"SOME PEOPLE... WELL, THEY *WOULDN'T UNDERSTAND*."

ONLY I DON'T THINK *KORIAND'R HEARD* WHAT I WAS SAYING.

AND THEY'VE BEEN *SEEING* EACH OTHER EVERY DAY FOR A *MONTH* NOW.

I DON'T THINK I'VE EVER SEEN KORIAND'R SO *HAPPY.*

SO WHAT'S THE *WORRY?* EVERYTHING'S *NIFTY!*

HEY! I'M *FAMISHED.* WANNA GRAB A HAMBURGER OR SOMETHING?

SURE. JUST LET ME STOP OFF AT MY *APARTMENT* FIRST.

YOU WANNA COME *WITH* US, VIC?

NAH! I GOT SOME *HEAVY READIN!*

Y'KNOW, LIKE HOW TA FIX YOUR *RUN-OF-THE-MILL CYBORG BODY* WHEN IT BREAKS DOWN.

'SOKAY, PAL. SEE YOU *LATER.*

SO EVERYTHING'S *NIFTY,* IS IT, SHORT-PANTS?

NOT FOR *THIS* SECOND-RATE ERECTOR SET, IT AIN'T.

KORY'S GOT HERSELF A NEW *GUY.* DICK 'N' LOGAN'S GOT A DOZEN GALS *EACH.*

WALLY'S GOT THE *WITCH,* AN' DONNA AN' THAT *TERRY LONG* DUDE ARE TIGHTER'N BROOKE SHIELDS' JEANS!

BUT ME, I GOT *ZILCH!*

CAN'T EVEN BRING MYSELF TA CALL *SARAH SIMMS* AN' TELL HER I'M BACK IN *TOWN*...NOT AFTER I JUST FLEW OFF WITHOUT LETTIN' HER KNOW.

BLAST! MEBBE *VIC STONE* WAS A BIG COLLEGE HERO, BUT *CYBORG'S* NOTHIN' MORE'N A CHROME-PLATED *CHICKEN!*

A SHADOW GLIDES THROUGH THE LIVING ROOM TOWARD THE BEDROOM BEYOND.

IT IS LOOKING FOR SOMETHING...

NO, NOTHING HERE.

BUT THEN...

DARK ROOM

DARK ROOM

DO NOT ENTER WHEN RED LIGHT IS ON!

...IT KNOWS!

6

THE RED GLOW OF DONNA TROY'S DARK-ROOM GIVES WAY TO THE GOLDEN GLOW OF A MID-AFTER-NOON SUN THAT CLEARLY EXISTS FOR ONLY THESE TWO...

NO, NOT *REALLY.* WHERE I'M FROM, I DIDN'T MEET MANY MEN.

YOU'RE *SPECIAL,* KORY...VERY *SPECIAL.* I DOUBT IF THERE'S ANOTHER ON EARTH *LIKE YOU.*

AND MAYBE THE GUYS WHERE YOU'RE FROM ARE *BLIND*--BUT I'M NOT. I'M NOT LETTING YOU GET *AWAY* FROM ME. I *LOVE* YOU.

OH, FRANK, I--

X'HAL!

I...I REALLY THINK I *CARE* FOR YOU, FRANKLIN.

I DON'T THINK I'VE EVER *FELT* THIS WAY BEFORE.

OH, COME ON, KORY, ANYONE WHO LOOKS LIKE YOU MUST HAVE A *HUNDRED* GUYS DROOLING AFTER YOU.

FRANKLIN-- GET BACK! THAT CAR IS *OUT* OF CONTROL!

SKEEEEEEE

SKRAK

BTRAKK!

HELP ME! HELP ME!! MY BRAKES WON'T HOLD!

I--I CAN'T STOP!

SPAM

SKREEEEEE

WHAK

OH, LORD, SHE'S GOING TO *CRASH!*

MAYBE *NOT,* FRANK.

I THINK I CAN DO THIS WITHOUT REVEALING WHO I AM.

THAT DOESN'T *MATTER* TO ME, BUT IT SEEMS SO IMPORTANT TO *DONNA!*

EVERYONE'S EYES RIVETED ON THE RUNAWAY CAR, NO ONE SEES STARFIRE UNLEASH A CRACKLING, BLAZING STARBOLT...

...WHOSE HEAT INSTANTLY MELTS BOTH RUBBER TIRE AND STREET TARMAC...

...FUSING BOTH TOGETHER...

...AND BRINGING THE RUNAWAY CAR TO A SLOW, STICKY HALT.

INCREDIBLE! THAT WAS FANTASTIC! DID YOU *SEE* THAT, KORY?

THAT WOMAN MUST HAVE A *GUARDIAN ANGEL!*

I GUESS SHE *DOES* AT THAT, FRANKLIN.

DOWNTOWN NEW YORK, ON THE CAMPUS OF MANHATTAN COLLEGE...

WELL, THIS IS IT, RAVEN.

I KNOW, WALLACE, AND I HAVE TO KEEP TELLING MYSELF THIS IS THE RIGHT THING TO *DO.*

ALL I KNOW ABOUT THE OUTSIDE WORLD IS FROM READING *BOOKS.*

BUT I MUST MINGLE WITH *REAL PEOPLE,* MUSTN'T I?

JUST EASE UP, KID, AND YOU'LL BE *FINE.*

SEE YOU AFTER CLASS. I'LL BE HERE *WAITING!*

SHE'S GOING, AND SHE DOESN'T REALIZE HOW ALL THIS CUTS ME UP.

BEING WITH HER, *LOVING* HER, AND KNOWING SHE WON'T COMMIT HERSELF TO ME UNTIL SHE UNDERSTANDS HERSELF.

WHY DOES IT HURT *LOSING* SOMEONE YOU NEVER REALLY EVER *HAD* IN THE FIRST PLACE?

8

AND NOW, LET US RETURN TO THAT EAST EIGHTIES PENTHOUSE, WHERE...

MY OWN APARTMENT GETS RIPPED OFF-- MY OWN APARTMENT!

I WANNA SCREAM!

THE LOCK WAS JIMMIED--NOT AT ALL A PROFESSIONAL JOB.

WHAT IN--? I-- I DON'T BELIEVE IT!

WHAT HAPPENS WHILE I'M OUT THERE, SWEATING, STOPPING CRIME ALL OVER NEW YORK?

I THINK I HAVE SOMETHING THAT CAN HELP US.

OH? A RADAR DETECTOR FOR BAD GUYS?

NOPE! DUSTING POWDER FOR FINGERPRINTS. MAYBE I WAS NEVER A BOY SCOUT, BUT NEVER LET IT BE SAID THAT I'M NOT ALWAYS PREPARED!

AN HOUR PASSES, AND AFTER A COMPLETE SEARCH OF THE PREMISES...

OKAY, THIS TAKES THE CAKE-- ONLY THING STOLEN IS ONE OF MY PHOTO SESSION CONTACT SHEETS.

WHO IN THEIR RIGHT MIND WOULD--

WE'LL FIND OUT AFTER THE POLICE COMPUTER RUNS A CHECK ON THESE PRINTS I LIFTED. C'MON, LET'S HURRY!

WITH LUCK WE'LL HAVE OUR WOULD-BE THIEF NAILED WITHIN THE HOUR.

I DON'T WANT TODAY TO END, FRANKLIN, IT'S BEEN HEAVEN!

I DON'T WANT ANY DAYS TO END, KORY, EVERY TIME I LEAVE YOU I GO CRAZY...

I'M JEALOUS THAT YOU'LL FIND SOMEONE ELSE.

FURIOUS AT SPENDING MY TIME ALONE!

KORY, CAN WE GO UP TO YOUR PLACE? I WANT TO ASK YOU SOMETHING...

OF COURSE... OF COURSE!

9

AND... DONNA?

STRANGE. SHE'S NOT *HERE* AND SHE SAID SHE *WOULD* BE.

AND THAT *MESS* ALL AROUND.

I'D BETTER *CHECK.*

TERRY? TERRY *LONG?* THIS IS, UHH... KORY ANDERS. IS *DONNA* THERE?

KORY? HEY, I WISH SHE WERE, CUTIE. I'M GOING STARK, RAVING *BONKERS* MARKING THESE TEST PAPERS.

SAY, WHEN YOU *SEE* HER, GIVE HER A BIG *KISS* FOR ME. HMMM, ON THE OTHER HAND, *I'LL* DO IT MYSELF AND GIVE 'ER *TWO* KISSES.

NOT THERE. HMMM. ODD, SHE'S ALWAYS SO WORRIED ABOUT *ME*... LEAVES A NOTE WHENEVER SHE GOES OUT. SHE TELLS ME *EVERYTHING.*

DO YOU *RECIPROCATE?* DOES SHE KNOW YOU'RE *STARFIRE?*

HUNH? YOU *KNOW?*

OHH, DONNA WILL BE *FURIOUS* WITH ME. HOW DID YOU *FIND OUT?* DID I MAKE A *MISTAKE?*

OH, I'VE KNOWN FOR *DAYS,* HONEY... YOU KNOW I FIRST CHALKED UP YOUR *COMPLEXION* TO BEING A MEDITERRANEAN *TAN*--

--BUT THEN THE OTHER DAY WHEN YOU WERE LEANING OVER--I SAW YOUR *EYES.*

BUT YOU DIDN'T *SAY* ANYTHING?

I FIGURED YOU DIDN'T *WANT* ME TO KNOW SO I DIDN'T *LET ON.* BUT I HAVE TO *NOW*...BECAUSE OF WHAT I WANT TO *ASK* YOU...

YOU MEAN YOU *STILL* LIKE ME EVEN KNOWING WHO I *AM?*

LIKE YOU? KORY ANDERS-- I *LOVE* YOU!

10

MANHATTAN COLLEGE...

MISS RAVEN-- UHH, IS THAT YOUR FIRST OR LAST NAME?

MY ONLY NAME, PROFESSOR HOLLIS.

YOU ARRIVED A BIT LATE. WE HAD BEEN DISCUSSING WHY YOU STUDENTS ENROLLED IN 'COMPARATIVE ANCIENT PHILOSOPHIES'.

WOULD YOU CARE TO ENLIGHTEN US AS TO YOUR REASONS?

PROFESSOR, FROM THE MOMENT WE ARE BORN WE ARE INUNDATED WITH PROPAGANDA.

MUCH OF IT BENEFICIAL, SUCH AS 'DO UNTO OTHERS'... GENERAL RULES TO LIVE BY.

WE LEARN COMMUNICATION THROUGH MUTUAL ACCEPTANCE OF THESE RULES. WE BUILD SOCIETIES BASED ON THIS MUTUAL ACCEPTANCE.

BUT SOME OF THOSE ANCIENT PHILOSOPHIES --THEIR PROPAGANDA HAS NOT ALWAYS BEEN FOR THE COMMON GOOD.

--OTHERS COMPASSIONLESS PACIFISM SUCH AS THE CULT OF AZAR.

MANY PHILOSOPHIES PREACHED INTOLERANCE. SOME JUSTIFY WANTON VIOLENCE--

BUT THESE EXTREMIST CULTS, THESE PHILOSOPHIES, ALL EXIST TO DESTROY A COMMON BOND OF GROWTH BY LIMITING PERSONAL FREEDOM AND PRODUCTIVE GOALS THAT--

OHH, I PRATTLE ON. I AM SORRY.

I HADN'T MEANT TO EMBARRASS MYSELF WITH.. NO, I STILL TALK TOO MUCH. I--

I AM SO SORRY... SO SORRY...

MISS RAVEN, SOMETHING TELLS ME THIS YEAR'S CLASS IS GOING TO BE ANYTHING BUT ORDINARY.

SIGHHH...

WOW! YOU WERE INCREDIBLE! YOU MENTIONED AZAR-- I THOUGHT NO ONE KNEW ABOUT THEM EXCEPT ME. I STUDED THEIR WAYS... EVEN PRACTICED--

EXCUSE ME. THE PROFESSOR HAS ASKED FOR YOUR ATTENTION.

OH.

AN HOUR PASSES BEFORE WE RETURN TO DONNA TROY'S PENTHOUSE...

DO YOU REALLY HAVE TO GO NOW, FRANKLIN?

PLEASE SAY YOU CAN STAY.

I WANT TO, HONEY. BUT I CAN'T. I'LL SEE YOU TONIGHT, THOUGH.

I CAN'T WAIT TO TELL THE OTHERS.

NO, PLEASE DON'T. NOT UNTIL I CAN BE WITH YOU.

I WANT TO SEE THEIR EXPRESSIONS.

OKAY. I PROMISE. BUT HURRY BACK.

GOSH.

DONNA, I NO LONGER ENVY YOU.

I'M IN LOVE!

LOVE!!

AND SUDDENLY, ANY PROBLEMS THAT MIGHT HAVE BEEN ARE GONE...

12

...BUT HARDLY FORGOTTEN...

FRANKLIN CRANDALL SAUNTERS AWAY FROM A SMALL, PRIVATE PARKING SPACE IN GREENWICH, CONNECTICUT...

HE WHISTLES MERRILY, PLEASE AT THE DAY GONE BY...

CRANDALL, YOU WERE GONE *LONGER* THAN YOU WERE SUPPOSED TO.

WHAT DO *YOU* CARE? STARFIRE'S *IN LOVE* WITH ME. ISN'T THAT WHAT *THE H.I.V.E.* WANTED?

THAT IS WHY *I* HAVE PAID YOU, CRANDALL.

HAVE YOU THE *INFORMATION* I WANT?

COME ON. I JUST TOLD HER I KNEW WHO SHE WAS. IT'LL TAKE *TIME* BEFORE I CAN ASK HER *THOSE* KINDS OF QUESTIONS.

I DO NOT *HAVE* THAT SORT OF *TIME*, CRANDALL.

I WAS BROUGHT INTO *THE H.I.V.E.* TO REPLACE THE MEMBER KILLED BY *THE TERMINATOR.**

*NTT #10. --LE

I WISH TO *DEMONSTRATE* TO THE OTHERS THAT THEY HAVE MADE A *WISE DECISION.*

LOOK, I REALLY DON'T LIKE DOING THIS TO KORY.

SHE'S A *GOOD KID* AND I FEEL LIKE *FILTH,* PLAYING HER THIS WAY.

YOU *ARE* FILTH, CRANDALL. YOU'VE MADE *HUNDREDS* OF WOMEN FALL IN LOVE WITH YOU-- ONLY TO TURN AGAINST THEM WITH *BLACK-MAIL.*

HEY, THOSE WERE ALL *RICH BROADS* CHEATING ON THEIR HUSBANDS.

KORY'S *DIFFERENT.* SHE'S INCREDIBLY SWEET, AND I ACTUALLY *LIKE* HER.

WHAT IF I PAY YOU BACK EVERYTHING YOU GAVE ME... CALL THIS *OFF*--

SWAK!

NO! YOU WILL NOT BACK AWAY AND MAKE ME LOOK LIKE A *FOOL.*

YOU WILL DO WHAT I *WANT,* OR I SWEAR THIS STARFIRE WILL BE THE *LAST* FEMALE YOU EVER LOVE.

DO YOU *UNDERSTAND* ME, CRANDALL?

AFRAID FOR THE FIRST TIME IN HIS LIFE, FRANKLIN CRANDALL NODS.

13

MEANWHILE, AS CLASS LETS OUT AT MANHATTAN COLLEGE...

HEY, RAVEN-- BEAUTIFUL. C'MON OVER HERE.

WHAT'S *WRONG* WITH YOU, GIRL? STUCK UP? I *CALLED* YOU.

PLEASE, I DO NOT WISH TO *TALK* NOW.

C'MON, *'COURSE* YOU DO. I HEARD YOU IN *CLASS*, THOUGHT YOU AND I COULD--

PLEASE, YOU'RE HURTING MY *ARM.* WON'T YOU *LET GO?*

NO, I CAN SEE YOU *WON'T.*

YOU GIVE ME *NO CHOICE* THEN.

HUH?

WH-WHAT DID YOU *DO* TO HIM? HE'S NOT *MOVING!*

I SIMPLY *CALMED* HIS INNER VIOLENCE. HE WILL BE *ALL RIGHT.*

HOLD IT, RUDY!

YOU LET RAVEN *ALONE,* YOU HEAR ME?

SWOK!

YOU *ALL RIGHT?* DID THEY *HURT* YOU?

YOU SAID YOU STUDIED THE WAYS OF *AZAR,* THAT YOU *BELIEVED* IN THEM.

IN *THIS* THE WAY YOU *SHOW* YOUR PACIFISM? BY *FIGHTING* FOR ME LIKE SOME COMMON *BRAWLER?*

YOU ARE JUST LIKE *THEY* ARE-- BATTLING FOR A PRIZE THAT DOES NOT *WANT* YOU.

STAY *AWAY* FROM ME. ALL OF YOU, STAY *FAR AWAY!*

14

THANK HEAVEN FOR THE COMPUTER. I'VE FIT ALL THE PIECES TOGETHER.

I KNOW WHO RIFLED THROUGH YOUR APARTMENT, DONNA.

VICTOR, BE SERIOUS. WHO WAS IT, DICK?

FIRST, LET'S GO OVER WHAT WE KNOW: THE ONLY THING STOLEN WAS CONTACT PROOFS ON ANGELA DOVE, A MODEL.

WE WENT TO ANGELA'S PLACE, AND SHE WAS GONE.

THERE WERE SIGNS OF A BREAK-IN AND A STRUGGLE. SHE WAS PROBABLY TAKEN.

NOW, ACCORDING TO THESE PICTURES, ANGELA WAS THE GIRLFRIEND OF ONE JASON SILVER, A SMALL-TIME NUMBERS RUNNER IN HARLEM.

SILVER WORKED FOR-- AND IS TESTIFYING NEXT WEEK IN COURT AGAINST-- MOB BOSS BIG PHIL CERULLO.

NOW SILVER'S ALSO DISAPPEARED. MY BET IS CERULLO TRIED TO GET TO SILVER THROUGH ANGELA--

PERSONALLY, BAT-BOY, I THINK IT WAS LOGAN-- SEARCHIN' FER SOME CHEESECAKE PICS OF STARFIRE!

--AND HE GOT ANGELA'S ADDRESS THROUGH YOU, KNOWING SHE WAS MODELLING FOR--

GUYS, GUYS, I'M SO GLAD YOU'RE ALL HERE!

I FEEL SO GOOD, AND I HAVE A SURPRISE.

LOGAN'S BACK FROM HIS VACATION WITH DAYTON AN' STEELE AN' HE'S GONNA RUIN OUR DAY, RIGHT?

OH, NO... A REAL SURPRISE, VICTOR, BUT I CAN'T TELL YOU YET. YOU'LL FIND OUT WHEN I TAKE YOU TO FRANKLIN'S APARTMENT TONIGHT.

DONNA, HE'S THE MOST UNDERSTANDING, GLORIOUS GUY IN THE WORLD. I MEAN, HE FOUND OUT WHO I AM AND HE STILL LOVES ME.

OBOY! KORY, YOU AND I HAD BETTER TALK.

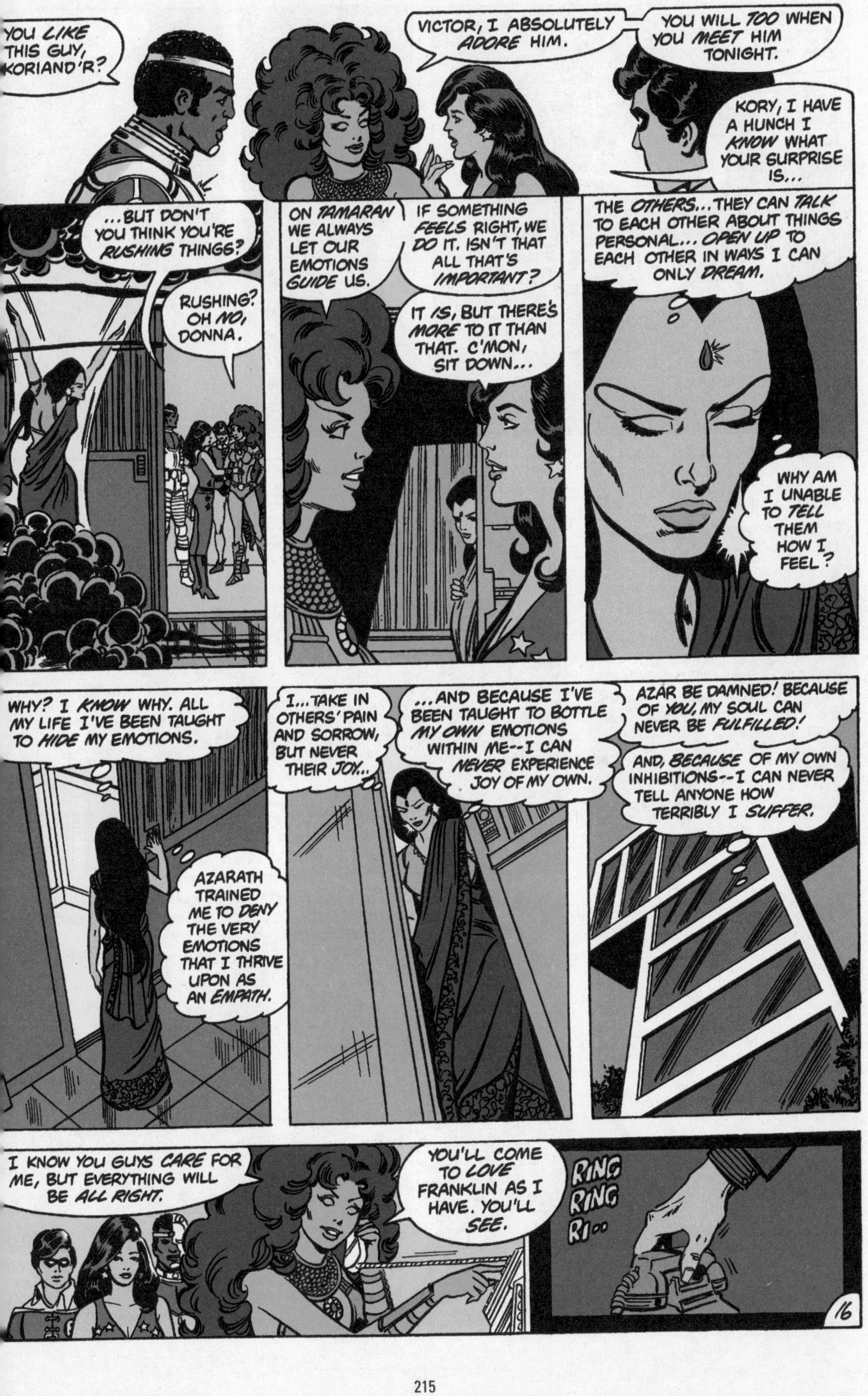
YOU LIKE THIS GUY, KORIAND'R?
VICTOR, I ABSOLUTELY ADORE HIM.
YOU WILL TOO WHEN YOU MEET HIM TONIGHT.
KORY, I HAVE A HUNCH I KNOW WHAT YOUR SURPRISE IS...
...BUT DON'T YOU THINK YOU'RE RUSHING THINGS?
RUSHING? OH NO, DONNA.
ON TAMARAN WE ALWAYS LET OUR EMOTIONS GUIDE US.
IF SOMETHING FEELS RIGHT, WE DO IT. ISN'T THAT ALL THAT'S IMPORTANT?
IT IS, BUT THERE'S MORE TO IT THAN THAT. C'MON, SIT DOWN...
THE OTHERS... THEY CAN TALK TO EACH OTHER ABOUT THINGS PERSONAL... OPEN UP TO EACH OTHER IN WAYS I CAN ONLY DREAM.
WHY AM I UNABLE TO TELL THEM HOW I FEEL?
WHY? I KNOW WHY. ALL MY LIFE I'VE BEEN TAUGHT TO HIDE MY EMOTIONS.
AZARATH TRAINED ME TO DENY THE VERY EMOTIONS THAT I THRIVE UPON AS AN EMPATH.
I...TAKE IN OTHERS' PAIN AND SORROW, BUT NEVER THEIR JOY...
...AND BECAUSE I'VE BEEN TAUGHT TO BOTTLE MY OWN EMOTIONS WITHIN ME--I CAN NEVER EXPERIENCE JOY OF MY OWN.
AZAR BE DAMNED! BECAUSE OF YOU, MY SOUL CAN NEVER BE FULFILLED!
AND, BECAUSE OF MY OWN INHIBITIONS--I CAN NEVER TELL ANYONE HOW TERRIBLY I SUFFER.
I KNOW YOU GUYS CARE FOR ME, BUT EVERYTHING WILL BE ALL RIGHT.
YOU'LL COME TO LOVE FRANKLIN AS I HAVE. YOU'LL SEE.
RING
RING
RI
16

OH, FRANKLIN, I'M GLAD I *CAUGHT* YOU. WHEN CAN WE COME *OVER?*

HOW'S *EIGHT O'CLOCK* SOUND, HONEY?

FINE, JUST FINE. I *LOVE* YOU.

I LOVE YOU, *TOO,* KORY.

I LOVE YOU, TOO.

IT'S STILL *EARLY*-- PLENTY OF TIME TO FIND YOUR *MODEL FRIEND,* DONNA.

IF I'M *RIGHT,* SHE SHOULD BE IN CERULLO'S HARLEM *DROP PLACE*... AN ADDRESS THE COMPUTER HAD ON *FILE,* FORTUNATELY.

NO, GIRL, YOU JUST TAKE IT *EASY,* EH? WE'RE NOT GONNA *HURT* YA NONE.

SURE WOULDN'T WANNA SCAR UP THOSE BEAUTIFUL *FEATURES* ANY...

...'CAUSE I GOT *PLANS* FER YA, YER GONNA MAKE ME A *BUNDLE*--

--YER GONNA BE ONE FINE PONY IN *MY* STABLE...

...PROVIDIN' YER BIG-MOUTH BOYFRIEND, *SILVER, COOPERATES* WITH ME WHEN TALKIN' TA THE *FEDS.*

YOU UNNERSTAND WHERE I'M *COMIN'* FROM, DON'T YA, BABE?

ANGELA DOVE, ORIGINALLY LUWANDA BROWN, NODS, SHE WILL AGREE WITH ANYTHING NOW... JUST SO LONG AS SHE ISN'T *HURT*...

17

A PROBLEM THAT WON'T BE MUCH OF A PROBLEM IN LESS THAN FIVE SECONDS...

PARTY'S OVER, CREEPS!

SKRASH!

AND THE NEXT TIME YOU SADISTS GET THE DESIRE TO *TORTURE* HELPLESS GIRLS--

--REMEMBER NOT ALL OF US ARE HELPLESS!

SWAK

C'MON, BOYS, LET'S SEE WHAT YA DO WHEN *YOU'RE* THE ONES WHO ARE *OUTNUMBERED!*

LET'S SEE WHAT KINDA *BIG SHOTS* YOU ARE WHEN SOMEONE *ELSE* HOLDS THE UPPER HAND!

CYBORG'S WHITE-SOUND BLASTER RIPS THROUGH THE CLOSEST OF ANGELA'S ABDUCTORS...

...WHILE ROBIN, THE ACROBATIC TEEN WONDER, EASILY MOPS UP THE REST...

WE USUALLY FIND OURSELVES FIGHTING *COSTUMED* CREEPS--

-- JERKS OUT TO *CONQUER THE WORLD* AND SUCH...

...BUT Y'KNOW SOMETHING, STOPPING SLUGS LIKE YOU IS MUCH MORE *SATISFYING!*

BECAUSE WHAT *YOU* PUNKS DO MAKES ME PERSONALLY VERY *MAD!*

NOT A BAD *SPEECH*, KID. MEBBE I'LL HAVE IT CARVED ON YOUR *GRAVESTONE!*

HUH?

ANGELA--?

18

YA MADE CREAM CHEESE OF MY *MOB*, BUT NOW YER JUST GONNA SPIN AROUND AN' *LEAVE*...

WHAT'S *MORE*, YA AIN'T GONNA *SAY* A *WORD* 'BOUT THIS, RIGHT?

'CAUSE IF YA *DO*... WELL, MISS *DOVE* HERE'S GONNA MAKE HER *LAST FLIGHT*, IF YA UNNERSTAN' WHERE I'M COMIN' FROM.

NO WE DON'T, *KILLER!*

ARRGH!

SKREEEE

OH, NO...

STARFIRE, DID YOU--?

YOU *SKRAG* 'IM, GOLDIE?

KILL HIM? OH, NO. I *WANTED* TO, BUT YOU KEEP TELLING ME TO *CONTROL* MY STARBOLTS.

I JUST *STUNNED* HIM.

HE *HURT* ME. H-HE WAS GOING TO *KILL* ME.

YOU'LL BE ALL *RIGHT* NOW. JUST TAKE IT *EASY.*

HOW *IS* HE?

BREATHING, BUT JUST *BARELY.* STARFIRE, YOU USED TOO MUCH *POWER.*

WELL, HE CERTAINLY *DESERVED* IT, WONDER GIRL. HE WASN'T EXACTLY A *GOOD* MAN.

OBOY, WE REALLY HAVE TO *TALK* ABOUT HOW YOU USE YOUR POWERS...AND TALK *SOON.*

19

MEANWHILE...

I'M CALLING OFF OUR DEAL.

AND YOU CAME HERE TO KILL ME?

I DID. BUT I'VE NEVER KILLED BEFORE...

... AND I'M NOT STARTING NOW, SO HERE--TAKE MY GUN--

--IT DOESN'T HAVE ANY BULLETS IN IT ANYHOW.

I'M SEEING THE TITANS TONIGHT AND I'M TELLING THEM EVERYTHING.

YOU WOULDN'T DARE, CRANDALL. YOU KNOW WHAT THE H.I.V.E. DOES TO TRAITORS.

HEY, STOW IT, WILL YOU?

I'M NO FOOL. I CHECKED AROUND.

YOU'RE WORKING ALONE ON THIS TO SCORE BROWNIE POINTS WITH THE OTHERS.

I... JUST HOPE KORY CAN FORGIVE ME. I REALLY DO LIKE HER.

THEY PROBABLY DON'T EVEN KNOW YOU'RE DOING THIS.

SO, GOODBYE, MISTER--AND GOOD RIDDANCE.

INDEED, MR. CRANDALL...

GOODBYE...

...AND GOOD RIDDANCE!

BAM!

20

219

I CAN'T *WAIT*. YOU'RE ALL GOING TO BE SO *SURPRISED.*

THAT DIDN'T TAKE *LONG*. WE'LL GET TO YOUR FRIEND'S PLACE *EARLY.*

WILL WE, KORIAND'R? I CERTAINLY *HOPE* SO.

BUT THEN, WHY AM I *WORRYING* SO MUCH?

THIS IS IT... HE'S WAITING *INSIDE.*

FRANK? FRANK--

OH, X'HAL! X'HAL!

FRANKLIN!

Y-YOU'RE *BLEEDING!* YOU'VE BEEN *HURT!* WHAT HAPPENED, FRANKLIN? WHO *DID* THIS TO YOU?

TELL ME WHO *DID* THIS?

K-KORY... *H.I.V.E.*... WANTED... YOU... 276 ARCHER-- TWO... TWO BLOCKS...

;COUGH; WANTED YOU...WAN-- OH, KORY--

I-I... LOVE... YOU...

OH, X'HAL-- D-DON'T TALK, FRANKLIN. DON'T *TALK*. WE'LL GET *HELP.*

DICK! DONNA! YOU'VE GOT TO *HELP* HIM.

I...LOVE... YOU...

AND I LOVE *YOU*, FRANKLIN... BUT PLEASE... PLEASE DON'T *TALK.*

YOU'LL BE *ALL RIGHT.* YOU WILL BE, I *KNOW* YOU WILL.

21

DICK, HE'S OKAY, ISN'T HE? HE'LL BE ALL RIGHT--?

YOU CAN *HELP* HIM, CAN'T YOU?

HE WON'T *DIE*, HE WON'T. I *KNOW* HE WON'T.

I'LL CALL GREENWICH HOSPITAL, TELL THEM WE'RE BRINGING HIM *IN*.

WONDER GIRL... DON'T *BOTHER*--

--IT'S *TOO LATE*.

NO! YOU'RE *WRONG*. CHECK HIM AGAIN AND YOU'LL SEE YOU MADE A DREAD-FUL *MISTAKE*.

HE'LL PULL THROUGH. I *KNOW* HE WILL.

KORY, HE'S *GONE*, THERE'S NO *CHANGING* THAT.

BUT YOU, I'M *WORRIED* ABOUT YOU. PLEASE, LISTEN--

NO!

I'VE *HAD IT* WITH LISTENING TO YOU, DICK!

SWAK!

ALWAYS TELLING ME WHAT TO *DO*... TELLING ME TO HOLD IN MY *POWER!*

WHERE DID IT *GET ME*, DICK?

THAT FILTHY *KILLER*--THE ONE WHO KILLED FRANKLIN--

--HE'LL SEE HOW *TERRIBLE* MY POWER IS, DICK. HE'LL SEE.

HE'S A *DEAD MAN!*

WE GOTTA *STOP HER!* SHE'LL *KILL* HIM!

NO, VICTOR, YOU TAKE CARE OF *DICK*.

I'M *AFRAID* THIS IS SOMETHING I'D BEST DO *MYSELF*.

SHE IS AN ANGRY, FIERY COMET BLAZING THROUGH THE CONNECTICUT SKIES...

22

NEVER HAS SHE FELT THIS WAY BEFORE; NOT WHEN RUTHLESSLY KIDNAPPED AS A FRIGHTENED TWELVE-YEAR-OLD...

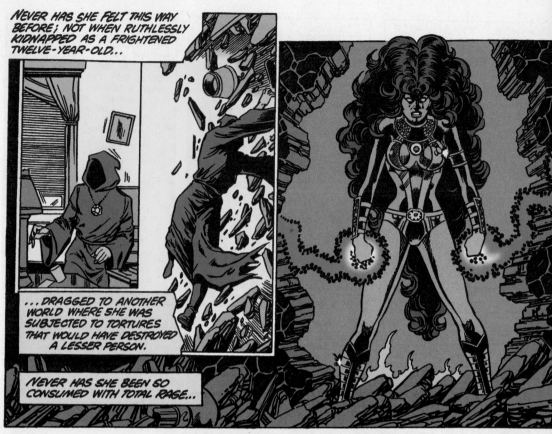

...DRAGGED TO ANOTHER WORLD WHERE SHE WAS SUBJECTED TO TORTURES THAT WOULD HAVE DESTROYED A LESSER PERSON.

NEVER HAS SHE BEEN SO CONSUMED WITH TOTAL RAGE...

NEVER HAS ONLY ONE DESIRE BURNED SO BRIGHTLY IN HER FURIOUS HEART:

PRINCESS KORIAND'R OF TAMARAN WANTS ONLY TO KILL!

STOP IT, GIRL. THAT WAS BUSINESS, THAT'S ALL.

I WANTED TO SHOW THE OTHERS THEY HAD CHOSEN WELL IN ME--

--THERE WAS NOTHING PERSONAL--

LORD!

SHE'LL KILL ME, UNLESS--

SKREEEEEE

SPAKK!

SHE STARES AT HER FALLEN FOE AND THERE IS NO PITY IN HER COLD HEART.

ALL SHE SEES IS THE MURDERER OF THE MAN SHE HAD LOVED.

ALL SHE SEES IS A MAN WHO IS GOING TO DIE!

23

SHE STEPS CLOSER...

THERE IS NO JOY IN HER WIDE OPEN EYES.

NO JOY, ONLY CASCADING TEARS OF SORROW.

STARFIRE-- STOP! DON'T DO IT!

X'HAL!

WHAT ARE YOU *DOING?* DO YOU KNOW WHAT THIS MADMAN *DID?*

I *DO.* AND I STILL CAN'T LET YOU *KILL HIM!*

YOU CAN'T *STOP ME!*

KRAK!

HE'S *MINE!* HE'S GOING TO *DIE!*

THEN YOU'LL HAVE TO KILL *ME* FIRST.

WE HAVE *LAWS* HERE, STARFIRE. IF YOU *STAY* ON THIS PLANET YOU'LL HAVE TO *OBEY* THEM.

BECAUSE IF YOU *DON'T,* NO MATTER HOW MUCH WE *LOVE* YOU AS A *FRIEND*--

--WE'LL BE FORCED TO *HUNT YOU DOWN.* WHAT IS IT GOING TO *BE?*

24

IT'S NOT FAIR!

IT'S NOT AT ALL FAIR!

I'M SORRY. I REALLY AM!

BUT IT HAD TO BE THIS WAY.

NO MATTER HOW THINGS ARE DONE ON YOUR WORLD, IT HAD TO BE THIS WAY!

EH? THE H.I.V.E. KILLER-- HE'S GONE!

HE GOT AWAY WHILE STARFIRE AND I WERE ARSUINS.

BUT I'LL FIND HIM FOR YOU, KORY... I SWEAR I'LL FIND HIM.

AND HE'LL PAY... BUT ACCORDING TO OUR LAWS...

THE WAY THINGS HAVE TO BE...

...WHETHER WE LIKE IT OR NOT.

NIGHT...

SO DARK AND CHILLING...

NOT AT ALL A NIGHT FOR COMFORTING A SUNDERED HEART... 25

...OR A GUILTY SOUL.

NUMBER SEVEN, YOU *DISOBEYED* THE RULES OF *THE H.I.V.E.*

BEHIND OUR BACKS, YOU WORKED AS AN *INDIVIDUAL!*

TO ACHIEVE OUR GOALS *THE H.I.V.E.* ALWAYS WORKS AS *ONE.* NO ONE MEMBER *DOMINATES* THE OTHERS. NO ONE EVER WORKS *ALONE.*

BUT I DID IT TO *PROVE* MYSELF TO YOU.

AND IT *WORKED.* I GOT INFORMATION ABOUT THE *TITANS...*

THEN YOU WILL *TAKE* THAT INFORMATION TO YOUR *GRAVE.*

YOU STAND NOW BEFORE US FOR *JUDGMENT.*

AND OUR *JUDGMENT* IS--

IT IS A LONG, *BLOODCURDLING* SCREAM THAT ALL-TOO-SLOWLY DIES UPON THE COLD NIGHT WINDS...

MORNING FINALLY COMES...

THEY FOUND HIS *BODY,* DICK. SIX *BULLETS--* ALL IN THE *HEART.*

HE *PAID...* AND IT WASN'T *KORY* WHO MADE HIM PAY. SHE DIDN'T *KILL* HIM--EVEN THOUGH, IN HER *HEART,* THAT'S ALL SHE *WANTED.*

I THINK SHE'S *GROWN* SOMEWHAT, DICK.

DO YOU THINK SHE KNOWS THE *TRUTH* ABOUT FRANKLIN?

NO. I THINK SHE THINKS HE WAS JUST CAUGHT BETWEEN HER AND *THE H.I.V.E.* SHE THINKS HE WAS AN INNOCENT *PAWN...*

AND, AS FAR AS *I'M* CONCERNED, SHE DOESN'T *EVER* HAVE TO KNOW ANY *DIFFERENTLY!*

HE DIED *LOVING* HER, AND AS KORY HERSELF SAID-- ISN'T THAT ALL THAT'S *IMPORTANT?*

DAILY N
GANGLA SLAYIN

DR. WILLIS DARROW SH TO DEATH FORMER CRIMINAL SCIENTIST FOUND SLAIN

26

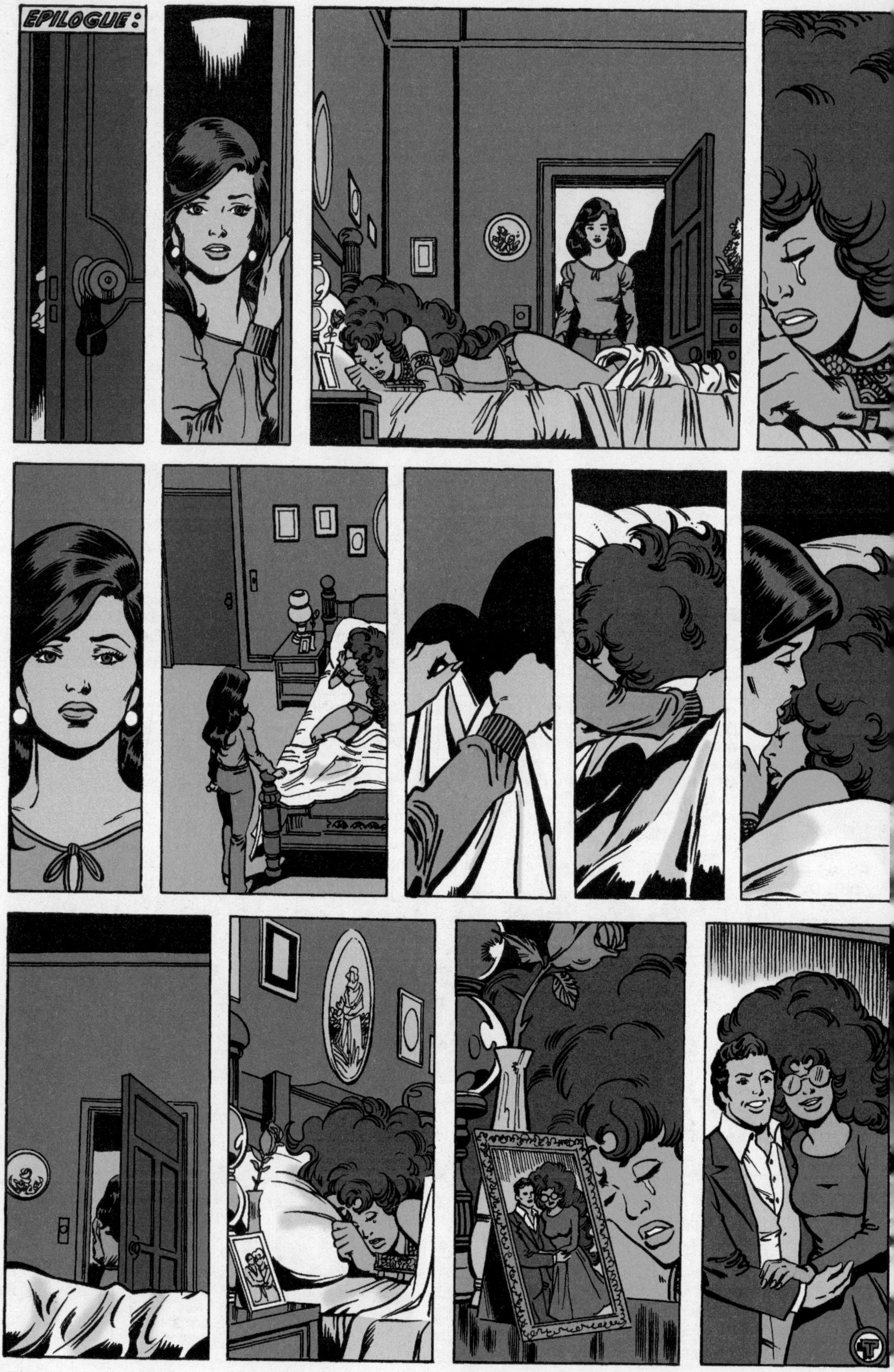
EPILOGUE:

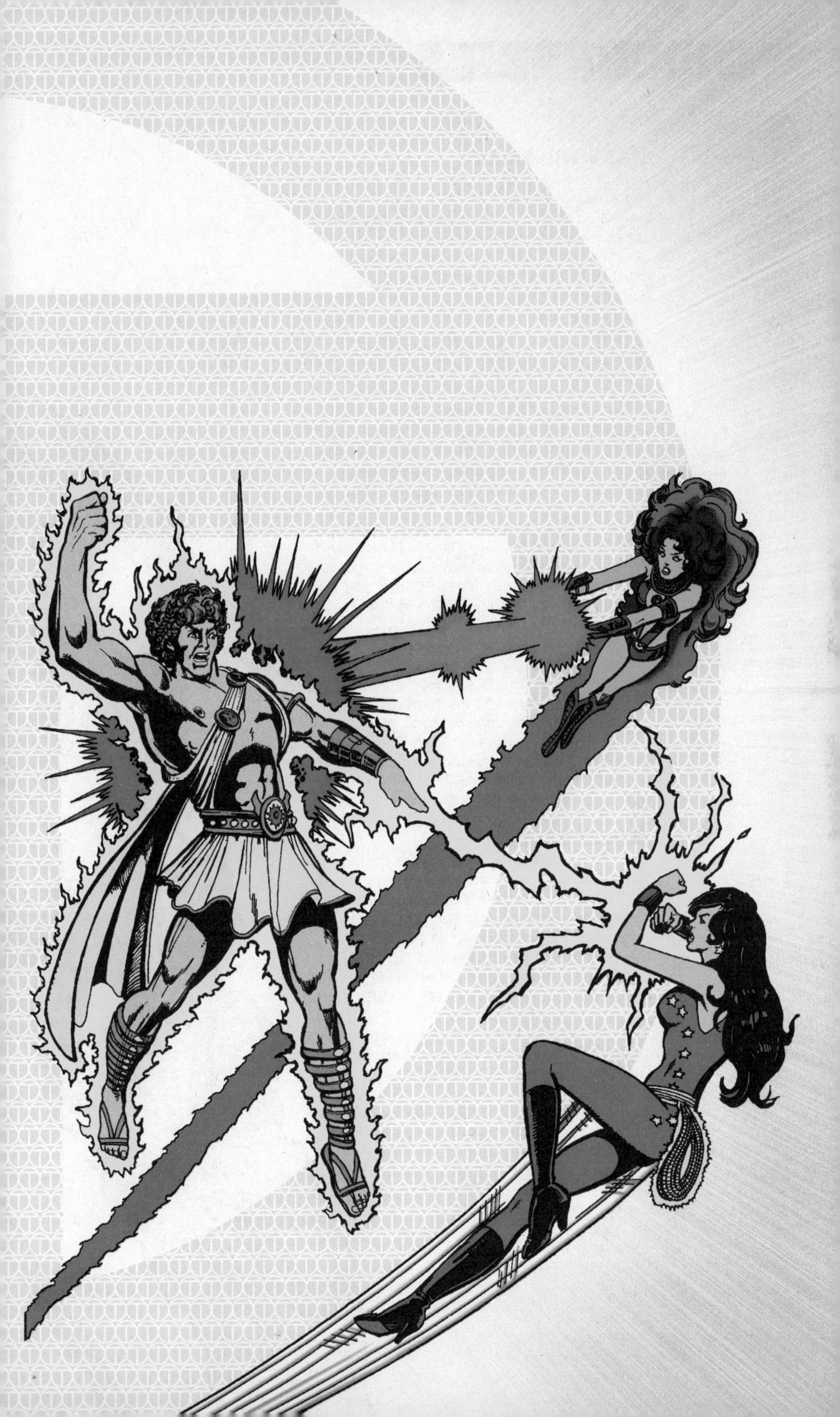

BIOGRAPHIES

MARV WOLFMAN

One of the most prolific and influential writers in modern comics, Marv Wolfman began his career as an artist. Realizing that his talents lay more in writing the stories than in drawing them, he soon became known for his carefully crafted, character-driven tales.

In a career that has spanned nearly 30 years, Wolfman has helped shape the heroic careers of DC Comics' Green Lantern, Blackhawk and the original Teen Titans, as well as Marvel Comics' Fantastic Four, Spider-Man, and Nova. In addition to co-creating THE NEW TEEN TITANS and the universe-shattering CRISIS ON INFINITE EARTHS with George Pérez, Wolfman was instrumental in the revamp of Superman after CRISIS, the development of THE NEW TEEN TITANS spinoff series VIGILANTE, DEATHSTROKE THE TERMINATOR and TEAM TITANS, and created such characters as Blade for Marvel, along with the titles NIGHT FORCE and the retooled DIAL "H" FOR HERO for DC.

In addition to his numerous comic book credits, Wolfman has also written several novels and worked in series television and animation, including the *Superman* cartoon of the late 1980s and the hit *Teen Titans* show on Cartoon Network. His novelization of CRISIS ON INFINITE EARTHS was published in the spring of 2005 by iBooks.

GEORGE PÉREZ

George Pérez started drawing at the age of five and hasn't stopped since. Born on June 9, 1954, Pérez began his professional comics career as an assistant to Rich Buckler in 1973. After establishing himself as a penciller at Marvel Comics, Pérez came to DC in 1980, bringing his highly detailed art style to such titles as JUSTICE LEAGUE OF AMERICA and FIRESTORM. After co-creating THE NEW TEEN TITANS in 1980, Pérez and writer Marv Wolfman reunited for the landmark miniseries CRISIS ON INFINITE EARTHS in 1985. In the aftermath of that universe-smashing event, Pérez revitalized WONDER WOMAN as the series' writer and artist, reestablishing the Amazon Princess as one of DC's most preeminent characters and bringing in some of the best sales the title has ever experienced. He has since gone on to illustrate celebrated runs on Marvel's *The Avengers*, CrossGen's *Solus* and DC's THE BRAVE AND THE BOLD.

ROMEO TANGHAL

Born and raised in the Philippines, Romeo Tanghal began drawing comics professionally after graduating from high school. He emigrated to the United States in 1976 and almost immediately began working for DC Comics. A prolific inker and occasional penciller, Tanghal contributed to a vast array of DC's titles over the next 25 years, including JUSTICE LEAGUE OF AMERICA, WONDER WOMAN, GREEN LANTERN and, of course, THE NEW TEEN TITANS.

DICK GIORDANO

A veteran of more than five decades in the comic book field, Dick Giordano began his career as an artist for Charlton Comics in 1952 and became the company's editor-in-chief in 1965, launching the short-lived but well-remembered Action Heroes line. In 1967 he moved to DC for a three-year stint as editor and became part of a creative team that helped to change the face of comic books in the late 1960s and early 1970s. Together with writer Dennis O'Neil and penciller Neal Adams, he helped to bring Batman back to his roots as a dark, brooding "creature of the night" and raise awareness of contemporary social issues through the adventures of Green Lantern and Green Arrow. The winner of numerous industry awards, Giordano later returned to DC and rose to the position of Vice President-Executive Editor before "retiring" in 1993 to once again pursue a full-time freelance career as a penciller and inker. He passed away on March 27, 2010.

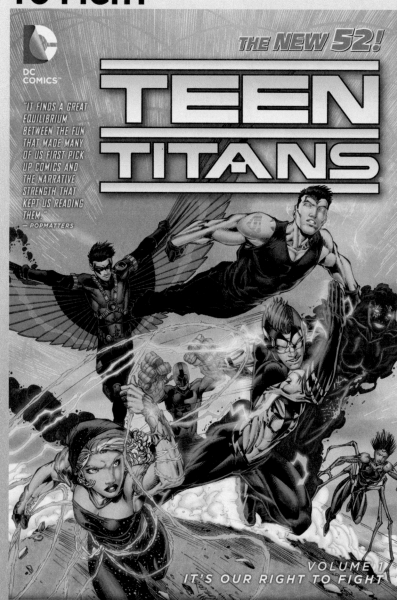

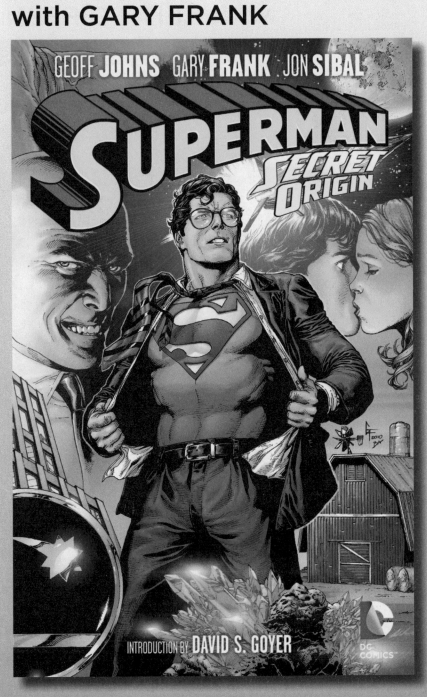